RETHINKING MASCULINITY

RETHINKING MASCULINITY

Philosophical Explorations in Light of Feminism

edited by
Larry May
and
Robert A. Strikwerda
with the assistance of Patrick D. Hopkins

Littlefield Adams Quality Paperbacks

LITTLEFIELD ADAMS QUALITY PAPERBACKS

a division of Rowman & Littlefield Publishers, Inc.
4720 Boston Way, Lanham, Maryland 20706

Copyright © 1992 by Rowman & Littlefield Publishers, Inc.

British Cataloging in Publication Information Available

Library of Congress Cataloging-in-Publication Data

Rethinking masculinity : philosophical explorations in light
of feminism / edited by Larry May and Robert A.
Strikwerda, with the assistance of Patrick D. Hopkins.
p.   cm. — (New feminist perspectives series)
Includes bibliographical references and index.
1. Men—United States.   2. Sex role—United States.
3. Masculinity (Psychology)—United States.   4. Feminist
theory.   I. May, Larry.   II. Strikwerda, Robert A.
III. Hopkins, Patrick D.   IV. Series.
[HQ1090.3.R48   1992b]
305.31—dc20   92–22297   CIP

ISBN 0–8226–3021–4 (pbk. : alk. paper)

Printed in the United States of America

 The paper used in this publication meets the minimum requirements of
American National Standard for Information Sciences—Permanence of
Paper for Printed Library Materials, ANSI Z39.48–1984.

For: Elizabeth, Avian, Brennin, and Linden.

Contents

Acknowledgments

"Sex and Social Roles: How to Deal with the Data" by Patrick Grim originally appeared in *Femininity, Masculinity and Androgyny,* edited by Mary Vetterling-Braggin (Lanham, Md.: Littlefield Adams, 1982). Reprinted by permission of Rowman & Littlefield.

"The Enduring Appeals of Battle" by J. Glenn Gray originally appeared in *The Warriors: Reflections on Men in Battle* (New York: Harcourt Brace, 1959). Copyright extended by Ursula A. Gray, 1987. Reprinted by permission.

"Gay Jocks: A Phenomenology of Gay Men in Athletics" by Brian Pronger originally appeared in *Sport, Men and the Gender Order,* edited by Michael Messner and Donald Sabo (Champaign, Ill.: Human Kinetics, 1990). Reprinted by permission of Human Kinetics Books and Michael Messner.

"Fatherhood and Nurturance" by Larry May and Robert Strikwerda originally appeared in the *Journal of Social Philosophy,* vol. 22/2, Fall 1991. Reprinted by permission of the *Journal of Social Philosophy.*

"Male Friendship and Intimacy" by Robert Strikwerda and Larry May originally appeared in *Hypatia,* vol. 7/2, Summer 1992. Reprinted by permission of the authors.

"Why Do Men Enjoy Pornography?" by Alan Soble originally appeared in *Pornography* (New Haven: Yale University Press, 1986). Reprinted by permission of Yale University Press.

"Pornography and the Alienation of Male Sexuality" by Harry Brod originally appeared in *Social Theory and Practice,* vol. 14/3, Fall 1988. Reprinted by permission of *Social Theory and Practice* and the author.

"Men, Feminism and Power" by Victor J. Seidler originally appeared in *Men, Masculinities and Social Theory,* edited by Jeff Hearn and David H. J. Morgan (London: Routledge, Chapman and Hall, 1990). Reprinted by permission of Routledge, Chapman and Hall.

Introduction

Several years ago we attended a lecture by Sandra Harding in which she spoke of a need for writings by men who are committed to feminism who "speak specifically as men, of themselves, of their bodies and lives, of texts and of politics, using feminist insights to see the world. . . ." She warned that the task would be "difficult and painful" but that it was tremendously important for men to come to a self-understanding of their experiences as men in a way that women had done in the early stages of the feminist movement.[1] This anthology owes its conception to Harding's words of inspiration.

The essays in this anthology all have the following in common: they are written by men, most of whom call themselves feminists; they are philosophical essays that attempt to come to terms with some issue or question arising out of the authors' experiences; they are exploratory, often merely attempting to survey an experiential terrain in conceptual terms; they approach the variety of experiences of being a male in Western culture in an attempt to find non-oppressive alternatives for men and for our children and grandchildren. The authors come from a varied set of backgrounds, yet all but one of us are academic philosophers, which explains our emphasis on conceptual analysis. Each of the authors has tried to write in a rigorous way that is nonetheless accessible to those not schooled in philosophy, and in a way that remains rooted in his experiences.

Feminist philosophers have shown how much philosophy has attempted to speak of "human experience" or "human nature" while ignoring or distorting the experiences of women. This has come about because Western philosophy has tended to ignore gender or failed to see the influence of gender on philosophy. And while it is true that philosophers have by and large ignored the experiences of women, it is also true that the experiences of many men have also not been taken seriously. Many male philosophers have been influenced by feminism, but have not seen it as requiring real change in how they do philosophy. Feminist philosophy has been viewed as being for, and about, women. Our anthology takes a different tack. Just as historians and anthropologists have realized the importance of the category of gender, so we believe that gender is a valuable analytic category.[2] We look to the experiences of men in our culture not to uncover the "essence" of maleness, but because we believe that good social philosophy needs to take gender fully into account.

Although there have been many popular books on masculinity, as well as many books in social science and literature, there have been very few books on philosophy and masculinity. Three of our authors in this anthology have written or edited the very few books in this field. Kenneth Clatterbaugh's book *Contemporary Perspectives on Masculinity*[3] surveys in a comprehensive fashion the spectrum of views that men currently take toward the topic of masculinity. Victor Seidler's book *Rediscovering Masculinity*[4] combines conceptual analysis and political theorizing about many of the central topics of our anthology. And Harry Brod's edited collection, *The Making of Masculinities*,[5] contains many interesting essays by men trying to construct a model of men's studies and to relate this model to current controversies in feminist theory. But there are very few other books on philosophy and masculinity.

In this brief introduction we will do two things. First, we will discuss two of the more popular books on masculinity, John Stoltenberg's *Refusing to Be a Man*,[6] and Robert Bly's *Iron John*,[7] in an attempt to locate our anthology. These two books represent two extreme poles of the current reaction to changes in gender roles inspired by feminism. Unlike some authors who reject or attack feminism, both claim to take feminism seriously and to respond to it supportively. Stoltenberg responds by claiming that men should give up completely on the traditional model of masculinity, and Bly proposes a return to an even more traditional model. Second, we will situate the various essays collected in our anthology and compare them with one another. But this will be very brief, for we want this anthology to stand on the strength of the voices of our authors' own words as they try to grapple with the incredibly difficult task of explaining, criticizing, and reconceptualizing what it means to be male in contemporary Western culture.

Denying and Affirming Traditional Male Roles

In his book, *Refusing to be a Man*, John Stoltenberg presents us with a very powerful popular call "for the end of manhood as we know it.''[8] He argues that manhood has been inextricably connected with patriarchy and injustice toward women. In one of the book's most powerful moments, Stoltenberg claims that ''The male sex is socially constructed. It is a political entity that flourishes only through acts of force and sexual terrorism.''[9] Stoltenberg describes the subtle and not-so-subtle ways that men force women to submit to gender roles. He contends that ''the act of prevailing upon another to admit of penetration without full and knowledgeable assent so sets the standard in the repertoire of male-defining behaviors that it is not at all inaccurate to suggest that the ethics of male sexual identity are essentially rapist.''[10]

But Stoltenberg also displays the more subtle side of male sexual identity that similarly forces women to do what men want:

> A ''he,'' being a he, can get away with murder—figuratively, and sometimes even literally—simply by virtue of the fact that he dissembles so sincerely, or he uses up someone's life with such single-minded purpose, or he betrays someone's trust with such resolute passion, or he abandons commitments with such panache. When men are held to account for what they do in their lives to women—which happens relatively rarely—their tunnel vision, their obliviousness to consequences, their egotism, their willfulness, all tend to excuse, rather than compound, their most horrific interpersonal offenses.[11]

All of this is part of a ''value system in which some acts are deemed 'good' and 'right' because they serve to make an individual's idea of maleness real, and others 'bad' or 'wrong' because they numb it.''[12]

Stoltenberg asks us to imagine that the variety of people's sex organs can be placed along a continuum, rather than falling into distinctly male or female sex organs. He also urges that men think of their penises as not significantly different from a woman's clitoris. And throughout this book he supports a view of eroticism that is polymorphic. While he does not say this explicitly, he seeks to replace the category of masculinity (as well as femininity) with that of androgyny. For, in the end, there are no differences between men and women that Stoltenberg allows to be a basis for differential sexual roles. At the end of one of the earlier chapters, he says, ''I invite you to become an erotic traitor to male supremacy.''[13]

While many of Stoltenberg's proposals are laudable, he leaves us with very little to grasp hold of once we have refused to be a man. What is positive in Stoltenberg's book is the ''idea'' that men can choose something different from the traditional roles they seem to be thrown into. But it is as if men should start from scratch, since all of their past conceptions of masculinity are to be rejected on this account. Yet we believe that many changes in gender roles have to be much more incremental to be successful. (There are exceptions—male recourse to violence, for example, should be stopped immediately.) One must recognize the powerful forces of socialization that must be overcome; and one must set intermediate goals that open the door for more moderate change to be regarded as "success." Relying on radical feminist insights, Stoltenberg persuasively criticizes many aspects of contemporary American masculinity. But there is very little attention to the positive aspects of masculinity that could be mined once the negative aspects have been rejected. Indeed, it is no accident that the title of Stoltenberg's book calls for a refusal not to be masculine in some of its manifestations, but a refusal to be a man. We are not convinced that such a step is necessary. As the papers that follow will indicate, there are many other positions one can take, also inspired by feminism, that offer more options to those who find it difficult or impossible to reject masculinity altogether.

Robert Bly has also provided a very popular recent book on masculinity called *Iron John*. Bly is primarily concerned to overcome the historical changes in men's relationships (centering on fathers and sons, but neglecting fathers and daughters) brought about by industrialization. But the current situation for men is often cast as a reaction to feminism's critique of contemporary masculinity; namely, that men no longer feel that they have the inner strength and self-assurance necessary to assume the leadership roles in society they traditionally played. Here is how he states this view:

> The women of twenty years ago were definitely saying that they preferred the softer receptive male. . . . Young men for various reasons wanted their harder women, and women began to desire softer men. It seemed like a nice arrangement for a while, but we've lived with it long enough now to see that it isn't working out.[14]

According to Bly, men who have chosen to reject the traditional role of the strong, aggressive male are now not happy because of a "lack of energy in them." They are anguished and unsure of themselves, incapable of making decisions and incapable of taking the lead on matters they consider important.

While Bly claims that he is not opposed to feminism, he nonetheless implies that the women's movement must bear some of the blame for the current state of emasculated manhood. Indeed, most of the myths that Bly retells place a woman, normally the mother, at the center of men's difficulties. Bly claims to provide a third alternative between the machismo male and the soft male in his stories of the "Wild Man." The Wild Man "resembles a Zen priest, a shaman, or a woodsman more than a savage," he tells us.[15] But it is women who have created the situation in which "Men are suffering right now—young men especially."[16] And it is only other men, especially older men like Bly himself, who can lead the way toward salvation.

What Bly envisions is a return to a much earlier tradition than that of the machismo male, a tradition in which "the divine also was associated with mad dancers, fierce fanged men, and being entirely underwater, covered with hair."[17] Unlike Stoltenberg, Bly thinks that there are essential differences between men and women, differences that we will deny at our own peril. "Geneticists have discovered recently that the genetic difference in DNA between men and women amounts to just over three percent. That isn't much. However the difference exists in every cell of the body."[18] We must move away from the rejection of masculinity, says Bly, and eventually reclaim all that was positive in the images of men as heroes and even men as "Lord."[19]

The model of masculinity that Robert Bly sketches has gone too far in the opposite direction from the model sketched by Stoltenberg. Instead of envisioning new ways for men and women to interact, ways that resolve the problems that Bly insightfully discusses, he turns uncritically to the past. As many other commentators have noted, Bly sets the stage for another round of blaming women for the problems in men's lives. And this sets the stage for another round of male violence against women. Why should we think that the boys and men Bly describes, who work so hard at being ferocious, will rein themselves in when confronted with women who do not wish to go along with their warlike games? Bly's image of masculinity is as one-sided as that of Stoltenberg. But surely there are more diverse and moderate views of a revised understanding of masculinity in today's society. Our anthology aims at just such a variety of reappraisals of traditional roles and constructive explorations of alternatives available to men today.

Assessments of, and Alternatives to, Traditional Masculinity

Our selection of readings begins with Patrick Grim's assessment of the scientific evidence used by those who claim that there are differences between men and women that justify various social practices. Grim begins by pointing out that for sexual differences to be supported by evidence, that evidence "must be something more than merely a record of how men and women raised in our society have happened to turn out." Some of the evidence used to buttress the claim that men and women should be assigned different roles in society misconstrues the social nature of the evidence. But even where there is good evidence for thinking that men have more of one natural trait than do women, aggressiveness, for instance, it is not clear that the society should require or encourage only men to pursue the role which is associated with that trait. As Grim argues, "we must consider whether differences ought to be exploited or compensated."

J. Glenn Gray's essay is the oldest in our anthology and the only one
not written in the light of feminism. It is included here because it is the
most provocative account ever written of the contradictions that men
have felt in wartime situations. Reflecting on his own experiences in
World War II, Gray says: "many men both hate and love combat.
They know why they hate it; it is harder to know and to be articulate
about why they love it." Gray examines three "attractions of war":
"the delight in seeing" that comes especially from the grand spectacle
of battlefield encounters; "the delight in comradeship" that comes
from the communal sense one achieves through mutual willingness to
engage in self-sacrifice; and "the delight in destruction" that is as
rooted in the psyche as is the delight in creation. In all three cases, it
is the ecstatic dimension of experience that is key. But the drives of
destruction and self-sacrifice are very problematic for most men. As
Gray puts it: "What our moral self tells us is abhorrent, our religious
self and our aesthetic self yearn for as the ultimate good." But
ultimately, the delights of war are passing and empty. As Gray concludes: "Our society has not begun to wrestle with this problem of
how to provide fulfillment to human life, to which war is so often an
illusory path."

Brian Pronger provides a fresh look at another paradigm of male
experience, athletics. Like Gray, Pronger is struck by both the positive
and negative sides of this experience. From the positive side, Pronger
is especially interested in the possibilities that are opened up when the
male athlete is envisioned as gay. "The popular images of the athlete
and the gay man are virtually antithetical . . . the image of the athlete
is quintessentially healthy and positive . . . unlike the judicial, medical,
and religious models that have categorized the homosexual man as a
criminal, pathological, degenerate sinner." Pronger critically discusses
the traditional characterization of the athlete and the gay man and then
explores the way that our conceptions of homosexual men might
change when these two worlds meet in the person of the "gay jock."

Hugh LaFollette examines one of the traditional roles assigned to
men, often characterized as being a "real man," that is, a man who
never shows weakness or emotion in personal relationships with
women. LaFollette explores various ways that men can relate to
women that would be liberating for the men as well as for the women.
He addresses issues of trust and equality, two of the most important
concepts in a feminist-oriented approach to the role of men in heterosexual relationships. LaFollette tackles the difficult question of how
much feminist men should "help" their spouses to overcome their own
gender socialization. And at the end of his paper, LaFollette tackles
the difficult question of whether the concept of justice should be
employed in describing and thinking about heterosexual relationships.

His provocative conclusion is that justice is inappropriate in reasonably egalitarian relationships.

Larry May and Robert Strikwerda examine another traditional role assigned to men, the role of father-as-provider. After explaining why the traditional model of fatherhood is harmful to both men and their families, we argue that father-as-nurturer is an appropriate model for many contemporary men in Western societies. (Leonard Harris's essay also discusses parenting, but with a different emphasis.) We counter the arguments from psychology and biology that have been given against men nurturing their children. Rather than finding it simply frustrating for men to take an equal role in childrearing, we argue that it can be enriching. We end by discussing the resources that many men already possess that would make them good nurturers of their children.

In a companion essay to the previous one, Robert Strikwerda and Larry May discuss the widely reported phenomenon that contemporary men have much less intimacy in their lives (especially in the company of other men) than do women (especially in the company of other women). Using some of J. Glenn Gray's insights, we distinguish comradeship from true friendship and then we point out parallels between Aristotle's understanding of friendship among males and our own. One of the chief obstacles to men's intimacy is the inability of men to be aware of their own feelings. At the end of the essay we suggest resources that many men already have that, when developed, could provide the groundwork for enhanced intimacy in their relationships.

Patrick Hopkins explores one of the concepts that is most likely to impede intimacy among men, namely, homophobia. Hopkins argues that homosexuality is a challenge to the very way that men define themselves. Hopkins draws on various continental approaches to sexuality (as does Brian Pronger in his essay) in an attempt to provide a working characterization of homophobia that does justice both to the central role that gender bifurcation plays in our culture and to some of the more extreme forms of violence perpetrated as a reaction to homosexuality. The main body of the paper concerns an exploration of three explanations of how homophobia develops and he relates those explanations to the correlation between masculinity and personal identity.

Alan Soble discusses pornography from a Marxist perspective, emphasizing the way that pornography causes alienation among men. Of central importance to his concerns is the notion that pornography overstresses the visual and eventually leads to the desensitization of the male body. But, nonetheless, men enjoy pornography because it gives them full control over their erotic worlds by allowing for a wide variation of fantasies. In this sense, men engage in an infantile escape from reality and this contributes to their increasing powerlessness over their own lives. Yet even as pornography alienates men from their bodies, Soble thinks there is a positive side to pornography. "If the vast consumption of pornography implies that a good deal of masturbation is going on, then men are rejecting the prevailing standards of masculinity . . . men are abandoning the idea that, to prove themselves, they need to seduce women."

Harry Brod takes a different look at pornography, especially at the way that pornography supports patriarchy and the subordination of women while also stressing the "negative impact on men's own sexuality." Brod criticizes Soble's somewhat positive assessment of pornography. We are left with the very disconcerting fact that pornography operates to the disadvantage of women and to the "disadvantage of the group it privileges, men." Drawing on socialist feminism, Brod explains how pornography alienates men from their own sexuality by creating an unreachable ideal of male performance and from the kind of need satisfaction that sex is supposed to provide. In place of patriarchy, Brod urges us to think of pornography as promoting fratriarchy, the rule of brothers, that is a kind of conspiracy to deny the way that the commodification of sex has led to increased violence against women and also the alienation of men from their bodies.

Kenneth Clatterbaugh takes the analysis of the relationship between men and feminism one step further. In his paper he argues that men have not been oppressed by feminism. Indeed, after a detailed analysis of what is right and wrong with various theories of oppression, he defends a theory of oppression that makes it impossible for a member of a dominant group in society to be oppressed. If oppression is understood as relative dehumanization, then men *as men* (not as Hispanic, or as gay) have not been oppressed by society at large or by feminism, but women *as women* have been oppressed. Even though only men are drafted and used as cannon fodder, given the high social status assigned to combat soldiers, men are not oppressed even by a system that sends them (and not women) out to be slaughtered on the battlefield.

Leonard Harris examines the concept of honor and tries to explain why this social good has been so elusive for African-American males. He contrasts the image of Malcolm X, the proponent of violence and tough-minded activism, with that of Martin Luther King, Jr., whose image is of a more passive and "feminine" role model. He asks what it would mean to honor King for his "feminine" characteristics of love, care, compassion, and sacrifice. Harris is interested in how honoring King might affect the tendency to perceive honor in strictly "masculine" terms. But Harris contends that racism continues to be pervasive in American society, virtually excluding African-American males from the moral community and thus from that group which is afforded honor. In spite of the honor bestowed on King, our society is reluctant to honor African-American males and this has contributed to their lack of empowerment.

Victor Seidler pursues the question of men's powerlessness, asking what role feminism has played in creating this feeling of a lack of power by men. Seidler contends that feminism is indeed "a threat to the way that men are," for feminists challenge the hierarchy of power that men have established. Relying on insights from post-structuralist philosophers, Seidler stresses "the importance of a social movement for change." In this context he calls for a new understanding of the way that men have traditionally oppressed women that will "illuminate the conditions and possibilities of changing conceptions of masculinity, if not also for the liberation of men."

These essays, written from a wide variety of philosophical perspectives, are all related in wanting to provide characterizations of masculinity that are empowering, or at least enlightening, for men, without contributing to the further oppression of women. We do not view this anthology as self-sufficient, standing by itself, for there are many more perspectives and issues of importance that we have not addressed than those that we have. Rather, our hope is that this anthology will stimulate other philosophers and social theorists to work on topics we have not been able to include, especially those who can draw on experiences quite different from those of our authors. And while the jury is still out, we believe that this collection of essays will strike its readers as providing reasonable analyses of what is wrong with the traditional model of masculinity and with plausible suggestions for change that will benefit both men and women today.

We are grateful to Jon Sisk and Rosemary Tong for encouraging this project. We would also like to thank Penny Weiss and Marilyn Friedman for providing many helpful suggestions at various stages in the process of completing this project. Patrick Hopkins, who constructed the bibliography and did valuable editing work, made it possible for us to meet our deadlines and to bring this project to completion.

Notes

1. See Sandra Harding's essay "After the End of 'Philosophy'," delivered at Purdue University's Matchette Conference in 1989.

2. See John Dupre's essay "Global versus Local Perspectives on Sexual Difference," in *Theoretical Perspectives on Sexual Difference*, edited by Deborah Rhode (New Haven: Yale University Press, 1990), pp. 47–62.

3. Kenneth Clatterbaugh, *Contemporary Perspectives on Masculinity* (Boulder, CO: Westview Press, 1990).

4. Victor J. Seidler, *Rediscovering Masculinity* (London: Routledge, 1989).

5. Harry Brod, *The Making of Masculinities: The New Men's Studies* (Boston: Allen and Unwin, 1987).

6. John Stoltenberg, *Refusing to be a Man* (Portland, OR: Breitenbush Books, 1989).

7. Robert Bly, *Iron John* (Reading, MA: Addison-Wesley, 1990).

8. Stoltenberg, op. cit., p. 4.

9. Ibid., p. 30.

10. Ibid., p. 19

11. Ibid., p. 17.

12. Ibid., p. 24

13. Ibid., p. 39.

14. Bly, op. cit., p. 3.

15. Ibid., p. x.

16. Ibid., p. 27

17. Ibid., p. 26.

18. Ibid., p. 234.

19. Ibid., p. 237.

PART ONE

Sex Differences

1

Sex and Social Roles: How to Deal with the Data

Patrick Grim

Women consistently score higher on verbal aptitude tests than do men, whereas males generally do better on tests involving "visual-spatial" skills: that is, depth perception, mazes, picture completion, map reading, and the like.[1] On questionnaires women rate moving, marriage, and loss of a job as more stressful than do men.[2] Women appear to be more sensitive to sound volume and higher frequencies than men, are better at fine coordination and rapid decisions,[3] and it has been proposed that women are able to "read" facial expressions more readily.[4] Men consistently test out as more aggressive.[5]

What are we to do with data of this sort? One way it is often used is as a justification for social practices involving a division of labor on sexual lines. If women are more sensitive to stress and less aggressive than men, it is argued, we should leave those tasks calling for aggression and tolerance of stress to men. If women are "communicative" animals and men are "manipulative" animals, we should leave the "communicative" tasks of childrearing to women.[6] If men excel at mathematical tasks and women have superior verbal skills, our engineers should be male and our telephone operators should be female. Fine coordination and rapid decision making qualify women as excellent typists, whereas better spatial perception indicates that jet pilots should be male.

I am grateful to Mary Vetterling-Braggin, David Pomerantz, and Kriste Taylor for their help with revisions on an earlier draft.

The form of this argument should be familiar: our data shows that men and women differ in certain ways, and those differences (so the story goes) justify a differentiation of social roles along sexual lines. The argument is quite clearly public property and appears with tedious regularity in common conversation. But it also appears in one guise or another throughout much of the literature on sex differences.[7] It is this form of argument I wish to attack.

My attack is in three parts. In the first section I hope to raise briefly some embarrassing questions concerning the data itself. The data on which arguments of this form rely may not always be as objective, nor as clearly indicative of fundamental differences, as is often made out. In the second section I hope to address a general practical problem regarding sexual differences and our own ignorance. In the final section I will argue that the inferences often drawn from data regarding sexual differences are neither as direct nor as tight as is commonly assumed. Even if we have appropriately hard data demonstrating clearly fundamental sexual differences, the data may not support the conclusions regarding social roles which it appears to support.

I. Questioning the Data

Without an authoritative appeal to scientific data regarding sexual differences, an argument of this type would not even get off the ground. The argument as a whole, in fact, might be seen as an attempt to transfer to its social conclusions the scientific respectability of the data on which it relies. In a later section we will consider whether the argument succeeds; whether the data, however good, supports the social conclusions it appears to. But for now let us consider the data itself. Is it always as tight as it appears to be?

In order for the data to supply appropriate support for the argument at issue, it must be something more than merely a record of how men and women raised in our society have happened to turn out. That alone would not tell us whether observed characteristics are fundamental characteristics, independent of social influence, and would not show that people might not turn out quite differently in some other social context. Thus it wouldn't show, as the argument is designed to show, that social roles should quite generally be distinguished along sexual lines. If the differences at issue are merely a reflection of our own social order, they are part of what can be changed, rather than invariables which dictate the form that social change can or should take. So any data relied on in arguing for general social role differentiation along sexual lines must give some indication that observed differences are more than mere social epiphenomena. Only data which in some way goes beyond a simple record of differences between women and men in the context of a particular status quo can do this.

It is because of this basic requirement that our data must in several ways be free of social influence. To the extent that our data reflects a given social situation rather than indicating sexual differences independent of social influence, it will be of little help in deciding, however indirectly, how society ought to be.

There are at least two ways in which data regarding sexual differences may be a reflection of our society rather than of something more. The data may not, first of all, be appropriately *hard* data; the apparent differences such data show may in fact be the result of social influences on or inherent in the ways in which the data are collected, counted, and represented. The data of a sexist observer might not be hard in this sense; the differences observed are in fact merely in the eye of the observer. But even if our data are appropriately hard—even if the ways in which it is accumulated are free from illegitimate social influence—the differences for which we then have evidence may themselves be the result of social influences. Given the systematically different ways in which children of different sexes are brought up in our society, it would be surprising indeed if no psychological differences showed up on our tests.[8] But this is not the data we need. Somehow we must have an indication that our data are not to be explained in social terms; that the differences objectively recorded are genuinely *fundamental* differences.[9]

Though in principle distinct, the requirement that our data be hard data and the requirement that recorded differences be genuinely fundamental differences tend to blur in practice. The concern I want to raise here tends toward worries regarding the hardness of some of our data, though questions of fundamentality are clearly at issue as well. My objections are not intended to impugn all data we have or might collect. But they are intended as a warning by example of how easily implicit operation of social factors may be overlooked.

Consider first the question of aggression. Is one sex more aggressive than the other? Perhaps no other question in the history of testing for sex differences has had so long a history involving such a variety of test procedures. But despite the apparent simplicity of the question, a bit of reflection shows that any attempt to put it to the test involves a number of pitfalls. That in turn is good reason to think that much of the testing already done has been subject to those pitfalls, and thus good reason to be generally suspicious of the data regarding sexual differences with regard to aggression.

One difficulty is what gets counted as aggression. In a sexist society such as ours it would not be surprising to find that male and female behavior is interpreted differently as aggressive. A guffawing, hand-clamping, back-slapping female is more likely to be considered aggressive than is her male counterpart, who is merely considered outgoing or friendly. A rumor-spreading male, on the other hand, may more readily be considered aggressive than his female counterpart, who is merely "catty." It may also be that whether or not an individual's behavior is perceived as aggressive depends on the sex (and social conditioning) of the perceiver; a female observer is more likely to see Joe's constant sexual overtures to women as aggressive than is another male. If "aggression" is socially loaded in these ways, it is hardly a proper tool for collecting or representing objective data; any tests we try to perform concerning the relative aggressiveness of the sexes will be shot through with social prejudices from the start. Another way of putting the point is this: "aggressive" may be a term which in subtle ways is applied differently to men than to women. If so, it is not a neutral characteristic which we can compare in the two cases. Asking whether one sex is more aggressive than the other is more like asking whether one is generally taller; neither "aggressive" nor "attractive" is applied to each group with the objective impartiality of a yardstick.

Consider another piece of data mentioned earlier; the fact that women generally rate moving, marriage, or loss of a job as more stressful than men. This has been taken as an indication that women are more sensitive to, and less tolerant of, stress.[10] But we might draw other conclusions instead. In a job market in which women are consistently discriminated against, the loss of a job is a greater disaster for a woman than for a man. Women may be more stressful about losing jobs, not because they are such delicate creatures, but because, things being as they are, the loss of a job is in fact a more serious matter for women than for men. Consider also marriage, the second item on the list. Given our social situation, the social burdens of marriage fall harder on the shoulders of women than men; a man often takes a wife on the side whereas a woman tends to enter married life like a career change. Small wonder that women find the prospect of marriage more stressful than do men. The statistics on sex, stress, and moving fit a similar pattern. Ozzie doesn't have to worry much about moving because moving, in its excruciating organizational detail, isn't his job; Harriet does it. Thus the fact that women rate particular tasks and situations as more stressful than do men may tell us more about those tasks and situations than about women and men; it may indicate simply that those tasks and situations are already distinguished along sexual lines. The problem noted above with testing for aggression was that "aggression" may not be a term applied sufficiently sex-neutrally to allow for legitimate comparison. The difficulty here is that job loss, marriage, and moving may not, as things stand, be sex-neutral tasks, and thus may not be suitable as neutral gauges of any fundamental differences between the sexes with regard to stress.

These cases are presented only as warnings of how our testing can go wrong in subtle ways and how as a result our data may in some cases be neither as hard nor as fundamental as it appears to be. It is easy to imagine similar difficulties in other tests, and perhaps pervasive difficulties with standard modes of testing in general. Because of social differences in upbringing, the environment of a laboratory or the phenomenon of being observed may not themselves be appropriately sex-neutral.

Does this indicate that all our data on sex differences is something less than hard data, or that there are insurmountable problems in testing the types of claims with which we began? Not at all. All that is indicated is that some data which might pass for hard data is not hard at all, that differences may appear fundamental when they are not, and that there are often deep and pervasive difficulties to be wary of in testing for sexual differences. This does, I think, justify a bit of skepticism in reviewing the accumulated research on sexual differences and calls for more than a bit of caution in trying to assemble better data. But it does not constitute a blanket objection to all such investigation, and I doubt that any a priori considerations alone could do so.

II. What to Assume When You Don't Know What to Assume

The arguments of the previous section can be understood as arguments that our ignorance is greater than our research might lead us to believe. Not all our data regarding sexual differences are genuinely hard data revealing genuinely fundamental differences. In this section I want to address the question of how we should act and what we should assume when we are to some extent ignorant as to how we should act and what we should assume.

Consider a case which appears quite frequently. We have, we think, objectively established a genuine difference between men and women in our test sample; men score higher on characteristic f_1, whereas women score higher on characteristic f_2. But we aren't sure how the difference is to be explained; whether as a fundamental and socially independent characteristic of men and women in general, or as merely a result of differences in the upbringing of men and women in our sample. In such cases we often have theorists at loggerheads; one group insists on explaining the differences as fundamental, whereas the other attempts to present plausible suggestions as to how the data might be explained as the result of social conditioning.

There are two questions we might raise concerning such cases: how the dispute is to be resolved, if it is to be resolved,[11] and how we should act and what we should assume in cases in which the dispute remains unresolved.

There is no easy answer to the first question. In order to establish whether or not an observed difference is a fundamental difference we might employ cross-cultural testing (on the theory that fundamental differences will be universal in ways in which socially inculcated differences will not), testing of newborns (if possible, given the characteristics at issue), or testing for development patterns at different ages (on the somewhat shaky assumption that social factors will show a more pervasive influence with time). We might also rely on links to other data. If we find that certain observed differences correlate very well with certain hormonal balances, and if we have independent evidence that hormonal balances of the right type are largely independent of social influences, we will have evidence that the difference at issue is a genuinely fundamental difference.

Thus in some cases we can expect the dispute to be resolvable in one way or another. But this point can easily be overstated as a conviction that all such disputes are in all cases easily resolvable by appeal to some decisive form of additional testing. They are not. Few of the phenomena to which appeal is made in order to settle such disputes are unambiguously decisive. Cross-cultural testing has pitfalls of its own, and there are various explanations for cultural universality short of innatist hypotheses. Some social influences may be constant in a way which does not show variation over time, and we know of many strictly physical characteristics which vary with age. The differential characteristics at issue are generally complex enough to make testing of newborns impossible, and the physical data to which we attempt to establish correlations cannot always be shown to be itself independent of social influences. Only in exceptional instances does some crucial experiment decide the case. Such disputes are resolved, to the extent that they are resolved at all, by a subtle accumulation of plausibility—none of it clearly decisive—on one side or the other. Often even this does not occur; the additional tests appealed to are themselves ambiguous enough to allow for either interpretation. A gray area remains and for the sake of unanimity each side may blur the dispute by speaking of what various data suggest rather than of what they show and by speaking of differential tendencies which may involve both social and fundamental factors, rather than of differential characteristics of solely one kind or the other.

To some extent we are presently ignorant of whether certain differences between men and women reveal fundamental differences or are to be attributed to social causes. To some extent, we will always be ignorant. Does this matter? If whether certain differences are fundamental or social in origin may be of moral relevance in shaping a society—an issue more fully considered in the following section—then our ignorance does matter. What we don't know may hurt us in the attempt to make our society what it ought to be.

This in effect saddles us with a quandary as to how to act in ignorance. There are differences between men and women which may be genuinely fundamental or which may be social in origin. How we ought to treat men and women may depend on which explanation is correct, but we cannot claim to *know* which explanation is correct. In that case which ought we assume; should we treat the differences at issue as fundamental until proven otherwise, or as social in origin until and unless the evidence indicates otherwise? The dilemma is both of practical importance and as unavoidable as our own ignorance.

It might be thought that in such a situation the decision we face is genuinely arbitrary; since the available evidence cannot tell us which alternative to choose, nothing can, and we might lose either way. I am not sure, however, that this is quite our predicament. Allow me to sketch in broad outlines a form of argument which would suggest that there are ethical reasons for treating men and women as if one explanation were correct even if we don't know which explanation is correct. Because of a number of fairly obvious complications the argument here is merely a sketch, and all I would claim for it at present is that it is suggestive. But it is, I think, an argument worthy of further development, and for that reason, although "merely suggestive," is not to be despised.[12]

The argument can be presented conveniently in the form of a gain-loss grid, similar to simple models of economic decision making. We might assume a fundamental explanation for differences at issue, and might be either right or wrong. We might assume a social explanation for the differences, and once again might be either right or wrong. My strategy will be to propose that the risks we run are less significant and the prospective gains greater on the assumption of a social explanation, and thus that to the extent that we are ignorant we should assume that observed sex differences are to be explained in social terms.

Theory True

		Fundamental	Social
	Fundamental	1	2
Theory Assumed	Social	3	4

There is one class of prospective gains and losses which appear to balance out between our alternatives: the promise of social efficiency and the threat of social disutility. If we assume either explanation for observed differences, and if we're right, other things being equal, we can expect the social programs we introduce or the social structures we build on the basis of our theories to work more smoothly overall. If our assumed theory is wrong, we can expect to suffer on the same score.[13]

But consider also the matter of social injustice. The treatment of differences which are in fact merely social as if they were fundamental—the outcome represented by (2)—seems to be a clear instance of socially unjust treatment. Standard paradigms of racism and sexism involve precisely this feature; that differences between individuals or groups, real or imagined, are taken to be inherent and fundamental which are not. The stereotypical black is thought to be *inherently* lazy and stupid, not merely socially handicapped, and racism would be quite a different matter were this not the case. The true sexist holds not just that some particular group of women are by force of circumstance scatter-brained and fragile, but that women are so by nature. Part of the injustice of racism and sexism is simply that the stereotypes don't fit. But even if they did, sexist and racist treatment would be unjust because the characteristics involved are not the *fundamental* characteristics they are assumed to be.

On this model, I think, we must envisage social injustice of an all-too-familiar sort as one of the potential losses to be entered against the assumption of a fundamental explanation for observed differences.[14] Is there a comparable threat of injustice on the other side?

It must be admitted that the outcome envisaged in (3) includes losses above and beyond mere social disutility. Two of the ethically most significant losses are the following. If we attempt to correct for differences which are not of social origin by social means, we can expect a disproportionate distribution of social goods. If we pour our social resources into attempts at social remedy for low scores on some characteristic among some particular group, and if the original low scores are in fact of social origin, we can in a sense see ourselves as distributing social goods with some form of equity. The low-scoring individuals were presumably shortchanged or handicapped at some point, and our attempts to correct the situation are both compensationally and distributively just. But if we end up "compensating" in this way for "social ills" which are not social ills at all, we will be allotting a greater share of our social energies to a particular group, those with low scores on the characteristic at issue.

By the same token, in such an outcome we may be doing more to develop the lower potential of some than we are doing to develop the higher potential of others. That individual with a greater fundamental potential will have his or her potential developed to a lesser degree (though not to a lower level) than will those with a less handsome fundamental endowment.

Both of these, I think, are indeed social and ethical losses. We do, all things being equal, regard equal treatment as a requirement of distributive justice. And we do hold as an ideal the full development of each individual's potential. But it should be noted that these losses can be entered against outcome (2) as well as against outcome (3). If we treat social differences as if they were fundamental we can expect a disproportionate distribution of social goods, simply because we will be dealing with differences here as well. Nor would it be at all surprising to find that the treatment of social differences as if they were fundamental results in the differential development of various potentials; the crippling and neglect of individual potential have been a constant feature of this form of treatment in the past. Thus the losses envisaged in (3) are also losses to be entered against (2), in addition to the quite basic injustice of (2) discussed above. The risks of (3) don't balance out those of (2) simply because those same risks, and more, appear in (2).[15]

A closely related point can be put in terms of the prospective gains, above and beyond social utility, to be entered in boxes (1) and (4). To the extent that observed differences are social in origin rather than fundamental, they can in principle be socially avoided; society might be constructed such that those differences did not appear at all. To the extent that differences are genuinely fundamental, as in (1), this is not possible. But there is another and more glowing way of expressing this difference. One of our standard social ideals is that of a truly egalitarian society, a society of equals. When that ideal is criticized, it is generally criticized as utopian or unrealistic. But it is not criticized, other than in corrupted forms, as ethically undesirable. This is important because, to the extent that differences at issue are merely social, an approximation of the ideal of egalitarianism is a real possibility. To the extent that differences are fundamental, we will always fall short of that goal. Thus in a sense the prospective gains of box (4) are greater than those of box (1); (4) allows a prospect of egalitarianism which (1) does not, and thus a closer approximation of a deeply seated ethical ideal.

If this argument is correct, there are ethical reasons to prefer a social explanation of observed differences over a fundamental explanation to the extent that we remain in ignorance. The prospect of social injustice is less on such an assumption, and the prospective gain in terms of approximating an egalitarian ideal is greater. Ethically, we have more to gain and less to lose.

The argument is, I think, a suggestive one. But I must admit that the presentation above is incomplete in a number of respects. Some of the intuitions regarding justice on which it relies call for a more complete examination than I am able to offer here, and there may be ethically relevant matters which have been neglected. So at present all I would claim for the argument is that it is a suggestive sketch. But what it suggests is of importance; that even our treatment of the data regarding sex differences, and of our own ignorance, is an ethical matter which calls for more than mere data.

III. What If It's All True?

In the previous sections we have raised some doubts concerning the data on which the arguments at issue rest and have suggested that there may be ethical reasons for treating differences as social rather than fundamental in cases in which we cannot claim to know which they are. But let us suppose that in some case we do have firm and unambiguous empirical evidence of differences between the sexes; let us suppose that we can *prove* that men are characteristically more aggressive, that women are generally more "communicative," and the like. What follows from suitably hard data revealing suitably fundamental differences even if we have it? Not as much, I think, as is often assumed.

Let us assume some fundamental characteristic of men f_1 and some fundamental characteristic of women f_2. Let us also suppose a set of tasks $t_1, t_2, \ldots t_n$ for which characteristic f_1 is a prime qualification, and a different set of tasks $t'_1, t'_2, \ldots t'_n$ for which f_2 is a prime qualification. Does it follow, as the argument at issue has it, that social roles ought to be distinguished along sexual lines such that men are assigned tasks $t_1, t_2, \ldots t_n$ and women are assigned tasks $t'_1, t'_2, \ldots t'_n$? It at least does not follow as night the day; allow me to catalog a number of major qualifications required in any such inference.

There are very few tasks indeed which call for one and only one simple qualification. Brain surgery demands dexterity, but not dexterity alone, and plumbing demands physical strength and a degree of limberness, but not these alone. The most dexterous of brain surgeons and the strongest and most limber of plumbers might nonetheless be a very bad brain surgeon and a very bad plumber; each might lack foresight, experience, spatial perception, and appropriate forms of mechanical imagination. The general lesson here is that qualification for most tasks is a complicated matter of balance of different abilities, some of which may be tied to fundamental characteristics and many of which may not be. Thus no single simple characteristic, and no small group of characteristics, however fundamental, can alone be expected to decide the question of who should be assigned which tasks; some other capacity or group of capacities, fundamental or social in origin, might always outweigh the significance of any inherent difference. Thus even given fundamental sexual differences, and even given that some of those differences involve characteristics which are qualifications for different sets of tasks, we cannot conclude that those tasks ought to be divided on sexual lines without considering *all* qualifications relevant to those tasks, including qualifications which are not tied to fundamental differences.

Consider also a second difficulty. There are precious few fundamental differences in the data which are not at best merely statistical differences, often very slight, which show up in testing large groups of men and women. A statistical difference of this type may not alone indicate very much. That women score higher on average in a characteristic f_1 is perfectly consistent with each of the following; that those who score most highly on f_1 are men, and that a finite number of occupational slots calling for only characteristic f_1 will best be filled entirely by men.[16] A statistical difference of this type is even consistent with the claim that your chances of selecting an individual satisfying a specific requirement for a high f_1 score are greater if you draw from a pool exclusively of men than from either a pool exclusively of women or from a randomly mixed pool.[17] A higher average score on f_1 among women does not entail that any woman scores above all men, that most women score above all men, that the highest score is a woman's or that the lowest is a man's, or that the majority of women score more highly than the majority of men.[18] Nonetheless the statistical difference in such a case is quite standardly represented by saying that "women score more highly with regard to f_1 than do men," and this latter phrase has a peculiar tendency to be misread (and misused in argument) as if it were the quite different claim that all women score more highly with regard to f_1 than all men. This subtle shift can, of course, make all the difference between truth and falsity.[19]

The importance here of this elementary error is that a *clear* justification of universally applied sex-role differentiation would require the stronger universal claim: that all women score more highly with regard to f_1 than do all men. From the mere fact that the average score for women with regard to f_1 is higher than the average score for men it simply does not follow that tasks calling for f_1 ought to be assigned to any particular group at all, unless we nominate those with high f_1 scores as such a group. Consistent with the truth of the statistical claim, and depending on the circumstances, that group might be composed exclusively of women, might be composed exclusively of men, or might be composed of any proportion of the two.

We are assuming, for the moment, that the data regarding sexual differences on which arguments of the type at issue rely are beyond reproach, i.e., genuinely hard data revealing genuinely fundamental sexual differences. But this is not the only data which is required if the argument is to go through. Given different characteristics f_1 and f_2, and sets of tasks t_1, t_2, . . . t_n and t'_1, t'_2, . . . t'_n, we must also have firm and objective data concerning the importance of those characteristics for those tasks. Oddly enough, those who present arguments for social role differentiation on the basis of sexual differences generally neglect to supply this second batch of data, substituting instead a form of armchair speculation which they would rightly reject in other contexts. From the fact (if it is a fact) that women have greater fine coordination and are better at rapid decisions, it is too often concluded that they would make good typists.[20] But why not brain surgeons or astronauts?; these too call for the characteristics in question. The fact (if it is a fact) that men are more aggressive is similarly taken to justify a role-assignment as soldiers and businessmen. But is not aggression also a qualification for the protective role of babysitters? In order for the link from fundamental traits to social roles to be a properly logical link, free from the corrupting influence of social prejudice, we would need independent demonstration of a correlation between certain traits and certain tasks or occupations. That data would have to be as hard as the data regarding the fundamental differences itself. At this point the argument for social role differentiation characteristically takes the form of armchair speculation as to what makes a good typist, a good businessman, and the like. But if we allow armchair speculation at this point, we might as well have allowed armchair speculation as to basic sexual differences to begin with.

Another group of major assumptions lies hidden in the argument as well. Let us assume that a particular characteristic—aggression, for example—is a salient characteristic of contemporary businesspeople and is perhaps even essential to the current structure of business itself. Let us also assume that men are more aggressive than women, and here we might even assume that men are *universally* more aggressive. Does it follow that businesspeople ought to be male? Only if we add an additional ethical premise: that contemporary businesspeople are as businesspeople ought to be, and that the current social structure of business is as it ought to be. What this shows is that no form of the argument at issue can be a pure extrapolation from data, however good; it must always involve a premise as to how society *ought* to be as well. In actual use, I think, the hidden assumption is always that our society is at least by and large as it ought to be. So it shouldn't be too surprising that the argument is generally used as a defense of the status quo; it relies on an assumption in favor of the status quo. But with different assumptions as to how society ought to be we would get different results. If aggression in business is a social handicap rather than a social strength—if, for example, it is that aggression which generates the ills of corporate capitalism—then we ought not encourage aggression in business, and perhaps quite generally ought not encourage aggression in positions of power. If males were universally more aggressive than females, we should do all we can to deny them a role in business and to keep them from occupying positions of power.

Consider finally the question of whether certain differences ought to be exploited or compensated. The fact (if it is a fact) that men and women differ in particular ways does not alone dictate how we ought to deal with those differences. Some differences between people are differences we rely on in constructing a social order—differences as to interests, needs, and desires, for example. But some differences are ones we attempt to correct or compensate for rather than to exploit. We don't give the curably ill different jobs simply because they are ill; we try to cure them. We don't simply arrange work for amputees which is better done without certain limbs; we at least attempt to supply mechanical replacements. If there are differences which *cannot* be corrected or compensated for, of course, we learn to live with them. But nothing has been said to indicate, and as far as I know none of the data shows, that any of the supposed differences between men and women are differences for which correction or compensatory treatment is impossible. The statistics on aggression do not show that males could not be trained to be less aggressive, or females to be more so. Superior verbal ability on the part of females does not mean that males could not, with proper compensatory training, reach the same level. Thus one might conclude from the data regarding sexual differences not that we ought to assign career-roles along sexual lines, but that we owe each group compensatory training as a corrective for its shortcomings, so that in the end the only determinant of social role will be individual interest and desire. The point here is simply that differences alone do not show that our society ought to be constructed so as to exploit those differences; we might equally well conclude that society ought to attempt to correct them or compensate for them.

This is, I am sure, radically incomplete as a catalog of weaknesses in the inference from data regarding sexual differences to recommendations regarding social roles. But it is sufficient to show that the argument with which we began is a simple non sequitur as it stands. We have assumed that the data at issue are suitably hard data revealing genuinely fundamental differences, an assumption challenged in the beginning. But even given that assumption the conclusions generally drawn regarding social roles do not follow. In order legitimately to conclude anything at all regarding the desirability of social role differentiation we must deal with a number of additional and complicating factors. We must consider whether differences ought to be exploited or compensated, we must make explicit and defend assumptions as to how society ought to be, and we need firm evidence rather than armchair speculation as to links between particular characteristics and effectiveness at certain tasks. We must be wary of misreading statistical generalizations as universal claims, and must avoid treating prima facie and partial qualifications for particular roles as if they were sole qualifications. Without these the argument simply falls short, no matter how tight our data regarding sexual differences.

Does this indicate that the data, even if legitimate, shows nothing which might be of significance to social decisions? That would be too strong. If there *are* fundamental sexual differences, that fact may be one of moral importance in deciding how society ought to be. Together with other claims and arguments it *could* even be part of a satisfactory justification of social role differentiation along sexual lines. But no data of this type, however good, would alone dictate the shape our society ought to take.

IV. Conclusion

The discussion above has a clear central theme, even if it does not build to a conclusive agrumentative climax. Contemporary data regarding sex differences is quite often taken as a justification for social recommendations involving social role differentiation on sexual lines. I have tried to detail a number of objections against the use of such an argument and against some assumptions behind it. The data on which such arguments rest is often data of which we should be suspicious, for a variety of reasons. In cases in which we are significantly ignorant, there may be ethical reasons for preferring a social explanation rather than the fundamental difference on which the standard argument relies. And even where the data is as tight and conclusive as one might like, the conclusion generally drawn is not one which follows in any rigorous sense.

It is not unusual for discussions of sex differences to end with an appeal for further testing. I will not make such an appeal. In light of the deep difficulties of attempting any satisfactory test, in light of the social dangers of a test gone wrong, in light of the inconclusiveness of the best of data for any social purposes, and given the variety of genuinely pressing demands on our social energies, I see little reason for continuing such testing.

Notes

1. See E.E. Maccoby and C.N. Jacklin, *The Psychology of Sex Differences* (Stanford: Stanford University Press, 1974). A more recent piece on visual-spatial abilities is L.J. Harris, "Sex Differences in Spatial Ability: Possible Environmental, Genetic, and Neurological Factors," in *Asymmetrical Function of the Brain*, ed. M. Kinsbourne (Cambridge: Cambridge University Press, 1979), pp. 405–522.

2. Monte Buchsbaum cites this difference and offers a biochemical explanation in "The Sensoriat in the Brain," *Psychology Today* 11 (May 1978): 96–104.

3. See Diane McGuinness and Karl H. Pribram, "The Origins of Sensory Bias in the Development of Gender Differences in Perception and Cognition," in *Cognitive Growth and Development: Essays in Memory of Herbert G. Birch,* ed. Morton Bortner (New York: Brunner/Mazel, 1979), pp. 3–56.

4. Sandra F. Witelson, "Sex and the Single Hemisphere: Specialization of the Right Hemisphere for Spatial Processing," *Science* 193, no. 4521 (1976), pp. 425–27.

5. Aggression is probably *the* standard sex difference, with more studies to its credit than any other. See E.E. Maccoby, *The Development of Sex Differences* (Stanford: Stanford University Press, 1966) and E.E. Maccoby and C.N. Jacklin, *The Psychology of Sex Differences,* op. cit.

6. The terms "manipulative" and "communicative," and various echoes of the argument, appear in Diane McGuinness and Karl H. Pribram, "The Origins of Sensory Bias," op. cit.

7. Some examples include Witelson, "Sex and the Single Hemisphere," McGuinness and Pribram, "The Origins of Sensory Bias," Monte Buchsbaum, "The Sensoriat in the Brain," and informal quotations from Jerre Levy in Daniel Goleman, "Special Abilities of the Sexes: Do They Begin in the Brain?," *Psychology Today* 11 (November 1978): 48–59, 120. A history of this and related arguments appears in Stephanie A. Shields, "Functionalism, Darwinism, and the Psychology of Women: A Study in Social Myth," *American Psychologist* 30, no. 7 (1975): 739–54.

8. Were our data to show no sex differences at all then it might be proposed that we would have a very strong case for there being fundamental differences somehow "compensated" by differential social treatment.

A distinction is sometimes drawn between biological and psychological sex differences; between height in inches, for example, and tendencies toward aggression. In what follows I concentrate for the most part on questions of psychological differences, simply because these seem the most interesting. But in most respects the argument would apply equally well to either type of trait, and I am wary of attempting a sharp demarcation between them.

9. One might also distinguish between psychological and behavioral traits on the grounds that the same psychological traits might have different behavioral manifestations in different settings or within different socially enforced roles. Though I have not relied on this distinction, and though it seems to me to be one very difficult to distinguish in practice, the discussion below of aggression and stress seems to emphasize this importance.

10. From Monte Buchsbaum, "The Sensoriat in the Brain," op. cit.

11. It might be suggested that in such cases the data can be of no help to us at all; that the data cannot decide between competing theories because it is that data which each of the theories is to explain. But this would overlook the dual role of scientific data vis-à-vis scientific theories. That which a theory explains (or seems to explain) is at the same time evidence for the truth of the theory.

The issue, of course, is which of the competing theories *better* explain the data, a matter involving the complexities and subtleties of breadth, ties with other bodies of theory and simplicity.

12. The argument has the general form of Pascal's wager, and like Pascal's wager shows strictly not that a particular alternative is true but that a particular alternative ought to be believed, or that one ought to act as if it is true. In "The Subjection of Women," J.S. Mill comes at least close to this form of argument in maintaining that given natural sex differences, there would be no need to enforce socially distinct roles. Since what women "can do, but not so well as the men who are their competitors, competition suffices to exclude them from . . ." we have nothing to lose in acting as if there are no fundamental differences. But the argument presented here differs from Mill's in a number of major respects. A convenient abridgment of Mill's essay is included in *The Feminist Papers*, ed. Alice R. Rossi (New York: Bantam Books, 1974), pp. 196–238.

13. Whether the loss of efficiency we risk in each case is the same is, perhaps, a more complicated question. Depending on how we (wrongly) treat certain differences and on what effects our incorrect treatment in fact has, these might not balance out. I am obliged to David Pomerantz for bringing this complication to my attention.

14. It should be noted, however, that all possible forms of treatment of social differences as if they were fundamental may not involve equal degrees of injustice. Exploitation of merely social differences as if they were fundamental, for example, may be a more extreme case than attempted correction of social differences as if they were fundamental.

15. Were these prospective losses *only* characteristic of (3), we might still argue that they fail to balance out the radical injustice of (2). But that would call for a more complex argument concerning the assignment of various weights to various social goals, which I have not attempted to provide here.

16. Consider, for example, a hypothetical sample such as the following, using W_1 through W_5 to represent five women and M_1 through M_5 to represent five men:

W_1	.75	M_1	1.0
W_2	.75	M_2	1.0
W_3	.75	M_3	.5
W_4	.75	M_4	.5
W_5	.75	M^5	.5
Average:	.75	Average:	.70

The average score for women is .75, and for men is a mere .70. But those two individuals who score highest are male, and if we have two openings best filled by highest scorers, with no other considerations at issue, they will best be filled by these two men.

17. Consider, for instance, the following sample:

W_1	.85	M_1	.85
W_2	.75	M_2	.85
W_3	.75	M_3	.85
W_4	.75	M_4	.85
W_5	.65	M_5	.10
Average:	.75	Average:	.70

Let us suppose that we have an opening which demands a high score, and that we have set .80 as a specific requirement. Our chances of drawing a satisfactory candidate from the pool on the left are 1/5, from a randomly mixed pool are 5/10, and from the pool on the right are 4/5, despite the fact that the average score for the right-hand column is lower than the average for that on the left.

18. The sample in footnote 16 is one in which the highest score is not a woman's. A sample in which the lowest score is not a man's, though the average male score is lower, can easily be constructed:

W_1	1.0	M_1	.70
W_2	.5	M_2	.70
Average:	.75	Average:	.70

The following sample is one in which the score of the majority of men is higher than the score of the majority of women:

W_1	.75	M_1	.80
W_2	.75	M_2	.80
W_3	.75	M_3	.80
W_4	.75	M_4	.55
W_5	.75	M_5	.55
Average:	.75	Average:	.70

For a somewhat simpler discussion of statistical frequencies and sex differences, see Joyce Trebilcot, "Sex Roles: The Argument From Nature," in *Feminity, Masculinity and Androgyny,* ed., Mary Vetterling-Braggin (Lanham, Md.: Littlefield, Adams, 1982) pp. 40–48. The general spirit of Trebilcot's discussion and mine are, I think, very similar.

19. Interestingly enough, "branching quantifiers" appear quite frequently in trying to represent the data. Some of the difficulties and ambiguities of grammatical and logical forms are made clear in Jon Barwise, "On Branching Quantifiers in English," *Journal of Philosophical Logic* 8 (1979): 47–80.

20. An example taken from Diane McGuinness and Karl H. Pribram, "The Origins of Sensory Bias." In "Sex Differences in Mental and Behavioral Traits," *Genetic Psychological Monographs* (1968), J.E. Garai and A. Schienfeld classify those abilities which favor females as "clerical skills" (pp. 169–299).

PART TWO

Traditional Roles for Men

2

The Enduring Appeals of Battle

J. Glenn Gray

I feel cheerful and am well-pleased. . . . What is ahead may be grim and dreadful but I shall be spiritually more at rest in the heart of the carnage than somewhere in the rear. Since I have lent myself to the war, I want to pay the price and know it at its worst. (War journal, January 31, 1944)

My friend wrote once late in the war that he often thought of me as *the soldier*. To him I had come to stand for the qualities that he associated with universal man at war. The idea, I recall, both flattered and insulted me a little at first but ended by impressing me with its truth, though I should never have conceived it on my own. I wrote in my journal: "Perhaps the worst that can be said is that I am *becoming* a soldier. To be a soldier! That is at best to be something less than a man. To say nothing of being a philosopher." Since then I have frequently wondered what it meant to be a "soldier" and why I regarded myself then, insofar as I was a soldier, as less than a man.

At the time I wrote these lines I faced the grim realization of how narrowed all our desires had become. The night before, one of the women in the town where we were staying had declared: *"Das Essen ist die Hauptsache."* Food is the main thing. And the words had burned into my brain with the force of a proverb. The majority of my fellows seemed content with the satisfaction of their natural urges—eating, drinking, and lusting for women. Interests and refinements that transcended these primitive needs, and that I had built up over the years, were rapidly falling away, and I felt that I was becoming simply one of the others.

In a German newspaper, taken from a prisoner, I read a letter from a soldier long years on the Russian front, who lamented that the war had robbed him of any sense of self-identity and that he no longer possessed an ego and a personal fate. I realize now, much better than I did then, that there was another force much more determining than simple need and desire. It was the emotional environment of warfare, more specifically, the atmosphere of violence. The threat to life and safety that the presence of the opponent, "the enemy," represented created this climate of feeling. Near the front it was impossible to ignore, consciously or unconsciously, the stark fact that out there were men who would gladly kill you, if and when they got the chance. As a consequence, an individual was dependent on others, on people who could not formerly have entered the periphery of his consciousness. For them in turn, he was of interest only as a center of force, a wielder of weapons, a means of security and survival. This confraternity of danger and exposure is unequaled in forging links among people of unlike desire and temperament, links that are utilitarian and narrow but no less passionate because of their accidental and general character.

In such a climate men may hold fast in memory to their civilian existence of yesterday and stubbornly resist, as I tried to do, the encroachments of the violent and the irrational. They may write home to their parents and sweethearts that they are unchanged, and they may even be convinced of it. But the soldier who has yielded himself to the fortunes of war, has sought to kill and to escape being killed, or who has even lived long enough in the disordered landscape of battle, is no longer what he was. He becomes in some sense a fighter, whether he wills it or not—at least most men do. His moods and disposition are affected by the presence of others and the encompassing environment of threat and fear. He must surrender in a measure to the will of others and to superior force. In a real sense he becomes a fighting man, a *Homo furens*.

This is surely part of what it means to be a soldier, and what it has always meant. *Homo furens* is, so to speak, a subspecies of the genus Homo sapiens. Obviously, man is more than a fighter and other than a fighter, in our age and formerly. In some generations—alas! too few as yet—organized war has been little more than an episode. Even those generations who have had to spend much time in combat considered themselves farmers, teachers, factory workers, and so on, as well as fighters. Man as warrior is only partly a man, yet, fatefully enough, this aspect of him is capable of transforming the whole. When given free play, it is able to subordinate other aspects of the personality, repress civilian habits of mind, and make the soldier as fighter a different kind of creature from the former worker, farmer, or clerk.

Millions of men in our day—like millions before us—have learned to live in war's strange element and have discovered in it a powerful fascination. The emotional environment of warfare has always been compelling; it has drawn most men under its spell. Reflection and calm reasoning are alien to it. I wrote in my war journal that I was obsessed with "the tyranny of the present"; the past and the future did not concern me. It was hard for me to think, to be alone. When the signs of peace were visible, I wrote, in some regret: "The purgative force of danger which makes men coarser but perhaps more human will soon be lost and the first months of peace will make some of us yearn for the old days of conflict."

Beyond doubt there are many who simply endure war, hating every moment. Though they may enjoy garrison life or military maneuvers, they experience nothing but distaste and horror for combat itself. Still, those who complain the most may not be immune from war's appeals. Soldiers complain as an inherited right and traditional duty, and few wish to admit to a taste for war. Yet many men both hate and love combat. They know why they hate it; it is harder to know and to be articulate about why they love it. The novice may be eager at times to describe his emotions in combat, but it is the battle-hardened veterans to whom battle has offered the deeper appeals. For some of them the war years are what Dixon Wecter has well called "the one great lyric passage in their lives."

What are these secret attractions of war, the ones that have persisted in the West despite revolutionary changes in the methods of warfare? I believe that they are: the delight in seeing, the delight in comradeship, the delight in destruction. Some fighters know one appeal and not the others, some experience all three, and some may, of course, feel other appeals that I do not know. These three had reality for me, and I have found them also throughout the literature of war.

War as a spectacle, as something to see, ought never to be underestimated. There is in all of us what the Bible calls "the lust of the eye," a phrase at once precise and of the widest connotation. It is precise because human beings possess as a primitive urge this love of watching. We fear we will miss something worth seeing. This passion to see surely precedes in most of us the urge to participate in or to aid. Anyone who has watched people crowding around the scene of an accident on the highway realizes that the lust of the eye is real. Anyone who has watched the faces of people at a fire knows it is real. Seeing sometimes absorbs us utterly; it is as though the human being became one great eye. The eye is lustful because it requires the novel, the unusual, the spectacular. It cannot satiate itself on the familiar, the routine, the everyday.

This lust may stoop to mindless curiosity, a primordial impulse. Its typical response is an open-minded gaping at a parade or at the explosion of a hydrogen bomb. How many men in each generation have been drawn into the twilight of confused and murderous battle "to see what it is like"? This appeal of war is usually described as the desire to escape the monotony of civilian life and the cramping restrictions of an unadventurous existence. People are often bored with a day that does not offer variety, distraction, threat, and insecurity. They crave the satisfaction of the astonishing. Although war notoriously offers monotony and boredom enough, it also offers the outlandish, the exotic, and the strange. It offers the opportunity of gaping at other lands and other peoples, at curious implements of war, at groups of others like themselves marching in order, and at the captured enemy in a cage.

However, sensuous curiosity is only one level of seeing. The word "see," with its many derivatives, like "insight" and "vision," has an imaginative and intellectual connotation which is far more expansive than the physical. Frequently we are unable to separate these levels of seeing, to distinguish the outer from the inner eye. This is probably no accident. The human being is, after all, a unity, and the sensuous, imaginative, and intellectual elements of his nature can fuse when he is absorbed. Mindless curiosity is not separated as much as we like to believe from what art lovers call the disinterested contemplation of beauty. The delight in battle as a mere spectacle may progress almost insensibly to an aesthetic contemplation or to a more dominantly intellectual contemplation of its awfulness. From the simplest soldier who gazes openmouthed at the panorama of battle in his portion of the field to the trained artist observing the scene, there is, I believe, only a difference of degree. The "seeing" both are engaged in is for them an end in itself before it becomes a spur to action. The dominant motive in both cases appears to be neither the desire for knowledge, though there is much that is instructive in the scene, nor the need to act, though that, too, will become imperative. Their "seeing" is for the sake of seeing, the lust of the eye, where the eye stands for the whole human being, for man the observer.

There is a popular conviction that war and battle are the sphere of ugliness, and, since aesthetic delight is associated with the beautiful, it may be concluded that war is the natural enemy of the aesthetic. I fear that this is in large part an illusion. It is, first of all, wrong to believe that only beauty can give us aesthetic delight; the ugly can please us too, as every artist knows. And furthermore, beauty in various guises is hardly foreign to scenes of battle. While it is undeniable that the disorder and distortion and the violation of nature that conflict brings are ugly beyond compare, there are also color and movement, variety, panoramic sweep, and sometimes even momentary proportion and harmony. If we think of beauty and ugliness without their usual moral overtones, there is often a weird but genuine beauty in the sight of massed men and weapons in combat. Reputedly, it was the sight of advancing columns of men under fire that impelled General Robert E. Lee to remark to one of his staff: "It is well that war is so terrible—we would grow too fond of it." . . .

As I reflect further, it becomes clear, however, that the term "beauty," used in any ordinary sense, is not the major appeal in such spectacles. Instead, it is the fascination that manifestations of power and magnitude hold for the human spirit. Some scenes of battle, much like storms over the ocean or sunsets on the desert or the night sky seen through a telescope, are able to overawe the single individual and hold him in a spell. He is lost in their majesty. His ego temporarily deserts him, and he is absorbed into what he sees. An awareness of power that far surpasses his limited imagination transports him into a state of mind unknown in his everyday experiences. Fleeting as these rapt moments may be, they are, for the majority of men, an escape from themselves that is very different from the escapes induced by sexual love or alcohol. This raptness is a joining and not a losing, a deprivation of self in exchange for a union with objects that were hitherto foreign. Yes, the chief aesthetic appeal of war surely lies in this feeling of the sublime, to which we, children of nature, are directed whether we desire it or not. Astonishment and wonder and awe appear to be part of our deepest being, and war offers them an exercise field par excellence. As I wrote:

> Yesterday morning we left Rome and took up the pursuit of the rapidly fleeing Germans. And again the march was past ruined, blackened villages, destroyed vehicles, dead and mangled corpses of German soldiers, dead and stinking horses, blown bridges, and clouds of dust that blackened our faces and filled our clothes. . . . Later I watched a full moon sail through a cloudy sky . . . saw German bombers fly past and our antiaircraft bursts around them. . . . I felt again the aching beauty of this incomparable land. I remembered everything that I had ever been and was. It was painful and glorious.

What takes place in us when we are under the spell of this powerful mood? It is often said that its deepest satisfaction lies in the sense of personal exemption from the fate of others. We watch them exposed to powers that overwhelm them, and we enjoy the feelings of superiority of the secure. When human beings are not involved, and feelings of the sublime steal over us at the majestic in nature, this can be traced to a heightened sense of the ego in one way or another. As spectators we are superior to that which we survey. In my journal are these words:

> This evening we watched a beautiful sunset over the Tyrrhenian Sea. From our window we looked out on the wall-enclosed gardens of Carano,

where flowers blossomed and peach trees made the air sweet with their white blossoms. Beyond them stretched fields and, farther, the mountains, Formia, Gaeta, the sea. As the sun sank behind the mountains, it illumined a cloud that was hanging low. As we watched the wonderful pageantry of nature, the sound of cannon was carried in on the evening air. We were forced to realize that a few miles away, in this area we were gazing at, men lurked with death in their hearts. We were looking over no man's land. As it grew dark, huge signs of fire appeared on the mountain. It was mysterious, but we had no doubt that it had to do with death and destruction.

The feeling of momentary depression, as Kant puts it, which we initially succumb to when looking through a telescope at the vastness of the heavens and the insignificance of ourselves in comparison is soon supplanted by the consciousness that we are the astronomers. It is we who know that the heavens are empty and vast, and the heavens presumably know nothing of us. The human spirit triumphs over these blind forces and lifeless powers of nature. Such scenes as I described above could be explained, by this view, as the exultation of the spectators that they were not actors or sufferers, for the sublime mood derives from a separation of the spectator from the spectacle, and its pleasantness consists in the superiority the ego feels.

But such a view is wrong, or, at the very least, one-sided. It is the viewpoint of an egoistic, atomistic psychology rather than the product of close observation. The awe that steals over us at such times is not essentially a feeling of triumph, but, on the contrary, a recognition of power and grandeur to which we are subject. There is not so much a separation of the self from the world as a subordination of the self to it. We are able to disregard personal danger at such moments by transcending the self, by forgetting our separateness.

Last evening I sat on a rock outside the town and watched a modern battle, an artillery duel . . . the panorama was so farreaching that I could see both the explosion of the guns and where their speedy messengers struck. . . . Several shells of replying batteries landed fairly close and made my perch not the safest of vantage points. But it was an interesting, stirring sight. After a while the firing died down and evening shadows came over the valley. A townsman carrying a pail of swill for his hogs came by, fell into conversation, and then asked me to await his return, when he would take me to his home for a glass of wine.

Perhaps the majority of men cannot become so absorbed in a spectacle that they overcome fear of pain and death. Still, it is a common-enough phenomenon on the battlefield that men expose themselves quite recklessly for the sake of seeing. If ever the world is blown to bits by some superbomb, there will be those who will watch the spectacle to the last minute, without fear, disinterestedly and with detachment. I do not mean that there is lack of interest in this disinterestedness or lack of emotion in this detachment. Quite the contrary. But the self is no longer important to the observer; it is absorbed into the objects with which it is concerned.

I think the distinctive thing about the feeling of the sublime is its ecstatic character, ecstatic in the original meaning of the term, namely, a state of being outside the self. Even in the common experience of mindless curiosity there is a momentary suppression of the ego, a slight breaking down of the barriers of the self, though insignificant in comparison with the rarer moods when we are filled with awe. This ecstasy satisfies because we are conscious of a power outside us with which we can merge in the relation of parts to whole. Feelings neither of triumph nor of depression predominate. The pervasive sense of wonder satisfies us because we are assured that we are part of this circling world, not divorced from it, or shut up within the walls of the self and delivered over to the insufficiency of the ego. Certain psychologists would call this just another escape from the unpleasant facts of the self's situation. If so, it is an escape of a very different sort from the usual. We feel rescued from the emptiness within us. In losing ourselves we gain a relationship to something greater than the self, and the foreign character of the surrounding world is drastically reduced. . . .

Another appeal of war, the communal experience we call comradeship, is thought, on the other hand, to be especially moral and the one genuine advantage of battle that peace can seldom offer. Whether this is true or not deserves to be investigated. The term ''comradeship'' covers a large number of relationships, from the most personal to the anonymous and general, and here I will consider only some essentials of military comradeship. What calls it into being in battle, what strengthens or weakens it, what is its essential attraction?

The feeling of belonging together that men in battle often find a cementing force needs first to be awakened by an external reason for fighting, but the feeling is by no means dependent on this reason. The cause that calls comradeship into being may be the defense of one's country, the propagation of the one true religious faith, or a passionate political ideology; it may be the maintenance of honor or the recovery of a Helen of Troy. So long as there is a cause, the hoped-for objective may be relatively unimportant in itself. When, through military reverses or the fatiguing and often horrible experiences of combat, the original purpose becomes obscured, the fighter is often sustained solely by the determination not to let down his comrades.

Numberless soldiers have died, more or less willingly, not for country or honor or religious faith or for any other abstract good, but because they realized that by fleeing their post and rescuing themselves, they would expose their companions to greater danger. Such loyalty to the group is the essence of fighting morale. The commander who can preserve and strengthen it knows that all other psychological or physical factors are little in comparison. The feeling of loyalty, it is clear, is the result, and not the cause, of comradeship. Comrades are loyal to each other spontaneously and without any need for reasons. Men may learn to be loyal out of fear or from rational conviction, loyal even to those they dislike. But such loyalty is rarely reliable with great masses of men unless it has some cement in spontaneous liking and the feeling of belonging.

Though comradeship is dependent on being together physically in time and space, it is not a herding animal instinct. Little can be learned, I am convinced, from attempting to compare animal and human forms of association. In extreme danger and need, there is undeniably a minimal satisfaction in having others of your own species in your vicinity. The proverb that "misery loves company" is not without basis, particularly in situations where defense and aggression are involved. But it is equally true that men can live in the same room and share the same suffering without any sense of belonging together. They can live past each other and be irresponsible toward each other, even when their welfare is clearly dependent on co-operation.

German soldiers who endured Russian prisoner-of-war camps in the decade after World War II have described convincingly how the Communist system succeeded in destroying any sense of comradeship among prisoners simply by making the results of individual labor the basis of food allotments. Under a system like this, men can not only eat their fill but also enjoy superfluity without any concern for a mate who may slowly be starving to death. This lamentable fact about human nature has too often been observed to require much further confirmation. The physical proximity of men can do no more than create the minimal conditions of comradeship. It no more explains the communal appeal of war than it explains why people love cities.

What then are the important components of comradeship, if physical presence is only a minimal condition? The one that occurs immediately is organization for a common goal. Even a very loose type of organization can induce many people to moderate their self-assertiveness and accommodate themselves to the direction of a superpersonal will. Everyone is aware of the vast difference between a number of men as a chance collection of individuals and the same number as an organized group or community. A community has purpose and plan, and there is in us an almost instinctive recognition of the connection between unity and strength.

Those who stand in disorganized masses against smaller groups of the organized are always aware of the tremendous odds against them. The sight of huge crowds of prisoners of war being herded toward collection centers by a few guards with rifles slung over their backs is one filled with pathos. It is not the absence of weapons that makes these prisoners helpless before their guards. It is the absence of a common will, the failing assurance that others will act in concert with you against the conquerors.

But organization is of many kinds, and the military kind is special in aiming at common and concrete goals. The organization of a civilian community, a city, for example, is not without goals, but they are rarely concrete, and many members are hardly aware of their existence. If a civilian community has goals with more reality and power to endure than military goals, as I believe it does, its goals are, nevertheless, unable to generate the degree of loyalty that a military organization can.

In war it is a commonplace of command that the goals of the fighting forces need to be clear and to be known. Naturally, the overall goal is to win the war and then go home. But in any given action, the goal is to overcome the attacking enemy or, if you are the attacker, to win the stated objective. Any fighting unit must have a limited and specific objective, and the more defined and bounded it is, the greater the willingness, as a rule, on the part of soldiers to abandon their natural desire for self-preservation. Officers soon learn to dread hazy and ill-defined orders from above. If the goal is physical, a piece of earth to take or defend, a machine-gun nest to destroy, a strong point to annihilate, officers are much more likely to evoke the sense of comradeship. They realize that comradeship at first develops through the consciousness of an obstacle to be overcome through common effort. A fighting unit with morale is one in which many are of like mind and determination, unconsciously agreed on the suppression of individual desires in the interest of a shared purpose.

Organization for a common and concrete goal in peacetime organizations does not evoke anything like the degree of comradeship commonly known in war. Evidently, the presence of danger is distinctive and important. Men then are organized for a goal whose realization involves the real possibility of death or injury. How does danger break down the barriers of the self and give man an experience of community? The answer to this question is the key to one of the oldest and most enduring incitements to battle.

Danger provides a certain spice to experience; this is common knowledge. It quickens the pulse and makes us more aware of being alive by calling attention to our physical selves. The thrill of the chase in hunting, of riding a horse very fast, or of driving an automobile recklessly is of this sort. But the excitement created in us by such activities has little communal significance. Its origin appears to be sexual, if we understand sex in the wide sense given to it by Freud. The increased vitality we feel where danger is incidental is due to awareness of mastery over the environment. It is an individualist, not a communal, drive.

The excitement and thrill of battle, on the other hand, are of a different sort, for there danger is central and not incidental. There is little of the play element about combat, however much there may have been in training for it. Instead, for most soldiers there is the hovering inescapable sense of irreversibility. "This is for keeps," as soldier slang is likely to put it. This profound earnestness is by no means devoid of lightheartedness, as seen in teasing and horseplay, but men are conscious that they are on a one-way street, so to speak, and what they do or fail to do can be of great consequence. Those who enter into battle, as distinguished from those who only hover on its fringes, do not fight as duelists fight. Almost automatically, they fight as a unit, a group. Training can help a great deal in bringing this about more quickly and easily in an early stage. But training can only help to make actual what is inherent. As any commander knows, an hour or two of combat can do more to weld a unit together than can months of intensive training.

Many veterans who are honest with themselves will admit, I believe, that the experience of communal effort in battle, even under the altered conditions of modern war, has been a high point in their lives. Despite the horror, the weariness, the grime, and the hatred, participation with others in the chances of battle had its unforgettable side, which they would not want to have missed. For anyone who has not experienced it himself, the feeling is hard to comprehend, and, for the participant, hard to explain to anyone else. Probably the feeling of liberation is nearly basic. It is this feeling that explains the curious combination of earnestness and lightheartedness so often noted in men in battle.

Many of us can experience freedom as a thrilling reality, something both serious and joyous, only when we are acting in unison with others for a concrete goal that costs something absolute for its attainment. Individual freedom to do what we will with our lives and our talents, the freedom of self-determination, appears to us most of the time as frivolous or burdensome. Such freedom leaves us empty and alone, feeling undirected and insignificant. Only comparatively few of us know how to make this individual freedom productive and joyous. But communal freedom can pervade nearly everyone and carry everything before it. This elemental fact about freedom the opponents of democracy have learned well, and it constitutes for them a large initial advantage.

The lightheartedness that communal participation brings has little of the sensuous or merely pleasant about it, just as the earnestness has little of the calculating or rational. Both derive instead from a consciousness of power that is supra-individual. We feel earnest and gay at such moments because we are liberated from our individual impotence and are drunk with the power that union with our fellows brings. In moments like these many have a vague awareness of how isolated and separate their lives have hitherto been and how much they have missed by living in the narrow circle of family or a few friends. With the boundaries of the self expanded, they sense a kinship never known before. Their "I" passes insensibly into a "we," "my" becomes "our," and individual fate loses its central importance.

At its height, this sense of comradeship is an ecstasy not unlike the aesthetic ecstasy previously described, though occasioned by different forces. In most of us there is a genuine longing for community with our human species, and at the same time an awkwardness and helplessness about finding the way to achieve it. Some extreme experience—mortal danger or the threat of destruction—is necessary to bring us fully together with our comrades or with nature. This is a great pity, for there are surely alternative ways more creative and less dreadful, if men would only seek them out. Until now, war has appealed because we discover some of the mysteries of communal joy in its forbidden depths. Comradeship reaches its peak in battle.

The secret of comradeship has not been exhausted, however, in the feeling of freedom and power instilled in us by communal effort in combat. There is something more and equally important. The sense of power and liberation that comes over men at such moments stems from a source beyond the union of men. I believe it is nothing less than the assurance of immortality that makes self-sacrifice at these moments so relatively easy. Men are true comrades only when each is ready to give up his life for the other, without reflection and without thought of personal loss. Who can doubt that every war, the two world wars no less than former ones, has produced true comradeship like this?

Such sacrifice seems hard and heroic to those who have never felt communal ecstasy. In fact, it is not nearly so difficult as many less absolute acts in peacetime and in civilian life, for death becomes in a measure unreal and unbelievable to one who is sharing his life with his companions. Immortality is not something remote and otherworldly, possibly or probably true and real; on the contrary, it becomes a present and self-evident fact.

Nothing is further from the truth than the insistence of certain existentialist philosophers that each person must die his own death and experience it unsharably. If that were so, how many lives would have been spared on the battlefield! But in fact, death for men united with each other can be shared as few other of life's great moments can be. To be sure, it is not death as we know it usually in civilian life. In the German language men never die in battle. They *fall*. The term is exact for the expression of self-sacrifice when it is motivated by the feeling of comradeship. I may fall, but I do not die, for that which is real in me goes forward and lives on in the comrades for whom I gave up my physical life.

Let me not be misunderstood. It is unquestionably true that thousands of soldiers die in battle, miserable, alone, and embittered, without any conviction of self-sacrifice and without any other satisfactions. I suspect the percentage of such soldiers has increased markedly in recent wars. But for those who in every battle are seized by the passion for self-sacrifice, dying has lost its terrors because its reality has vanished.

There must be a similarity between this willingness of soldier-comrades for self-sacrifice and the willingness of saints and martyrs to die for their religious faith. It is probably no accident that the religions of the West have not cast away their military terminology or even their militant character—"Onward, Christian soldiers! Marching as to war . . ." nor that our wars are defended in terms of devotion and salvation. The true believer must be ready to give up his life for the faith. And if he is a genuine saint he will regard this sacrifice as no loss, for the self has become indestructible in being united with a supreme reality. There are, of course, important differences. The reality for which the martyr sacrifices himself is not visible and intimate like the soldier's. The martyr usually dies alone, scorned by the multitude. In this sense his lot is infinitely harder. It is hardly surprising that few men are capable of dying joyfully as martyrs whereas thousands are capable of self-sacrifice in wartime. Nevertheless, a basic point of resemblance remains, namely, that death has lost not only its sting but its reality, too, for the self that dies is little in comparison with that which survives and triumphs. . . .

It is true that we in the West are frequently infatuated with the idea of sacrifice, particularly self-sacrifice. Why are some people so strongly repelled and others again and again attracted by the impulse to self-sacrifice? Or why do both attraction and repulsion have place in the same breast at different moments? As moralists, we are repelled, I suspect, because the impulse to sacrifice is not subject to rational judgment and control. It takes hold of us and forces us against our will, later claiming justification from some higher authority than the human. As often as not, it puts itself at the service of an evil cause, perhaps more frequently than in the service of the good. The mysterious power that such leaders as Napoleon, Hitler, and Stalin had in their being that enabled them to create a love for self-sacrifice perplexes us endlessly. We cannot condemn it with full conviction, since it seems likely that both leaders and led were in large degree powerless to prevent the impulses that dominated them.

Yet such power is appalling beyond measure and from a rational viewpoint deserving of the deepest condemnation. The limits of free will and morality are transgressed, and man is forced to seek religious and metaphysical justification for self-sacrifice, even when committed in an evil cause. As in the aesthetic appeal of war, when we reach the impulse of the sublime, so in the communal appeal of comradeship, when we reach the impulse to self-sacrifice, we are confronted with contradictions that are deeply embedded in our culture, if not in human nature itself. What our moral self tells us is abhorrent, our religious self and our aesthetic self yearn for as the ultimate good. This is part of the riddle of war.

If we are truly wise, perhaps we should not want to alter these capacities of our human nature, even though we suffer from them immeasurably and may yet succumb to their threat. For the willingness to sacrifice self, like the attraction of the sublime, is what makes possible the higher reaches of the spirit into the realms of poetry, philosophy, and genuine religion. They prevent our best men from losing interest in and hope for our species. They stand in the way of discouragement and cynicism. As moralists, we can condemn Saint Paul and Saint Augustine for their mystical conviction that without sacrifice no purgation from sin is possible. But we should be cautious in so doing, for they were convinced that without the supra-moral act, we human beings are not able to lead even a normally moral existence. Though they were not disposed to believe that God was without moral qualities, they were quite certain that there was more in His universe than the determinations of good and evil. For them the "I am" preceded logically and in time the "I ought." And vast numbers of people have agreed with them that the religious order is superior to the moral, though they continue to be confused about how the two are related.

Are we not right in honoring the fighter's impulse to sacrifice himself for a comrade, even though it be done, as it so frequently is, in an evil cause? I think so. It is some kind of world historical pathos that the striving for union and for immortality must again and again be consummated while men are in the service of destruction. I do not doubt for a moment that wars are made many times more deadly because of this striving and this impulse. Yet I would not want to be without the assurance their existence gives me that our species has a different destiny than is granted to other animals. Though we often sink below them, we can at moments rise above them, too.

If the lust of the eye and the yearning for communication with our fellows were the only appeals of combat, we might be confident that they would be ultimately capable of satisfaction in other ways. But my own observation and the history of warfare both convince me that there is a third impulse to battle much more sinister than these. Anyone who has watched men on the battlefield at work with artillery, or looked into the eyes of veteran killers fresh from slaughter, or studied the descriptions of bombardiers' feelings while smashing their targets, finds hard to escape the conclusion that there is a delight in destruction. A walk across any battlefield shortly after the guns have fallen silent is convincing enough. A sensitive person is sure to be oppressed by a spirit of evil there, a radical evil which suddenly makes the medieval images of hell and the thousand devils of that imagination believable. This evil appears to surpass mere human malice and to demand explanation in cosmological and religious terms.

Men who have lived in the zone of combat long enough to be veterans are sometimes possessed by a fury that makes them capable of anything. Blinded by the rage to destroy and supremely careless of consequences, they storm against the enemy until they are either victorious, dead, or utterly exhausted. It is as if they are seized by a demon and are no longer in control of themselves. From the Homeric account of the sacking of Troy to the conquest of Dienbienphu, Western literature is filled with descriptions of soldiers as berserkers and mad destroyers.

Perhaps the following account from the diary of Ernst Juenger in World War I may stand for many because it is so concise and exactly drawn. It describes the beginning of the last German offensive in the West.

> The great moment had come. The curtain of fire lifted from the front trenches. We stood up.
>
> With a mixture of feelings, evoked by bloodthirstiness, rage, and intoxication, we moved in step, ponderously but irresistibly toward the enemy lines. I was well ahead of the company, followed by Vinke and a one-year veteran named Haake. My right hand embraced the shaft of my pistol, my left a riding stick of bamboo cane. I was boiling with a mad rage, which had taken hold of me and all the others in an incomprehensible fashion. The overwhelming wish to kill gave wings to my feet. Rage pressed bitter tears from my eyes.
>
> The monstrous desire for annihilation, which hovered over the battlefield, thickened the brains of the men and submerged them in a red fog. We called to each other in sobs and stammered disconnected sentences. A neutral observer might have perhaps believed that we were seized by an excess of happiness.

Happiness is doubtless the wrong word for the satisfaction that men experience when they are possessed by the lust to destroy and to kill their kind. Most men would never admit that they enjoy killing, and there are a great many who do not. On the other hand, thousands of youths who never suspected the presence of such an impulse in themselves have learned in military life the mad excitement of destroying. The appetite is one that requires cultivation in the environment of disorder and deprivation common to life at the front. It usually marks the great difference between green troops and veterans. Generals often name it "the will to close with the enemy." This innocent-sounding phrase conceals the very substance of the delight in destruction slumbering in most of us. When soldiers step over the line that separates self-defense from fighting for its own sake, as it is so easy for them to do, they experience something that stirs deep chords in their being. The soldier-killer is learning to serve a different deity, and his concern is with death and not life, destruction and not construction.

Of the many writers who are preoccupied today with man's urge toward destruction, Ernest Hemingway stands out as one who has succeeded in incorporating the spirit of violence in his men and women. In his *For Whom the Bell Tolls*, he has his hero say at one point: "Stop making dubious literature about the Berbers and the old Iberians and admit that you have liked to kill as all who are soldiers by choice have enjoyed it at some time whether they lie about it or not." And his old colonel in the more recent book *Across the River and into the Trees* is as profound a portrait of the soldier-killer as we have seen in recent literature. The colonel is so far aware of this impulse to destruction in himself that he tries to counterbalance it by the contrary appeal, namely, Eros, in the form of the young and beautiful countess. This latter book has been harshly criticized from an artistic point of view, and not many have seen, I believe, how well Hemingway grasps the two primordial forces that are in conflict within the colonel, as within many a professional warrior, conflicts that can be resolved in a fashion only by death.

Sigmund Freud has labeled these forces in human nature the Eros drive or instinct, the impulse within us that strives for closer union with others and seeks to preserve and conserve, and the Thanatos (death) drive or instinct, the impulse that works for the dissolution of everything living or united. Freud felt that these two are in eternal conflict within man, and he became, consequently, pessimistic about ever eradicating war as an institution. Men are in one part of their being in love with death, and periods of war in human society represent the dominance of this impulsion.

Of course, this idea of an independent destructive force in life is age-old. The early Greek philosopher Empedocles gave imaginative form to a cosmology in which two universal principles explain the universe. Empedocles taught that the universe is in ceaseless change, in generation and decay, because Love and Strife are ever at work in the animate and the inanimate. Love unites all forms of life, for a period holding the upper hand, and Strife tears them apart and breaks down what previously belonged together. The original components are not annihilated, but simply dispersed in various forms by Strife. They are able to form new unions once more, and the endless process of composition and decomposition continues. Empedocles conceived both forces as of equal strength, both eternal, and both mixed equally in all things. In this imaginative vision of the world process, he sees, also, a necessary relationship between these cosmological powers, an insight that is sounder and more fruitful than most modern conceptions.

We are tempted under the influence of Darwinian thought to explain away man's delight in destruction as a regressive impulse, a return to primitivism and to animal nature. We picture, sometimes with the help of Freudians, all our cultural institutions as a kind of mask covering up the animalistic instincts that lie beneath the surface of all behavior. Such a view tends to explain all phenomena of human destructiveness, from the boyish pleasure in the tinkle of broken glass to the sadistic orgies of concentration camps, as a reassertion of man's animal nature under the veneer of culture. Man when he destroys is an animal; when he conserves he is distinctively human.

I cannot escape the conviction that this is an illusion, and a dangerous one. When man is at his destructive work, he is on a different plane from the animal altogether. And destructive urges are as capable of being found in highly cultivated natures as in the simpler ones, if not more so. The satisfaction in destroying seems to me peculiarly human, or, more exactly put, devilish in a way animals can never be. We sense in it always the Mephistophelean cry that all created things deserve to be destroyed. Sometimes there is no more concrete motive for destroying than this one, just as there is no expressible motive for creating. I described this kind of wanton behavior in my journal one night.

> It was an unforgivable spectacle. They shamed us as Americans, as colleagues and junior officers, they shamed us before our hired people. Our President lay on his bier in Washington, boys from our Division lay wounded and dying on the battlefields round about, and these lordly colonels drank themselves senseless and wantonly destroyed property with their pistols. It was a commentary on the war, on the uselessness of fighting for ideals, on the depravity of the military life.

Indeed, there are many important similarities, I feel, between the creative and destructive urges in most of us. Surely the immediate sense of release that is the satisfaction in accomplishment and mastery is not very different in the two impulses. One may become a master in one field as in the other, and there are perhaps as many levels of accomplishment. Few men ever reach superlatives in the realm of destruction; most of us remain, as in the domain of creation, moderately capable.

But artistry in destruction is qualitatively different in its effects upon the individual, in a way that minimizes similarities. It loosens one by one our ties with others and leaves us in the end isolated and alone.

Destruction is an artistry directed not toward perfection and fulfill-ment, but toward chaos and moral anarchy. Its delights may be deep and within the reach of more men than are the joys of creation, but their capacity to reproduce and to endure is very limited. Just as creation raises us above the level of the animal, destruction forces us below it by eliminating communication. As creativity can unite us with our natural and human environment, destruction isolates us from both. That is why destruction in retrospect usually appears so repellent in its inmost nature.

If we ask what the points of similarity are between the appeal of destruction and the two appeals of war I have already examined, I think it is not difficult to recognize that the delight in destroying has, like the others, an ecstatic character. But in one sense only. Men feel overpowered by it, seized from without, and relatively helpless to change or control it. Nevertheless, it is an ecstasy without a union, for comradeship among killers is terribly difficult, and the kinship with nature that aesthetic vision often affords is closed to them. Nor is the breaking down of the barriers of self a quality of the appeal of destroying. On the contrary, I think that destruction is ultimately an individual matter, a function of the person and not the group. This is not to deny, of course, that men go berserk in groups and kill more easily together than when alone. Yet the satisfaction it brings appears to lie, not in losing themselves and their egos, but precisely in greater consciousness of themselves. If they hold together as partners in destruction, it is not so much from a feeling of belonging as from fear of retaliation when alone.

The willingness to sacrifice self for comrades is no longer character-istic of soldiers who have become killers for pleasure. War henceforth becomes for them increasingly what the philosopher Hobbes thought to be the primal condition of all human life, a war of every man against every man. That soldier-killers seldom reach this stage must be attrib-uted to the presence of other impulses in their nature and to the episodical character of battle and combat. I can hardly doubt that the delight in destruction leads in this direction.

This is not the only melancholy consequence of this impulse, for its very nature is to be totalitarian and exclusive. Unlike other delights, it becomes, relatively soon in most men, a consuming lust which swal-lows up other pleasures. It tends to turn men inward upon themselves and make them inaccessible to more normal satisfactions. Because they rarely can feel remorse, they experience no purgation and cannot grow. The utter absence of love in this inverted kind of creation makes the delight essentially sterile. Though there may be a fierce pride in the numbers destroyed and in their reputation for proficiency, soldier-killers usually experience an ineffable sameness and boredom in their lives. The restlessness of such men in rest areas behind the front is notorious.

How deeply is this impulse to destroy rooted and persistent in human nature? Are the imaginative visions of Empedocles and Freud true in conceiving that the destructive element in man and nature is as strong and recurrent as the conserving, erotic element? Or can our delight in destruction be channeled into other activities than the traditional one of warfare? We are not far advanced on the way to these answers. We do not know whether a peaceful society can be made attractive enough to wean men away from the appeals of battle. Today we are seeking to make war so horrible that men will be frightened away from it. But this is hardly likely to be more fruitful in the future than it has been in the past. More productive will certainly be our efforts to eliminate the social, economic, and political injustices that are always the immediate occasion of hostilities. Even then, we shall be confronted with the spiritual emptiness and inner hunger that impel many men toward combat. Our society has not begun to wrestle with this problem of how to provide fulfillment of human life, to which war is so often an illusory path.

The weather has been unspeakably bad also, and what with the dawning realization that the war may continue through the winter, it has been sufficient to lower my previous high spirits. Perhaps "high spirits" is not the proper term for the nervous excitement and tension of this war front. I experience so much as in a dream or as on a stage, and at times I can step aside, as one does in a dream, and say: Is this really I? "Sad and laughable and strange" is the best combination of adjectives to describe these twilight days of our old world—the words that Plato used to describe his great myth at the end of *The Republic*. I would say, first strange, then sad, then laughable—but the laugh is not the same as the laugh of one in love when his beloved has delighted him with some idiosyncrasy of love. It is the laugh of the fallen angels who have renounced heaven but find hell hard to endure. (War journal, October 2, 1944)

3

Gay Jocks: A Phenomenology of Gay Men in Athletics[1]

Brian Pronger

Imagine walking into the crowded reception area of a major athletic facility at an international swimming competition. You have spent the last year training intensively, expecting that today you are going to swim faster than ever before. The foyer is packed with athletes, all of whom are at their peak of physical fitness, ready to race. The place is exciting.

On the deck just before the race the energy is amazing. So much power and speed in one place is awe-inspiring. Everywhere you turn there are men stretching and shaking the tension out of their powerful muscles— lithe bodies being tuned for the last time before the final event. You, too, are ready to fly into action at the sound of the gun. Bang! In less than a minute the race is over. You swam your personal best—victory.

The last event in the meet is the relays, in some ways the most exciting part of any meet. Team spirit is at its height, and these guys are ready to tear up the water. As each swimmer flings himself into the pool there is a burst of energy, lane after lane. These are men pushing themselves to the limit; every fibre of every body feels itself to be the consummation of power and masculinity. The race is over. The mood is ecstatic.

Relief. You, with your teammates, hit the showers with the hundred or so other swimmers. Everyone is exhausted and delirious from the racing. This time in the showers, overwhelming with steam and muscle, marks the end of an athletic experience. These powerful men know what it means to be men and athletes.

You exchange an ironic glance and a knowing smile with the blond swimmer from Thunder Bay next to you. The two of you, in the midst of this concentrated masculinity, also know a great deal about what it means to be athletes and men. As gay men, you and your friend from Thunder

Bay have experienced many things in common with the other men at the competition, most of whom are probably straight. Other experiences, however, have been and will be different. The following is an exploration of some of those unique differences.[2]

This chapter uses a phenomenological perspective to shed light on those experiences that gay men have in athletics that are unlike those of nongay men. It is essential to remember that many of the experiences of men who are not gay are also open to gay men. I will argue that the experience of being gay is a matter of context, that is, of understanding oneself in the light of socially constructed sexual and gender categories. These are contexts through which one can pass through different periods of life, from day to day and from moment to moment. This fluidity of context can predispose some men to a special way of interpreting the world that is ironic. This ironic point of view can shape the experiences that gay men have in athletics.

Historical and Theoretical Introduction

The first problem faced in any investigation of gay men is defining about whom we are speaking. When we discuss the anthropology or sociology of women, it is fairly clear to whom we refer. However, when we talk about gay men, we are presented with a moving target. Definitions of sexuality have changed over the years.[3] Michel Foucault and Jeffrey Weeks have suggested that the heterosexual and homosexual categories are not ahistorical and unchanging; they depend upon complex historical circumstances. The homosexual category emerged in the 18th and 19th centuries, and its creation was related to the development of capitalism and the triumph of the positive sciences.[4] Before that time there were no homosexuals, only homosexual acts. Foucault and Weeks argue that the creation of sexual categories such as *heterosexual, homosexual, pedophile*, and *transvestite* comprise a form of social control.[5] Through confinement of legitimate sexuality to heterosexuality and the family, and through the marginalization of other machinations of sexual expression, the social behaviour of individuals has, by and large, been controlled in the service of social order and economic productivity.

Most recent research on homosexuality has focussed on the social historical forces that have shaped and conceptualized the lives of contemporary men and women. The concern has been with the creation of sexual categories.[6] This phenomenological investigation, as a study of the way in which athletic experience emerges for gay men, is concerned not so much with the categories themselves as with the ways that individuals interact with historically constructed sexual categories in athletic settings.[7] In conjunction with my study of gay men in athletics, I conducted indepth interviews with 30 gay-identified men and two heterosexually identified national coaches. There was no attempt to obtain a statistically valid sample; such an approach is impossible in the study of gay men, because the meaning of being gay is highly subjective and therefore ambiguous.

Contemporary gay men, like anyone else, find themselves in a world of meaning, a world that has changed over time under the influence of a multitude of historical and cultural circumstances. The anthropologist Clifford Geertz said that "man is an animal suspended in webs of significance he himself has spun."[8] Culture, Geertz says, is such a web, and the study of it is a search for meaning. As gay men approach an athletic experience, they may confront athletic culture and find meaning in it through a special gay sensibility which has developed out of a unique web of significance drawn from the experience of being gay in a straight world. As we shall see, the world of athletics is a gymnasium of heterosexual masculinity. The unique experience that gay men can have of athletics involves the special meaning they find in masculinity.

Power, Masculinity, and Athletics

In their review of the sociological literature on masculinity, Carrigan et al. write, "One of the central facts about masculinity, is that men in general are advantaged by the subordination of women."[9] One of the techniques for the subordination of women by men is a complex semiotic of masculine and feminine behaviours that communicate power. As Foucault[10] has explained, power is

- a multiplicity of force relations,
- a process that transforms, strengthens, or reverses those relations,
- the support that those force relations find in one another, and
- the strategies that these relations employ.

In patriarchal society, men have power over women; the practice of masculine behaviour by men and feminine behaviour by women is the semiotic instrument of this power.

A common understanding of the difference between masculinity and femininity can be seen if we look at the dictionary; a number of important themes emerge. Power is the distinguishing feature of masculinity, whereas lack of power is the distinguishing feature of femininity. The *Oxford English Dictionary* (OED) defines *masculine* as "having the appropriate excellences of the male sex; manly, virile, vigorous, powerful." Interestingly, whereas *masculine* is defined in terms of "excellences," the OED offers a depreciative use of *feminine*, which is "womanish, effeminate." In this depreciative use, the powerlessness that is associated with femininity is borne out. The OED defines *effeminate* as "to make unmanly; to enervate. To grow weak, languish."

One form of masculine behaviour is the development and display of physical strength, an important phenomenon in the world of athletics. The masculine development and display of physical strength by men, in conjunction with its lack in women, embody Foucault's conception of power. Power, as a multiplicity of force relations, can be seen in the dominant and subordinate positions of men and women, respectively. As a process that transforms, strengthens, or reverses those relations, the masculine development of physical strength certainly fortifies the power relations between men and women. The complementarity of masculinity and femininity, of strength and weakness, functions as a system of support that the force relations betweeen men and women find in one another. The actual development and display of physical strength is one of the many strategies that these force relations employ.[11] Masculinity, then, is a strategy for the power relations between men and women; it is a strategy that serves the interests of patriarchal heterosexuality. Athletics, as a sign of masculinity in men, can be an instrument of those power relations.

Gay Men and Masculinity

Given the patriarchal heterosexual significance of masculinity, it can have a special meaning for gay men. In their personal lives, many urban gay men do not benefit significantly from the hegemony that masculinity is meant to afford men; some live their lives in virtual isolation from women. Others experience their relations with women as ones of equality. Women are sensitive to the difference between men who may see them as potential lovers, sexual partners, or victims of rape and those men who have no sexual interest in women and pursue them as friends on an equal basis. All the gay men I interviewed told me their relationships with women are very good; the men feel themselves to be on equal terms with women, and women seem to trust these men more than they do other men. A rower told me:

> My involvement with women is extremely important. I would guess that a lot of my closest friendships are with women, and it's a very central thing to what I am doing, doing things with women and being close to women, very important. I would guess it would be a very even split between women friends and men friends. . . . I don't notice anything unequal any more so than with my men friends.

This ease of social intercourse makes possible personal relations with women that are not patriarchal. The patriarchal signification of the masculine/feminine spectrum of behaviors, therefore, has little meaning to gay men in their personal lives. I am not suggesting that gay men are immune to patriarchal advantage. In a partriarchal society, certain things are automatically accorded men, such as privileged professional and financial advantage over women in economic life. But here I am describing the personal experiences that gay men have with women. In gay men's personal interactions with women, masculine patriarchal semiotics are generally inappropriate and insignificant.

Although gay men are not actively involved in hegemonic relations with women, these men are not unaware of the use of the masculine/ feminine spectrum of behaviours. Because gay men grow up in a predominantly heterosexual world, they have learned the standard language of masculinity. In coming out, which is a process of becoming gay-identified in some public contexts, one becomes resolved that one is not part of the mainstream of society and that, in some way, one fits the socially constructed category of the homosexual or gay man. In this often-long process, we reinterpret the predominantly heterosexual world in which we find ourselves.

One of those reinterpretations, I propose, is of the meaning of masculine and feminine behaviour. Gay men can come to see that the power relations for which the semiotics of masculinity and femininity constitute a strategy have little to do with their lives. The meaning of masculinity, consequently, begins to change. Although masculinity is often the object of sexual desire for gay men, its role in their lives is ironic. Said one of my interviewees:

> For gay men, masculinity has this kind of double edge to it; on the one side it's something they find erotically attractive to them in some ways, but on the other side it's the area which they are least able in some ways to perform correctly. For me to be masculine in my real life [like many gay men, he has developed muscles so that he can pretend to be masculine while pursuing sex] is a very difficult feat—it's something I'd have to work at constructing.

Like this man, many gay men may consciously employ masculine behaviours, yet I have also noticed that other gay men, shortly after coming out, start to show more effeminate mannerisms.[12] As one man told me, "Gay men are aware of more flexibility in these things than others." Indeed, for many gay men, masculinity and femininity cease to be experienced as what one *is,* and they become, quite consciously, ways in which one *acts.*

Gay Men and Effeminacy

Early theories of homosexuality were concerned with its aetiology.[13] Homosexuality was categorized by 19th-century medicine as a psycho-social disorder. The source of this disorder was in what was then considered to be the biological formation of gender. It was thought that homosexuality was a symptom of gender confusion. Many gay theoreticians maintain that the old conception of homosexuals as effeminate is simply fallacious. Gay men, theoreticians claim, are just as masculine as heterosexual men.[14] Any sense of incongruity, therefore, between homosexuality and athletic participation would be a misunderstanding of the true case of homosexuality. Such a reading ignores both the intrinsically heterosexual meaning of masculinity (as a semiotic instrument for the subordination of women) and the historical influences that have shaped homosexuality. My research suggests that this meaning and history cannot be so easily dismissed. Gay men are aware of the popular effeminate image of homosexuality. This image is important as a point of reference for the sense of identity and behaviour of many gay men. Furthermore, there are gay men who intentionally employ effeminate behaviour. Effeminate behaviour in men is clearly seen to signify homosexuality, and gay men who want to call attention to their sexuality can do so by behaving effeminately. Said Quentin Crisp "Blind with mascara and dumb with lipstick, I paraded the streets of Pimlico. . . . My function in life . . . was to render what was already clear, blindingly conspicuous."[15]

Gay men can employ masculine and feminine behaviours at will, depending on the social context and what they are trying to express. Most gay men have had the experience of "butching it up" when trying to hide their homosexuality. Likewise, many know what it means to, "let your hair down" and "camp it up" among friends. This variability in the use of masculine and feminine behaviours indicates an important dimension to the experience of being gay, which is the experience of fluidity.

The Fluidity of Being Gay and Passing as Straight

Whereas Foucault and others have argued that the homosexual category has come to define the entire person, I suggest that gay men experience substantial fluidity in the application of the category to themselves. Gay men contextualize their experiences. They apply culturally received categories of homosexuality at different times and under different circumstances. In a comment that was similar to those of many of the men I interviewed, one said:

Basically, my day-to-day life is quite straight, except for lunch, the informal social occasions when I can let loose with a gay reference. Socially, maybe 2 or 3 times a week, it's getting together for dinner or going to a bar, just me and my lover; we don't live together yet. There are gay times in the week and not gay times of the week. There is a fluidity to being gay.

By the implementation of gay sensibilities (which I will describe shortly), in reference to the historically constructed category of the homosexual, gay men can create gay cultural contexts not only in gay-community settings but also in nongay settings, such as mainstream athletics. Gay culture is not limited to life in the more or less formal institutions of the gay community such as bars, sports clubs, political groups, and churches. Gay culture (keeping in mind that culture is a "web of significance") is the world in which gay people meet—socially, intellectually, artistically, emotionally, politically, sexually, spiritually, and athletically. Gay culture can be expressed wherever there are gay people.

Gay men pass in and out of gay contexts, moment to moment, day to day, and through different periods of their lives. Gay contexts are created not only by the presence of gay men but also by their decisions to interpret a situation as gay. Consequently, it is possible for a gay man to go to a gymnasium, be completely involved in the athleticism of his workout, and experience that time as being simply athletic, devoid of any gay significance as far as he is concerned. Another day, he may go to the same gymnasium and find the same men there doing much the same exercises as they were previously; this time, however, he sees the experience as a gay experience. That is, he may find the situation sexy; he may find it ironic (as I will explain shortly); he may decide that he is with only other gay men and experience a sense of gay fraternity. The gay context depends on the man's interpretation. Self-concept also depends upon personal interpretation. A man who is a runner may enter the Boston Marathon, an event that he considers to be very important to himself athletically. His concerns are whether he will finish, what his time might be, or how painful the experience will be. Here, his concept of himself is overwhelmingly that of a runner. The same man could enter the same marathon another year, and having decided to wear a singlet with a large pink triangle emblazoned with the word *gay,* he sees himself as a gay runner and his participation in this race as an expression of his pride in being gay.

The fluidity of homosexuality is enhanced by the fact that gay men can and often do pass as straight men. In a society that assumes that everyone is heterosexual, it is relatively easy for homosexual men to "pass." This ability is a distinguishing feature of the homosexual minority; people of colour cannot easily pass as white, and women

have a difficult time passing as men. Passing is particularly important
in mainstream athletic culture where heterosexuality is expected.[16]
Certainly, it is usually necessary for gay men to pass as straight in the
potentially sexual situations of men's locker rooms and showers. ·

Afraid of losing their positions on teams, as a result of the compulsory heterosexuality of sport, many gay athletes find it necessary to
hide their homosexuality by passing as straight. I interviewed an
international competitive rower who said it was essential to seem to be
heterosexual:

> You did everything you could to hang on to your seat, to make the crew,
> that you would never jeopardize—you wouldn't even tell the coach you
> had a cold. You could be *crippled* and you'd hide it from the coach,
> because if there's any perceived weakness, they'll put somebody else in
> the boat. So to hint that I was gay was to kiss rowing goodbye.

The Ironic Gay Sensibility

The experiences of fluidity and passing can dispose gay men to a
special way of understanding the world. This can lead one to a special
knowledge that is uniquely gay. Schutz[17] argues that a phenomenological account of knowledge reveals that it is basically social. This, he
says, leads to the notion of the "social distribution of knowledge,"
which is demonstrated in the different knowledge that men and women
have in our society. I argue that just as gender in sexist society affords
people special knowledge that emerges from their positions in society,
so too sexual orientation, in a society that is divided along those lines,
privileges people with characteristic knowledge. Gay irony is a unique
way of knowing that has it origins in the social construction of heterosexist society. The ways that gay men think are very much the results
of having to deal with homophobia. To avoid suffering in potentially
homophobic settings like athletic teams and locker rooms, gay men
learn to pass as straight. Passing predisposes gay men to a sense of
irony.

From an early age, gay men are aware of this important irony—they
seem to be heterosexual when in fact they are not. Most social relations
are organized around heterosexuality. For boys, the social side of
sports is heterosexual. One's teammates form a "boys-wanting-girls
club." When a young male athlete socializes with his teammates,
inside or outside the locker room, talk is often about sex with girls and
the problems of dating. Bars, clubs, or athletic dances held to mark
the end of a sporting season or a school victory are always heterosexual functions. In their early years, most young gay people follow this
social pattern.

A gay man may follow these patterns, but because he is not really part of the heterosexual action, the budding gay man is aware of himself as an outsider, an observer. The position of the observer is an ironic stance.[18] A young homosexual person can be aware of himself as an outsider without having understood himself as homosexual. In fact, this sense of being an outsider may lead to one's self-identification as homosexual. During this time the foundation for a young gay person's sense of irony develops. In his position as an observer, the young gay man, probably unconsciously, masters some of the basic skills of the ironist. As he grows older he becomes increasingly aware of himself as the observer who seems to be part of the action. Although he may never define his world as ironic, the gay man may, nevertheless, employ irony unwittingly. (One need not analyze and define the formal structure of a way of thinking or being in order to use that structure in day-to-day life.) Growing up in a world in which heterosexuality is taken for granted, then, gay people may be introduced to the rudiments of irony. By developing this sense and seeing his world as ironic, the gay man can manipulate the socially constructed incompatibility of the appearance and the reality of his sexuality.

Wayne Booth[19] says that fundamental to irony is its invitation to reconstruct something deeper than what is apparent on the surface. While inviting one to see deeper than the superficial appearance and thereby understand what is actually meant, irony preserves the appearance. The total truth includes both appearance and reality. This technique for understanding reality while maintaining a cosmetic appearance is very useful to gay men while passing as straight. It is a technique that many of us learn to use at very young ages simply in order to survive. Because gay men feel at home with irony, even when "the closet" is not an issue, they continue to interpret their worlds ironically. Because irony brings with it a sense of superiority, a sense of looking at the world from a higher place, each gay ironic experience is a sublime reaffirmation of a gay worldview.

Gay irony is a way of thinking, communicating, and being that emerges out of the experience of being gay in a society in which people tend to believe that everyone is straight. It is a sensibility that is essentially fluid both through the lives of individuals and throughout society. The phenomenon of being gay is a matter of context; so too is the invocation of gay irony. Not all homosexual people see themselves as "gay," and not all gay people use irony. Being gay and the use of irony are conceptual dispositions and techniques that people use to think about themselves and interpret their worlds. Irony is a form of interpretation, a way of understanding that develops out of the experience of individuals' interactions with sexual and gender categories. Gay irony, therefore, is best understood as a tendency to interpret experience ironically rather than a consistent standpoint shared by all gay men.

The Ironic Experience of Gay Men in Athletics

In our society, which places great importance on sex and restricts "legitimate" sexuality to heterosexuality and the family, the assumption is that virtually everyone is heterosexual. This is almost universally the case in athletics, where, for example, men and women's locker rooms are always segregated. The assumption is that the heterosexual desires of men and women may be stimulated if male and female athletes were to see each other naked. The fact that men may find it sexually stimulating to be in a locker room full of other naked male athletes is either ignored or sublimated through aggressive, homophobic, and sexist humor.

The popular images of the athlete and the gay man are virtually antithetical. The history of homosexuality has constructed a less than positive and healthy conception of the homosexual man, whereas the popular image of the athlete is quintessentially healthy and positive. Many writers have suggested that athletics and healthy heterosexual masculinity are popularly equated: Bob Connell, David Kopay, and Don Sabo, to name only a few. Certainly, the popular image of the athlete as a healthy model citizen is unlike the judicial, medical, and religious models that have categorized the homosexual man as a criminal, pathological, degenerate sinner.[20] Being both athletic and gay presents a seeming contradiction, one of which many gay athletes are aware. Many of the gay athletes to whom I spoke said that when they were younger, they thought it was impossible to be both athletic and gay. This juxtaposition of the popular models of athletics and homosexuality, of appearance and reality, in the lives of gay athletes is a significant contribution to the ironic experience of gay men in athletics.

Anagnorisis

Gay men subtly communicate their shared worldview by using irony. This subtlety has important implications for gay men; it allows them to remain undiscovered by the uninitiated, thereby affording them some protection from the expressions of homophobia that frequently accompany detection. Especially important in gay irony is *anagnorisis,* which is the observer's recognition of the ironist as an ironist with a deeper intent than that which is immediately apparent on the surface. Anagnorisis occurs when the interpreter of the irony realizes the irony in the situation. In anagnorisis, the gay ironist not only reveals meanings that have been concealed by appearances, he also reveals himself. Eye contact is the way gay men usually recognize each other in nongay settings. One manifestation of this eye contact can be a subtle, knowing look, which can be the clue for mutual anagnorisis. One man told me about being in a university weight room and watching an athlete to whom he was attracted lifting a weight. To most observers, the scenario would appear to be quite straight. A man whom he didn't know was standing nearby and watching the same athlete. Moving from the athlete to each other, their admiring eyes met, and with no more obvious gesture than a slight pause in their gazes, they became aware of their secret fraternity. In their sententious exchange of glances, having as novelist John Fowles said, "the undeclared knowledge of a shared imagination," their worlds touched. They uttered not a word.

Acting Versus Being

As a result of coming out in some contexts, gay men become more consciously aware of passing in others; gay men can start to see others' uses of masculinity as a technique for passing. This insight can bring them to a heightened awareness of their uses of masculinity as an ironic form. Rather than thinking of themselves as being masculine, gay men can come to think of themselves as acting masculine. In the 1970s, the disco group "The Village People" epitomized this masculine (and I think intensely ironic) act. Their outfits were ironic caricatures of masculinity: construction worker, policeman, Indian, and a hyper-masculine-looking man with a mustache (a style known as the "clone"). One of their hit songs had the lyrics, "Macho, macho, man; I wanna be a macho man." The clue to their irony lies in the fact that they don't say they are macho men; rather, they "wanna be" macho men. That is, they look like macho men when in fact they are not. The macho look, especially that of the clone, became very popular in gay ghettos across North America and parts of Europe. The deep and sometimes subliminal irony of the gay masculine clone style[21] may best be appreciated in the light of Wallace Stevens: "The final belief is to believe in a fiction, which you know to be a fiction, there being nothing else. The exquisite truth is to know that it is a fiction and that you believe in it willingly."[22]

Two Ironies of Muscular Bodies

The attraction that many gay men have for masculine men presents a uniquely gay male interpretation of masculinity. Athletic, muscular bodies are masculine bodies. The popularity of muscles among gay men is evidenced by the predominance of muscular iconography in gay liberation magazines, erotica, and soft-core and hard-core pornography. Over the last 15 years or so, there has been a substantial migration of gay men to gymnasiums, so much so that some major cities have gymnasiums where the majority of members are gay men. The development of muscular bodies by gay men presents two important ironies. In the *Leviathan,* Hobbes says that "Forme is Power, because being a promise of Good, it recommendeth men to the favour of women and strangers."[23] The well-defined muscular body is a sign of strength, an indication of the power that has historically been given to men. The armour of Roman centurions was an exaggerated sculpture of a muscular male torso. The intention, no doubt, was to create the appearance of considerable strength, which would inhibit those who wished to usurp the officer's power. The truly masculine man with his muscular body asserts his authority over women and inhibits other men; his muscular appearance is meant to deter other men. This signification of muscular bodies is commonly understood. A gay man with a muscular body, however, has little intention of asserting his authority over women and may well have every intention of attracting other men. The significance that gay men give to the athletic body is ironic in that the masculine appearance that normally is meant to inhibit men emerges as an invitation to men.

The second irony of gay muscular bodies involves a dualism of mind and body. The muscled athletic male body is an expression of a powerful masculine mental disposition. John Hoberman points out that many prominent fascist leaders have exploited the athletic body (not necessarily their own bodies; i.e., they surround themselves with athletes) to express their power. Idi Amin, 6 feet and 4 inches, who before ascending to power in Uganda was the Ugandan heavyweight boxing champion, used his considerable athletic build to dramatize his political power.[24] Someone who has developed a powerful body is perceived as also having the mental resolve to mobilize his body into masculine action. By masculine action, I mean seizing patriarchal opportunities as they are presented and inhibiting other men. Some muscular gay men can be effeminate; here we have the irony of an effeminate mind in a masculine body. One man I interviewed did weight lifting exclusively as a masculine sexual lure. Pinpointing the fluidity, superficiality, and therefore irony of this masculinity, he said he used it

> as a tool to pick up men. I think I tend to exempt myself from, well, as I think a lot of gay people do, from the standard deviation [of] male and female, masculine and feminine. That we can make up our own rules and borrow from one and the other equally, according to what you find palatable or useful or stimulating or interesting.

This gay ironic play with masculinity is highlighted in radical drag. A man with bulging biceps and thunderous thighs wearing a slinky dress and a tiara is, through the juxtaposition of a masculine body and feminine clothes, expressing the overt irony of seeming to be "masculine" when he is also "feminine."

Conclusion

In conclusion, because being gay is a fluid experience and because gay men are in the unique position of being able to pass as straight in a society that assumes that everyone is heterosexual, some gay men have developed a special way of interpreting the world that is based on the manipulation of appearance and reality (i.e., the ironic gay sensibility). This is a view of the world that many gay men can apply at will and with which they feel very comfortable. It is an instrument of understanding that plays on the subtleties of life and reveals meanings that are particularly close to the unique experiences of gay men.

The semiotics of masculinity and femininity reveal an intricate spectrum of behaviours for the communication of power in the service of patriarchal heterosexual relations. Although gay men do not benefit significantly in their personal lives from the hegemony that masculinity is meant to afford men, gay men do employ masculine behaviour. The meaning that gay men find in masculinity is distinctive in its sexual and ironic signification.

The gay experience of athletics is a matter of context. Entering into an athletic situation, a gay man can be an athlete whose world is dominated by purely athletic experience: pain, sweat, exertion, the joy of movement. He can be an earnest gay person running a race as a representative of gay pride. He can be a national swim team member covertly communicating with his gay teammates through ironic innuendo. He can be a solitary gay person working out in a crowded university weight room, privately savoring the ironic fact that he is in the midst of a macho temple that for him is almost exploding with sexuality.

At the beginning of this chapter, you were invited to imagine yourself as a swimmer at an international competition. You may remember that after the meet, in the showers, you exchanged an ironic glance and a knowing smile with a friend from Thunder Bay. As gay athletes, your worlds met. In those glances and smiles were distilled personal and cultural histories of homosexuality, masculinity, femininity, sex, and irony.

Notes

1. An earlier version of this paper was presented to the Canadian Sociology and Anthropology Association on June 3, 1987, at the Learned Societies Conference at MacMaster University, Hamilton, ON.

2. Gay men are involved in both mainstream and gay community athletic milieux. Gay athletic clubs, which can be found in major cities across North America (see C. Rowland, "Games People Play: The Burgeoning World of Gay Athletics," *The Advocate,* 462, December 23, 1986, pp. 42–47, 108–109), constitute a major aspect of gay community life. These clubs offer gay men and lesbians a unique experience of athletics. Because space here is limited, I will devote this chapter to the experience of gay men in mainstream athletics. The phenomenology of gay men in athletics is an entirely new field of inquiry, both in regard to its approach and its subject. This paper is a simplified and brief outline of a complex and extensive phenomenon.

3. See M. Foucault, *The History of Sexuality: Vol. I. An Introduction,* translated by R. Hurley (New York: Vintage Books, 1978); J. Katz, *Gay/ Lesbian Almanac: A New Documentary* (New York: Harper and Row, 1983); J. Marshall, "Pansies, Perverts and Macho Men: Changing Conceptions of Male Homosexuality," in K. Plummer, editor, *The Making of the Modern Homosexual* (London: Hutchinson, 1981), pp. 133–54; K. Plummer, "Building a Sociology of Homosexuality" and "Homosexual Categories: Some Research Problems in the Labeling Perspective of Homosexuality," in K. Plummer, editor, Ibid., pp. 17–29 and 53–75; J. Weeks, *Sexuality* (Chichester, England: Ellis Horwood, 1986).

4. J. Weeks, "Discourse, Desire, and Sexual Deviance: Some Problems in a History of Sexuality," in K. Plummer, editor, ibid.

5. Ibid.

6. K. Plummer, op. cit.

7. My approach to phenomenology is drawn from Martin Heidegger (see his *Being and Time,* J. Marquarrie and E. Robinson, translators (New York: Harper and Row, 1926), pp. 49–62. He says that the term *phenomenology* refers to a method of inquiry, whereas *sociology, anthropology* and *psychology* refer to what is to be studied. Phenomenology, he says, directs us to the "how" of an investigation; it is the study of the way in which things appear to us.

8. C. Geertz, *The Interpretation of Cultures* (New York: Basic Books, 1973).

9. T. Carrigan, R. Connell, and J. Lee, "Toward a New Sociology of Masculinity," *Theory and Society,* vol. 4/5 (1985), p. 590.

10. M. Foucault, op. cit.

11. M. Foucault, ibid., pp. 92–93.

12. I am not suggesting that all gay men behave effeminately. In fact, nowhere in this paper do I suggest that gay men behave in a uniform fashion. As the reader will see, the fluidity of being gay precludes such a notion.

13. J. Marshall, op. cit.

14. M. Levine, "Gay Ghetto," in M. Levine, editor, *Gay Men: The Sociology of Male Homosexuality* (New York: Harper and Row, 1979), pp. 183–203.

15. Quentin Crisp, *The Naked Civil Servant* (London: Jonathon Cape, 1968), p. 114.

16. B. Kidd, "Sports and Masculinity," in M. Kaufman, editor, *Beyond Patriarchy: Essays by Men on Pleasure, Power, and Change* (Toronto: Oxford University Press, 1987), pp. 250–65; and D. Kopay and P. Young, *The David Kopay Story: An Extraordinary Self-Revelation* (New York: Arbor House, 1977).

17. R. M. Zaner and H. T. Englehardt, Jr., *Structures of the Lifeworld* (Evanston, IL: Northwestern University Press, 1974).

18. D. Muecke, *Irony and the Ironic* (London: Methuen, 1982).

19. Wayne Booth, *A Rhetoric of Irony* (Chicago: University of Chicago Press, 1974).

20. See K. Marshall, op. cit., and J. Weeks, op. cit.

21. The fluidity of being gay should be kept in mind here; that is, there are men who may practice homosexuality who view their masculine behaviors not in this gay context but in a traditional patriarchal one. Moreover, they may switch from a traditional context to a gay one from time to time, depending on the situation.

22. Wallace Stevens, *Opus Posthumous* (New York: Knopf, 1977), p. 163.

23. Thomas Hobbes, *Leviathan,* C. B. Macpherson, editor (Harmondsworth, England: Penguin Books, 1968 (1651)), p. 151.

24. John Hoberman, *Sport and Political Ideology* (Austin, TX: University of Texas Press, 1984).

PART THREE

New Roles for Men

4

Real Men

Hugh LaFollette

"Ah, for the good old days, when men were men and women were women." Men who express such sentiments long for the world where homosexuals were ensconced in their closets and women were sexy, demure, and subservient. That is a world well lost—though not as lost as I would like. More than a few men still practice misogyny and homophobia. The defects of such attitudes are obvious. My concern here is not to document these defects but to ask how real men, men who reject stereotypical male-female roles—men who are sensitive to the insights of feminism—should relate with women. In particular, how should men and women relate in intimate, sexually oriented, i.e., "romantic," relationships.

The Problem of Relationships

Intimate (close personal) relationships are relationships in which each person relates to the other as a unique individual whose interests she wishes to promote. Such relationships are exemplified by care, trust, sensitivity, and mutual support. In the best of circumstances, intimacy is difficult to establish and arduous to maintain. Even when we have the noblest of intentions, we often despoil our closest relationships. We know that from experience. The task of the philosopher is to explain why this is so, hoping thereby that we can learn how to overcome these difficulties.

Relationships falter for any number of reasons. For instance, intimate relationships can be neither established nor maintained unless the partners know and trust one another. Unless they know each other, they cannot promote each other's needs. Unless they trust each other, their fear of being hurt will circumscribe communication. Moreover, their interests—although they need not be identical—must be sufficiently overlapping so neither continuous conflict nor absolute acquiescence is inevitable.

Even when two people know, love, and trust one another and have reasonably similar interests, external conditions can undermine intimacy. Job pressures, family illness, or difficulties with children make regular and sustained conversations between partners difficult. Without intimate communication to nourish them, they will grow apart. Small troubles evolve into big problems. Big problems become insurmountable hurdles. Relationships are dashed on the rocks of miscommunication and misunderstanding.

Other relationships suffer because the partners are so desirous of intimacy that they squelch their own interests. For instance, Joan may strive to make Betty happy, even if she (Joan) is thereby unhappy. In and of itself there is nothing wrong with Joan's behavior. Altruism of some form must infuse every successful relationship. But it is far too easy for well-intentioned altruism to run amuck, particularly between partners who are not honest with one another. Each may accommodate to the other so often that she becomes angry. Each may accommodate so often that she does not know what she really wants.

These are substantial hurdles for anyone wishing to establish or preserve an intimate relationship. But these are especially problematic for a man and a woman—and perhaps even more so for a man and a woman engaged in a romantic relationship. We are products of a pervasively sexist culture. The sexism in which we were all acculturated is especially difficult to escape. It permeates our society. It pervades our attitudes. It haunts and—if allowed to run wild—devours our heterosexual relationships.

If the sexist culture had merely erected legal obstacles to equality, the battle against sexism would be relatively easy. Legal obstacles, being visible, can be attacked. The women's movement has made considerable effort to remove the most onerous legal barriers to equality. It has had considerable success.[1]

The primary engines of sexism, however, are veiled, subconscious forces. The dominant culture promulgates sexist stereotypes that pervade television, movies, books, and music. These embody well-defined gender roles that infuse the relationships children see at home, at school, and when visiting their friends. They establish expectations to which all of us are subject, images to which all of us respond—to some degree or another. They shape our desires, interests, and perspectives, thereby making informed, unbiased choice difficult if not impossible.

For instance, as men we are encouraged to be determined, strong, and perhaps even aggressive. We are taught to be interested in math and science, to crave success, to be competitive. We are discouraged from developing interests or personality traits that are deemed "feminine," e.g., an interest in children or a tendency to cry. Conversely, women are taught to fear math, to enjoy literature and art. They are encouraged to be giving, supportive, soft, maternal, and if need be, subservient.

Of course not every man or woman was shaped in precisely these ways or to this extent. But even children reared in relatively liberated, non-sexist homes are shaped, at least in part, by these dominant cultural stereotypes. The effects of such shaping cannot be obliterated. Those of us reared in a pervasively sexist culture will never be entirely free from those early influences. Even those of us sensitive to the insights of feminism will still hear sexist voices from the past. They inevitably modulate our interpersonal interactions, even as we seek to free ourselves from their influence.

Consider. Trust is important in intimate relationships. Trust involves, among other things, trusting that your partner will not intentionally harm you or your interests. Such trust requires vulnerability: I cannot trust you unless I am willing to be vulnerable with you—unless I am willing to put myself in a position where you can harm my interests.

The influences of our sexist culture make trust difficult for most men. We can "trust" our bankers and we can "trust" our colleagues: we are good at institutionalized, impersonal trust. However, our fear of being really vulnerable, of personally trusting another, has often made close relationships difficult. The cardinal sin for men is to be weak, vulnerable. We are supposed to be made of iron, spartans all. We were told we must know what to do, or, short of that, to act as if we did, since we must be "kings in our castles." We may occasionally be weak with our spouses; that is acceptable. But such weakness must be contained; most assuredly it must not be public. In short, men dominated by these standard images of masculinity cannot establish relationships as close as can those who are willing to be vulnerable.

Even those of us who are relatively free of these images, those of us who are willing to be emotional, to cry, to be vulnerable, are not free for our sexist upbringing. We often find—at the most inopportune times—that our fathers' urgings "to be strong" dominate the more informed voices that tell us to be vulnerable, to be a human being. Sexism harms men as well as women. It makes genuine, intimate, and fulfilling heterosexual relationships exceedingly difficult—as if they were not difficult enough on their own.

Or suppose you and I have a long-term relationship. At some point in our lives, I become dissatisfied with my job; I want to seek employment elsewhere. You, on the other hand, are pleased with your employer and are convinced you will have difficulty finding similarly rewarding employment in the town to which I wish to move.

Obviously there are any number of considerations we might think relevant. If we are especially concerned about financial security, perhaps we will consider the options that have the highest combined salary. Or we might concern ourselves with issues of "fairness"—you have had a job you liked for ten years, now it is my turn to have a job I like. Perhaps we might look at other amenities of the respective communities; the type of neighborhood in which we can raise our children, the climate, the nature of the public schools, or the proximity to ailing parents.

Regardless of what considerations we bring to bear, our final decision will be shaped by our desires, interests, and attitudes, and these were formed by the sexist culture in which we grew up and currently live—a culture not of our choosing. Consciously or unconsciously I may expect you to be willing, if not eager, to move. I may be uncomfortable baldly asserting that my male interests are superior. I may be uncomfortable even entertaining such thoughts—after all, I am supposedly liberated. So perhaps I find, instead, some way to rationalize my choice. You, on the other hand, may want to remain with your current employer, but the image of a dutiful spouse standing by her man may lead you to suppress your interests and to acquiesce. Perhaps neither of us will succumb to these urges, but they are likely operative, even if in attenuated form. And, although they do not dictate the outcome of our deliberations, they will likely affect it.

These urgings—what I like to think of as an internal gender police—will likewise influence our decisions about child care. Suppose we decide (perhaps on good medical grounds) to breastfeed our infant. You will inevitably be required to take additional responsibility for child care, at least for the first six months. It may then be all too easy for us to use this as an excuse for letting you continue to be the primary caregiver once the child has been weaned—after all, our upbringing has likely "convinced" us, albeit subconsciously, that this is the way it should be since, after all, you are better with children.

Escaping the Sexist Culture

If both of us wish to minimize the detrimental effects of social conditioning, we must be especially attuned to the influence our upbringing exerts over us. Then we must contain those influences. That is easier said than done. For *ex hypothesi* the sexist culture shaped not only our first-order desires—for example, the desire to be a successful professional or to play football—but also our second-order desires and abilities: our values and our ability to reason. These second-order desires govern how we evaluate and subsequently modify our first-order desires. They thereby influence the contours of the people we become.

If we wish to free ourselves from these culturally induced desires, we must first identify them. That is difficult since they are amorphous, indefinite. To the extent that we can identify them, we can do so only after careful and sustained self-examination. Consequently, we cannot easily excise them nor restrain their undesirable effects.

The difficulty of identifying and controlling these impulses has led some women to separate themselves from the sexist culture.[2] Separatists think that only by starting a new culture—constituted by new ideas, new beliefs, and new ways of relating—can they escape the mental bonds with which the sexist culture has shackled us. It is easy to see why separatists might reach this conclusion.

I am inclined to believe, however, that we cannot escape the power of the culture by separating ourselves from it. The same forces that control those of us who remain will operate on those who leave. Since the culture perpetuates itself by shaping desires, values, and attitudes, removing ourselves from the culture after these have been formed will not free us from their sway. Being physically removed from the dominant culture may even make it more difficult to identify and control these forces. Consider, for instance, an individual reared in a pervasively racist culture. Merely moving to an area of the country devoid of overt racists will not purge her of racist sentiments, although it may remove her from circumstances that elicit them. The best way to eradicate racism and sexism is to transform the dominant culture that formed and sustains them.

Perhaps, though, the separatists are correct. Perhaps we can change the dominant culture only by disengaging from it. But I would like to think them mistaken. Some of us men deeply want intimate relationships with women and would suffer a substantial loss were such relationships impossible. Some of us think women have a perspective and emotional maturity from which we can learn a great deal. Some of us sexually prefer women. It is not that we think homosexuality or bisexuality wrong, immoral, or inferior. Rather we are sexually attracted to women and think it would be more effort than it is worth to try to change our orientation. Needless to say, I cannot discuss separatism in any detail here. Consequently, I will assume for the remainder of the paper that separatism is not the only way to cope with the influences of our sexist culture. I will further assume that non-sexist male-female romantic relationships are possible, albeit difficult.

We return to the original question: how do we establish intimate heterosexual relationships within a sexist culture without succumbing to that culture's detrimental influences? We cannot immediately destroy the culture's power, nor can we eradicate its influence. We can, however, contain that influence and control its most detrimental effects.[3] However, deciding that we should rid ourselves of our sexist baggage is just the first step. We must also find a strategy for doing so. There is no algorithm for freeing ourselves from sexist stereotypes, no potion we can take to make us immune to this devastating mental virus. Yet we must find ways to control its symptoms if we wish to establish genuinely intimate relationships.

Equity

Women who choose to remain in the dominant culture, yet wish to free themselves of its sexist influence, may resort to the powerful moral tools of rights, obligations, and equality. It is easy to see why. For millennia women were systematically deprived of rights and legal standing. They could not vote, hold personal property, earn a fair wage, hold public office, or serve on a jury. The women's movement has fought to gain legal recognition for women by asserting that women had *rights* to social and political goods. That is exactly what women's advocates should have done. Rights are the appropriate medium of exchange within the impersonal political arena.

Given the power of rights to battle injustice and mistreatment within the political arena, women are naturally inclined to appeal to rights and equity to battle mistreatment in personal relationships. All too often women do the bulk of the work around the house, care for the children, etc. Even when some male partners do an equal portion of the work, that is sufficiently unusual to be worthy of comment. Such men are said to be "helping" their mates—which assumes, of course, that housework and child care are women's responsibility, work in which these great-hearted men share. Despite some positive changes in the treatment of women, this still captures standard practice within most households in the United States.

If I were a woman, I would be ticked off. Men *should* carry their share of housework. Something is fundamentally wrong if they don't. The question is: How should men understand and describe our responsibilities? Do we have an obligation to do an equal portion of the work? Do our partners have rights that we violate if we don't? It is tempting to say that we each have a right not to have to carry more than our "fair share" of the load. However, that, I think, is a grave mistake. Although talk of rights and equity is appropriate within the political domain, it is anathema to personal relationships.

Traditional wisdom says otherwise; it holds that successful personal relationships must be equitable. However, a growing minority of psychologists disagree. In a series of studies Margaret Clark found that although people expect equity in impersonal (exchange or trade) relationships, they do not expect it in personal (what she calls "communal") relationships.[4] Within exchange relationships, she claims, we are expected to benefit those who have benefited us. Such relationships continue only as long as each reciprocally benefits the other. For instance, an employer and employee exchange money for labor. As long as each receives what she or he considers fair, the relationship will likely continue.

Within close personal relationships, however, people are expected to respond to each other's needs—not to reciprocate benefits. More strongly, they are expected *not* to reciprocate benefits. For instance, if I try to return a benefit from someone with whom I have a communal relationship, I may thereby destroy the relationship—even though I would be acting exactly as expected had I been in an exchange relationship.

Moreover, we must remember that the studies which suggest that equity is important for interpersonal relationships are correlative: people claim to be satisfied in relationships they deem equitable; dissatisfied in those that aren't. That may well be true. However, that does not show that people are satisfied *because* the relationship is equitable. It may well be that they deem it equitable because they are satisfied. Perhaps many people in close relationships never consciously consider if theirs is equitable, although, if asked, they surmise that it must be since they are satisfied. Conversely, if one partner is dissatisfied, she will likely seek the cause of the dissatisfaction. In the current ideological environment, being exploited seems a plausible candidate.

Even if this does not account for all of the correlation—even if we grant that perceived inequity will lead to relationship dissatisfaction—there are two divergent explanations of why this is so. According to the first, an individual enters personal relationships *in order to obtain* specified benefits from the other but is also willing to give in return: that is, she wants an equitable exchange. When or if the exchange is no longer equitable—when the relationship ceases to be a good bargain—she is dissatisfied.

According to the second interpretation—which I endorse—people enter close personal relationships not in search of a good bargain but a good friend. Both partners expect to promote their intimate's interests, to respond to her needs. Nonetheless, given each person's belief that intimates respond to the needs of people for whom they care, it is not surprising if each expects something approximating equity.

Let me explain. We are in a relationship. You have settled views about how intimates should treat each other, namely, that neither person will take advantage of her intimate; moreover, you expect each will spontaneously satisfy one other's needs. Finally, you plausibly assume that any two people will have *roughly* equivalent needs and *roughly* equivalent abilities to satisfy another's needs.

Given these beliefs, you would reasonably expect that you and your partner will benefit and give *roughly* the same. Now suppose the relationship is notably inequitable; that is, that you have contributed much and received little. You will understandably infer that I do not really love you. Equity is the likely result of a close relationship. It is not the relationship's goal.

Still others have argued not that successful relationships *are* equitable, but that they should be. On this view, inequitable relationships are not merely unsatisfying (though usually they are); rather, they are unjust. People who take advantage of their intimates have acted unjustly or immorally, they have wronged or violated the rights of their intimates.[5] At one level this claim seems eminently reasonable, even indisputable. If Jeff lets Patty carry a full-time job, do all of the housework, and completely care for the children, while he spends his evenings watching television and his weekends golfing, then Jeff has wronged Patty. What more can be said? As it turns out, a great deal.

Doubtless one partner's behavior in a "personal" relationship may be so exploitative that we can only conclude that she has acted unjustly. On this point most people will agree. That does not show, however, that close relationships are best evaluated by standards of justice or by an appeal to rights. Rather, we should conclude that such relationships are properly evaluated by criteria of justice precisely because they are no longer close or personal. If one person regularly ignores the interests of the other, the relationship is not, properly speaking, intimate. It may have trappings of close relationships: the people may spend time together or even live together. They may have fond things to say about each other. However, these trappings in an abusive relationship are not the hallmarks of intimacy but of mere familiarity.

Let's look at the flip side of the issue. Even if rights managed to protect us from gross abuse from our intimates, they would still fail to provide what we want and expect from intimates. Rights are both too stringent and too lenient. Rights are too stringent because our friends have a license to treat us in ways we would not tolerate from strangers. Close friends may borrow from us without asking; in fact, we expect them to do so. A close friend, for instance, may enter my office in the evening to borrow a book; I would feel free to do likewise. Or, a friend may plausibly expect me to help her cope with personal trauma, even though the cost to me might be substantial; I would expect her to do the same. Or a depressed friend might become angry at me in ways I would not tolerate from a stranger. I assume I could do likewise. That is just what we expect from our good friends.[6] In these cases talk of rights is simply out of place. It does not capture the nature of the relationship. A friend who borrows a book without asking has not violated my property rights; nor have I waived my rights. A friend who interrupts me to talk about her problems has not invaded my privacy; she has done what I would have expected.[7]

On the other hand, we have higher expectations of our intimates than of strangers. We expect our intimates to care. That is something rights cannot provide. If I have a right, it is merely a claim that others accord me some minimal level of decent treatment. I do not have a right that others care for me or trust me or love me.

Additionally we also expect our intimates to have "better" motives than strangers. We expect strangers to respect our rights and to fulfill their obligations to us. We expect them, for example, not to steal our property (or to steal anyone else's, for that matter) or hit us over the head or kill us. But we will not settle for abstract respect from our friends; we want personal affirmation and affection.

Imagine how repugnant it would be to have a spouse or friend who *merely* respected us. Consider, "Don't worry, honey, I will fulfill my conjugal duties to you even though I do not want to." Or, "Sure, we will talk this evening; I realize I am obliged to do so." Such behavior makes a mockery of the relationship. We do not want our friends motivated by a sense of justice, but by the desire to be with us, to talk with us, to care for us, and to promote our interests.[8]

Of course sometimes the fact that you love someone and desire to satisfy their interests may lead you to do something you do not, for other reasons, particularly want to do at that moment. Patty may not want to listen to Jeff's problems right *now*. But she may do so because she loves him. That is rather different, however, from listening to him because she is obliged to do so. Of course intimates may occasionally be motivated by a sense of duty; perhaps that is unavoidable. But duty should not become a relationship's staple. If it does, our relationship is transformed from a close relationship into an exchange relationship. And an exchange relationship, no matter how good, can never satisfy our longing for love and personal affirmation that an intimate relationship provides.

Nonetheless, someone might say, considerations of justice must be operative in the background of personal relationships, even if they are not invoked or explicitly considered. That is true in one sense, namely, that people might appeal to considerations of justice when the relationship is seriously inequitable. But that does not show that those considerations are operative in well-functioning relationships; still less does it show that they should be.

In fact, I think that appealing to or even conceiving of our personal relationships in terms of rights is to misconstrue them and will likely subvert them. If we begin to construe our personal relationships in terms of justice or rights we will see our partner's interests as limitations on us (as we would in impersonal relationships) rather than as interests we wish to promote (as we should in personal relationships).

Rights talk is intended to govern interactions between strangers, between people who do not care for each other and who may even be in overt conflict. Thus Patty's right to property limits Jeff's ability to use that property, even if he wants or needs it. Jeff's right to life limits Patty's options; Patty cannot swing her new bat in an area occupied by Jeff's head. Rights tell us what we cannot do to each other. They thereby emphasize—or create—distance between us. Consequently, if in our personal relationships we begin to think in terms of rights, we begin to think about the other as placing limitations on us. We begin to ask: "What *must* I do for my intimate?" rather than "What *can* I do for them?" Thoughts of justice or rights constrain personal relationships.

None of this should be taken to suggest that people in personal relationships never, in fact, think it terms of rights, justice, or equality. Certainly we do. Given Western civilization's preoccupation with rights it would be surprising were it otherwise. What I am suggesting is that we would be better off if we didn't; if, instead, intimates conceptualized and dealt with their differences as two people who care about one another rather than as two people who must treat each other justly.

Consider a situation where we have an apparent clash of interests. We are trying to decide, for example, which car to purchase, where to take our vacation, or where to live. If we judge our relationship by standards of justice or rights, each of us will likely become preoccupied with our rights and our responsibilities. If there is no obvious solution to our "conflict," we will likely compromise. Compromises over important issues, however, rarely satisfy either person. Each of us will feel we sacrificed to the relationship.

Suppose, instead, that we focus on our mutual care, on the fact that I take an interest in you and you in me. I want to promote your interests as well as my own; you want to promote mine as well as yours. If we can conceive of our differences in these ways, there is no straightforward way to identify a conflict of interest between us.

Of course this does not eradicate our differences. The shift in perspective does not make disagreements vanish the way some dime store novels might suggest. It does, however, change the way we view those differences, the parameters within which we make a decision. Thus, I may recognize that my interest in you is more important than my interest in buying a new Prelude. Or you may decide that your interest in me is greater than your interest in visiting Orlando.

Even if this maneuver does not result in a quick solution, it will encourage us to consider alternative solutions that might satisfy us both, rather than settling for a compromise that satisfies neither. If we are intimates we will benefit from the resulting decision. We will each understand that our interests in ourselves and one another will be advanced. So considerations of justice, though they may in some sense lie in the background of personal relationships, are best ignored by parties within them.

Finally, if we emphasize love and care rather than rights and equity, we will be better able to cope with some of the effects of our sexist culture. At least that is what I argue in the next section.

Constraining the Sexist Influences

How, then, can we establish intimate relationships that limit sexist influences without relying on equality or rights? If we are sensitive to the insights of feminism we likely need not worry about controlling overtly sexist sentiments—presumably we do not openly advocate keeping women "barefoot and pregnant." (One who openly advocates *that* view will have no interest in limiting the effects of sexism.) For us the principal obstacles to non-sexist relationships arise from subconscious attitudes and from institutionalized practices that sustain them. Long-established practices make it all too easy for us to fall into sexist patterns of relating. Liberated partners must be cognizant of these patterns and must take steps to ensure they do not mindlessly fall into them.

Consider, for example, a common occurrence: a couple meets early in college and marries (or establishes a long-term relationship). The woman quits school and finds a job to support her man, all the while assuming she will return to school herself after he finds permanent employment.

He graduates and finds a job; she returns to college to finish her degree—unless, of course, they have had a child in the meantime, which will further delay her return to school. When she finishes, he has a two or more year "jump" on her in the job market. Thus, he likely makes more money than she does. If an opportunity later arises to relocate for a better position, they will likely move to advance his career, since he is already better established economically. Having moved, she now seeks new employment, putting her still further behind him in the competition for jobs. Their future is writ: he has become the breadwinner; she has become the little woman dependent on him.

Sensitive couples must be alert to these possibilities and must work to constrain them. However, talk of rights will not serve them well in this situation. It would be difficult to say where, in the above-cited scenario, that the woman's rights were violated; each decision seems reasonable. If, however, the partners emphasize their mutual care, they should act to ensure they do not get locked into this pattern, no matter how "reasonable" it seems. They must ensure that her opportunities are not limited. For instance, both might go to school part-time. Or perhaps he could guarantee that she will finish school and find suitable employment before he furthers his career. A man should act in these ways because he cares for his partner. That is how she should expect him to act—not because she has a right that he do so, but because she knows he cares. People who care for one another do not act in ways that close off options for the other. In short, in situations where both parties recognize the tendency for sexist institutions to direct them down pre-established gender paths, they must find ways to route themselves in more productive directions.

What happens, though, if one of the parties thinks the other is subject to sexist stereotypes in ways she does not recognize? Consider this most troubling form of the case. A woman, reared in a very traditional home, maintains the conviction that her husband should "rule the home." What should she—and her spouse—do? Should they merely let her maintain this conviction unchallenged? I think not. The woman *should* try to alter these beliefs, even if she is comfortable with them and even if she thinks it would be difficult to change them. For, if she blindly accedes to her husband's judgments, she is effectively abandoning her autonomy. This is a remnant of the sexist culture she should not tolerate.

A caring spouse should likewise urge her to change, even if she does not want to. Moreover, he should act in ways that will help her change. Doing so inevitably involves elements of paternalism—and paternalism within intimate relationships is always risky. On a rights' view, paternalism is not merely risky; it is absolutely prohibited. Yet I think that to exclude paternalism in such cases, especially since the goal is to free the woman from undue sexist influences, is to damage her and the relationship. If she always accedes to his interests and preferences, then they are not on sufficiently level footing to have a genuine relationship. Thus, the man should not permit his partner to be dependent on his judgment. That, I think, is not only unobjectionable, it is the only loving option.

This should not be taken as an across-the-board endorsement of paternalism. For as I noted, unconstrained paternalism of men toward their female partners is a sexist rut we must avoid. The only circumstances where it is permissible are in dramatic situations like those just described. In other, seemingly parallel, circumstances, paternalism is clearly out of order. For instance, I think relatively liberated people may legitimately leave remnants of our sexist upbringing in place. After all, we cannot plausibly eliminate all of them in one generation. Moreover, other effects might be alterable, but only by making efforts that "cost" more than they are worth.

Consider Ralph, a twenty-year-old man who is preparing for a career in mathematics. His father was a mathematician who imbued him with a love for math. Perhaps it is a shame the father influenced Ralph in this direction. Perhaps, with different parents, Ralph would have considered being a nurse, an accountant, an elementary school teacher, or a lawyer. But the fact is, he loves math. For him to try to alter his desires because he recognizes that, had other parents reared him he might have chosen differently, would be ludicrous. Of course if the parents had wanted him to become a criminal he should try to change (although I suspect he would have trouble doing so). But as long as it is a worthwhile and personally satisfying line of work, there is nothing wrong should he pursue math as a career. Likewise, there would be nothing wrong if Ralph decided he wanted to be a nurse. It is up to Ralph.

The problem becomes stickier, though, if we imagine a similar situation that many women face. Imagine a twenty-year-old woman completing her training to be an elementary school teacher. Although there is absolutely nothing wrong with her chosen career—it is a noble profession indeed—she likely developed her interest in teaching young children because of the gender roles into which she was inculcated. Perhaps she would have selected the same career had she been reared in a non-sexist culture; perhaps not. We will never know. Although she might have had different interests and desires, she is now the person whose first-order interests were shaped by her sexist upbringing. Under such circumstances she may decide that it would be counterproductive to try to develop different career interests. She might determine that she could not alter those interests. Or perhaps she might reason that she could alter her interests only by changing "who she is." She could diminish her desire to teach elementary school only by diminishing her interests in young children. That is something she does not want to do.

The woman does nothing wrong if she continues her preparation for teaching elementary school. Even though she (and Ralph) realize they might have pursued different careers had their upbringing been different, each decides that the cost of trying to alter their interests is either impossible, unnecessary, or imprudent.

If we are partners with a woman facing such a dilemma, it would be foolish *and* paternalistic to try to change her desires, even though these desires were largely formed by her sexist upbringing. (Of course if *she* wishes to change them, then her partner should support her in whatever way possible.) For, although the culture shaped her first-order desire to be a teacher, her second-order judgment is that her first-order desire need not be changed. If, under the circumstances, her male partner were to force her to change her career plans, it would be unacceptably paternalistic.[9] Notice, though, this case is relevantly different from the previous case in which I endorsed paternalism. There what was at issue was not some first-order desire, but rather, an all-pervasive second-order desire, which, if allowed to persist, would diminish if not eliminate her ability to make informed decisions.

Experiments in Relating

Abandoning talk of rights, equity, and egalitarianism may be especially frightening for men and women who want to relate in non-sexist ways. We all know how people encased in rights are supposed to relate—our entire culture is based on such ways of relating. We have brilliant models of people claiming their rights, demanding that they be treated justly or equitably. But, if we abandon sexist role models and refuse to build a relationship on rights, then we must establish new ways of relating. What are those new ways? We may be tempted to assume there is a preferred way of relating, a way we only need find. There is, however, nothing to find. There is no predetermined way of relating waiting to be discovered. There are no models we can emulate. We must *create* successful ways of relating through experiments in relating. We must try various arrangements, styles, and patterns, and we must critically evaluate our efforts. We must revise our efforts in light of that evaluation. There is no other way to have successful heterosexual intimate relationships. There is no well-trodden path for us to follow.

Conclusion

Having a close heterosexual relationship is difficult for those who seek to escape the constraints of sexist stereotypes. If such relationships are possible, it is only through the concerted efforts of both partners to identify and excise the sexist remnants. But the attempts to free ourselves from sexist bonds is a path rutted and full of brambles, ready to trip or ensnare us. For although we must regularly scrutinize our heterosexual relationships to ensure they are (relatively) free of sexist influence, we should not constantly scrutinize them. Constant analysis of ourselves and our relationships will make our actions stiff, ingenuine. Love involves spontaneously responding to the needs of our intimates. That is something we cannot do if we are constantly assessing our actions, motives, and relationships. We may expend so much energy ensuring that we have a non-sexist relationship that we do not have a relationship at all: we do not talk about things that are important; we cannot enjoy each other's company.

Self-reflection certainly plays an important role for humans; it is crucial for healthy personal relationships. It allows us to critically evaluate and subsequently modify our actions so they are more meaningful and productive. But its value can be fully achieved only if we are already active, if we already have a life worth evaluating. To put a twist on the well-known Socratic slogan: "the unlived life is not worth examining." Meaningful self-reflection is important. But it can all too easily become the purpose of the relationship, especially when people are on a holy crusade to excise the demons of sexism.[10]

Notes

1. I am well aware, however, that women have not made the legal and economic strides some politicians would have us believe. See Susan Faludi's *Backlash: The Undeclared War Against American Women* (New York: Crown Publishers, 1991).

2. For a philosophically sophisticated defense of separatism, and an account of a separatist ethic, see Sarah Lucia Hoagland's *Lesbian Ethics* (Palo Alto, CA: Institute of Lesbian Studies, 1988).

3. Perhaps eventually we can destroy all remnants of sexism. But doing so will take generations. For those of us who wish to have heterosexual relationships *now*, what can or will happen in a century is of little help. We must deal with the fact that we live in a sexist culture and that each of us at least partly embodies that culture.

4. "Perceptions of exploitation in communal and exchange relationships," *Journal of Social and Personal Relationships* 2, 403–18 (1985); "Record-keeping in two types of relationships," *Journal of Personality and Social Psychology* 47, 549–57 (1984); "Interpersonal attraction in exchange and communal relationships" *Journal of Personality and Social Psychology* 37, 12–24 (1979).

5. Marilyn Friedman, "Justice Among Friends," American Philosophical Association, Eastern division (1986). See Chapter 5 of her book, *What are Friends For? Feminism, Personal Relationships, and Moral Theory* (New York: Cornell University Press, forthcoming in 1993).

6. Perhaps the reader is not comfortable with the particular illustrations provided. Perhaps, you do not want *anyone* taking your books without permission. Or perhaps you do not want *anyone* to get angry with you—even if he or she is a friend. These examples, though, are just that: examples. My point is merely that there are some things that intimates can do without explicit permission—actions that, if performed by a stranger, would constitute a violation of your rights.

7. If I discovered that a good friend did not call when she desperately needed my help because she did not want to violate my privacy . . . I would be upset. Among other things, I would doubt whether our friendship was as important to her as it was to me.

8. In this section I draw heavily from John Hardwig's "Should Women Think in Terms of Rights," *Ethics* (1984).

9. This may be one more casualty of our sexist culture. In a completely non-sexist culture, intimates might well be justified in acting paternalistically toward their partners—at least in some cases. After all, we assume our

intimates *really do* wish to promote our best interests; likely, too, they know what those interests are. But, given the tendency of males to dominate, paternalism should be avoided in all but the most extreme cases.

10. I would like to thank the editors for their encouragement and criticism of an early draft of this paper.

5

Fatherhood and Nurturance

Larry May and Robert A. Strikwerda

I myself am still in doubts about matters concerning fathers.
—Sigmund Freud (1897)[1]

Shortly after the birth of our first children in the late 1980's, we were asked by several close friends how we liked "fatherhood." We found this question to be a bit puzzling. Why hadn't these people asked how we liked *parenthood*? What sort of things did they have in mind that we were expected to have done, as fathers, that would form the basis of our answers? At the time there were few if any experiences or feelings that we could put a finger on that would count as distinctly "fatherly." (Note the different connotations evoked by "mothering" a child versus "fathering" a child.) Yet, our lives certainly had changed. We had made a commitment to share equally in the raising of our children with our partners. But what was involved in being a parent was unknown. We did have some idea of the amount of *time* that was to be required, but the emotional and attitudinal changes that were, and continue to be, required were very much *terra incognita*. This paper is an attempt to frame some of our reflections on trying to be fathers who share equally in the parenting role.

There have been philosophical discussions of what fatherhood or parenthood should *not* be, in particular, not abusive, as well as discussions of the *duties* and responsibilities of a parent. But these establish limits, without developing a more positive sense of what fatherhood can be. It seems clearer what a bad father is than what a good father should be.[2] In this paper, we wish to advance the notion that being a father today, given our contemporary conditions, is best understood in terms of nurturance.[3] We take this notion of "fatherhood as nurturance" to be an *ideal,* not something which is necessarily

75

obligatory. Our philosophic experience has made us skeptical of trans-historical, trans-cultural claims about such things as ideals, and we recognize the limits of our personal experiences: white, male, hetero-sexual, middle-class. Nonetheless, we do think that the issues we raise have a wider relevance.

In arguing that fatherhood should today be ideally conceived in terms of nurturance we will first provide a brief history of modern conceptions of fatherhood. Second, we will analyze the notion of nurturance and argue that more traditional conceptions of fatherhood that are not drawn in terms of nurturance are quite anemic. Third, we will respond to several arguments against our thesis from biology and psychology. And finally we will explore some of the significant advantages to fathers, their children, their partners, and to society that will accrue when fathers see themselves as, and become, nurturers.

We will draw on philosophical works as well as our own experiences and those reported in social science literature. Our focus is philosophical: to see how the conception of fatherhood will change when men view themselves as nurturers, and to see how the conceptualization of nurturance may change when it is recognized that fatherhood, and not just motherhood, can be defined primarily by reference to nurturance. In discussing the ideal of fatherhood as nurturance we will be guided by parallels with the way feminists have come to reconceive mother-hood.[4]

I. Conceiving Fatherhood

There are at least two alternative ideals of fatherhood that have been historically important: the father as ruler and the father as educator. Sir Robert Filmer, author of the 17th-century tract in political theory entitled *Patriarcha,* uses a conception of fatherhood to dispute the growing movement of the time toward equality and natural liberty. He contends that it cannot be true that all are created equal, for God created one man, Adam, before all others, and made this man the father of us all. As Filmer states it, "not only Adam, but the succeeding Patriarches had, by right of fatherhood, royal authority over their children."[5] Filmer continues, "I see not then how the children of Adam, or of any man else, can be free from subjection to their parents."[6] And while he here uses parent rather than father, it is clear, as John Locke ably demonstrated, that Filmer was not thinking of female parents.

It was Filmer's intent to develop an analogy between a king and his subjects, on the one hand, and a father and his children, on the other hand. The father had absolute right over his children because of his legacy from Adam and also because he was, supposedly, the first cause of the conception of the child. These factors gave to a father a kind of property right in the child that the mother did not have. Similarly, a king had an absolute right to rule as a legacy from Adam, as first ruler, and as the literal father of all people, a right which could not be shared by others. Today, it is hard to see what kind of analogy could be drawn from family life. Perhaps, just as we have turned increasingly to democratic forms of rulership so there has been an increasing interest in role-sharing among parents.

Nine years after Filmer's book first appeared in print, John Locke began his *Two Treatises of Government* by soundly criticizing Filmer. He attacks Filmer's contention that "all power was originally in the father"[7] and that this gives fathers "absolute power over their children."[8] But, Locke argues, it is a mistake to focus so exclusively on only one of the two necessary parties in the procreative act. Rather, both mothers and fathers have an absolute claim on their children, since both performed necessary roles in begetting. It is parents rather than merely fathers that can lay claim to their children as property. And hence fathers and mothers are equals, Locke argued, in that they are equally absolute rulers over their children. Despite their differences, for Locke as well as for Filmer, parenthood is still conceived as rulership.

Rousseau develops a different ideal by extending Locke's point about equality and softening his conclusion about the consequences of this equality. In the *Discourse on the Origin and the Foundation of Inequality Among Men,* Rousseau talks of the "gentleness" of paternal authority:[9]

> by the Law of Nature the Father is the Child's master only as long as it needs his help, that beyond that point they become equal, and that then the son, perfectly independent of the Father, owes him only respect and not obedience. . . .

Freedom is characterized as a "gift of Nature" of which "Parents had no right to divest" their children.[10] In his *Emile,* Rousseau is quite strident in opposing the tradition which Filmer and Locke had embraced:[11]

> A father who engenders and feeds children, does with that only a third of his task. He owes to his species men; he owes to society sociable men; he owes to the state citizens. Every man who can pay this triple debt and does not do so is culpable, and more culpable perhaps when he pays it halfway. He who cannot fulfill the duties of a father has no right to become one.

Rousseau rails against fathers who find substitutes to fulfill their duties, whether these be hired caretakers or their wives. A major fear is that multiplying caregivers will lead to conflicting interpretations of right behavior, thus weakening the respect for the rule of law that Rousseau stresses fathers should be inculcating. He expects good fathers to show love and benevolence to their children, but his ideal is the father as educator, an educator of "sociable men" and citizens,[12] not the father as nurturer.

Historians have pointed out that there is a significant shift in the way that the family is organized and conceptualized with the onset of the 19th century. Previously, the family was typically a unit that sought to provide for the needs of its members by joint collaboration, epitomized by the cottage industries of the early industrial revolution, and by family-run farms. In the 19th century, it became possible and often necessary for one member of the family to support the family by working long hours outside the home. And it was almost always the man who left the home to find a job, and the woman who stayed at home with the children. Various theorists reflected this situation in their conceptualization of the roles of mothers and fathers.[13]

The effects of these changes were evident as we grew up in the 1950's. Parenting was what women did, and it was characterized as mainly involving the nurturance of children. Men worried about the financial security of their families, but rarely did they think of themselves as parents, except when it came to disciplining a recalcitrant child and introducing one's male children into various male activities. Fatherhood meant earning money, fixing the sink, and cutting the grass. Being a father had little to do with interacting with children. Except for an apparent greater emphasis on "providing," fatherhood was pretty much as it had been conceived in the 17th-century rulership ideal, with little understanding of even the educative roles that Rousseau had assigned to fathers.

II. Contemporary Types of Fatherhood

Today, due in part to the feminist movement, many heterosexual relationships aspire to be egalitarian (indeed many prefer the term "partnership" over marriage to describe significant relationships). Fathers don't breast-feed or give birth, but otherwise some fathers perform most if not all of the childrearing tasks that were once the exclusive domain of traditional mothers. Most fathers are involved to a greater extent in child-raising than their fathers were. Given these new realities for men, the door is now open for conceiving of fatherhood as nurturance.

We see our inability to think of our care-taking as "fatherly" as due to a conceptual disorder, a gap between what we were doing and how we thought of ourselves, and our activities. On reflection, though, it seems clear that what we are doing as fathers is quite similar to what, when done by mothers, is called nurturance. We see nurturance as a complex, multi-level notion. To be a nurturer is 1) to display caring behavior for an extended period of time, 2) to have an intellectual commitment to that caring, and 3) to identify oneself as a nurturing person. Nurturance is not simple caring, since as we will argue, nurturance requires a sustained effort toward a goal, and at least in practice, we do not think these activities can be sustained without a conscious effort and emotional identification.

The Oxford English Dictionary gives a number of related senses of nurturance. One is that of providing life-sustaining food, especially for an infant, probably the most common usage today. A second sense of nurturance is the support and rearing which leads to maturity. The first of these etymological stems is clearly linked to the mother's role in breast-feeding. But the second also has this identification in some cultures since it is the mother who raises the child to maturity as well. In the latter sense, nurturance is more than simply caring since it must proceed over a lengthy time-frame, from infancy to maturity. In addition, the dictionary definitions also list "to discipline and chasten" as a now obsolete meaning of nurture, implying that there is a sense of responsibility to nurturance that goes beyond that of simple caring.[14] We think that it is important to reinstate the idea that some forms of nurturance will typically involve discipline, a traditional domain of fathers.

The concept of nurturance has been closely linked to that of caring, and both have been closely identified with the experiences of women as mothers. In an influential study, Nel Noddings talks of three main components to caring: "receptivity, relatedness, and responsiveness."[15] But while important, these characteristics do not quite capture what is distinctive in nurturing. For the nurturer is not just receptive, but receptive in a particular way. And likewise the responsiveness is necessarily of a particular sort, which is based on the fact that the nurturer is related to a child, or an elderly parent, or a sick person as someone who has assumed the role of, and now identifies oneself as, a primary provider of what the child, parent or sick person needs. Thus nurturing involves fulfilling a responsibility to care for the other. The responsibility is normally defined in terms of a social role, such as parent or teacher, involving socially ascribed expectations, although this need not be true as is seen in the case of a mentor. These responsibilities of nurturing, in distinction from simple caring, also involve a commitment over some appreciable period of time, the time necessary to bring the subject to some end state such as health or adulthood.

Since fathers have often been given the role of disciplinarian and, following Rousseau, have sometimes been seen as chief educators of young children, they have engaged in some nurturing behavior toward their children. But they have not conceived of themselves as nurturers because there has been an overemphasis on the "to feed" dimension of nurturance. If we lay stress on nourishment as metaphor rather than literal meaning, then we come away with an understanding of nurturance as: sustained care including education and discipline, toward mature development. Such a definition of nurturance leaves ample room for fathers today, and gives us the opening we need to reconceptualize fatherhood in terms of nurturance.

It may be helpful if we situate our ideal of the nurturant father over against three other contemporary "types" of fathers. Two of these we could call "ideal types" since they incorporate an identifiable ideal, just as we found in the ideals of father as nurturer or educator. But at least one of these types, "the augmented traditional father," will be criticized precisely because it is incoherent in its "ideal." We freely admit that these "ideal types" are idealizations. Many contemporary fathers do not represent anything like the idealizations we will characterize. Some are either abusive to, or neglectful of, their children. In other families, finances are constrained to the point that one or both parents have to work such long hours that it is impossible for them to be the sort of parents they may otherwise wish to be. Our concern, though, is with what is the proper goal to which contemporary fathers should aspire.

The first contemporary type is that of *the traditional father,* working outside the home, understood in terms of pursuing a job or profession away from the hearth as well as in terms of maintaining the exterior of the house, the yard and the car. Such a father promotes a conventional image of strength, the provider and arranger of all things in the public realm. The older ideal of father as ruler has mutated into that of bureaucratic manager. Here there is a neat division between mother and father, what might be called separate spheres. Mothers are supposedly sovereign in the home, fathers are sovereign, as far as their family is concerned, outside the home. In the home itself, the father's major responsibility is that of disciplinarian, and secondarily one of role model for male children.

The second "type" of father is *the augmented traditional father.* Here the central aspects of the traditional father are maintained but with an acknowledgment of the pressures of the dual career family. This father cooks dinner when his partner is working late, or at least takes the kids out to dinner. He also does the laundry occasionally, and a bit of light housekeeping when things get really bad. He consoles and cares for his children on occasion, but perhaps as much to help out his partner as for the sake of the children directly. She is the one who worries about the children's overall development, their clothes and the household. Even if the time commitment of such a father to non-traditional male parenting activities is considerable, it is not a commitment that is central to his self-conception.

Third, there is what Calvin Trillin has called a SNAG, a sensitive new age guy.[16] Diane Ehrensaft describes one typical pattern of men who are trying to be fully equal parents. One sign of this is that some men claim to want a female rather than a male first offspring. Here's a bit of dialogue:[17]

> I really wanted a girl. I absolutely abhor male culture and have since I was a young boy. I do not like that kind of teasing, aggressive boys' play.

These men typically recall "the pain of their own boyhood and their early alienation from boy culture." Ehrensaft points out that if a boy was born to these men, they "discovered great joy and fulfillment in their relationships with their sons."[18] However, their bias against most things male very likely influences how such fathers parent. Ehrensaft also finds an interesting difference between the way that these fathers differ from mothers in the families she studied. "The man describes his relationship with his child as 'intimate.' The woman instead chooses the term 'nurturant.' "[19] Women typically see and describe their role as one of "protective bonding toward a small, helpless human being." The new age men studied have what Ehrensaft calls a "hunger for intimacy."[20] One father describes his relationship as follows:

> Kids are so spontaneous. No layers of social conventions. You can laugh, make silly jokes. You can't do that with adults. . . . With children, you can be a child with them.

This third "type" of father often seeks the kind of fulfillment in his children that he hasn't found in any of his other relationships.

We find all three of these types to be inadequate. The "traditional father" presupposes an economic division of labor which is quickly becoming obsolete. In addition, as feminists have long maintained, it perpetuates a stifling split of responsibilities along gender lines. Such a split deprives mothers of rewarding lives outside the home just as it deprives fathers of the rewards of nurturance. The traditional father may have known his place, but he barely knew his children, and more often than not was isolated from them when they were children and when they became adults.

The "augmented traditional father" is a bit harder to critique, especially if one sharpens the picture of the type. Suppose such a father devotes an extensive amount of time to child-care, an amount at least equivalent to that of his partner, and he thereby plays a major role in satisfying the needs of his children. But if he still does not see himself as a nurturing person, if nurturance has not entered into his self-conception, he will not be able to appreciate his accomplishments as a good father, nor will he attain the kind of satisfaction *within* the home that will free him from the need constantly to seek accomplishment only *outside* the home.

In this context consider the case of Stuart, a history professor who spends a lot of time caring for his infant child. Asked what he does when the baby is awake he says:[21]

> I try to do something constructive still, maybe a little reading or some project around the house . . . sometimes I'll be in the same room with him, other times I'll just let him play by himself.

Stuart seems to think that the time he spends in caring for his child is not constructive time. It is not enough for him to be intellectually committed to parenting, for this is not adequate for sustaining oneself in this role over time, or so has been our experience. The augmented traditional fathers, like Stuart, will not identify themselves as nurturers and they will have difficulty being motivated to be other than mere helpers, even though they may actually do as much child-rearing work as their partners.

The third type which conceives of fatherhood in terms of intimacy is also seriously flawed. There certainly are wonderful moments of spontaneity and personal directness in our relationships with our children, but this intimacy needs to be securely placed in a larger context. For example, Bob and the kids were having great fun jumping in the waves at Lake Michigan, reliving one of Bob's favorite childhood memories. But he did not notice that his daughter was moving quite close to a log, and suddenly a big wave propelled her against the log. The moment encapsulates the need to protect one's children, to remember to move them further down the beach out of the range of debris so they can continue to grow toward maturity. Communing with them is hardly enough.

We see nurturant fathers as closer to the mothers than to the new age fathers in Ehrensaft's study, especially given the stress on reciprocity and intimacy rather than caregiving. Personally, we would choose "nurturance" over "intimacy" in describing our roles as fathers. Do sensitive, new age fathers give up on those children who don't reward their fathers with intimate relationships? Fatherhood would not be worth much if this were the case. Intimacy involves full reciprocity; intimates know each other and reveal themselves to each other as equals. Nurturance can involve reciprocity, although it is not a necessary condition for it. But most often the kind of reciprocity involved in nurturance is partial rather than full. While our children normally display love in return for the love we show toward them, we continue to love them even when they are immersed in the nihilism and rebelliousness of the terrible two's. Also, while our children clearly add considerably to the growth process of their adult parents, this is not, nor should it be expected to be, comparable to what parents add to the development of their children.

To pick just one domain where much attention has recently been focused, it is clear that parents should not view their children as intimates in the sense of satisfying sexual or other emotional needs for the parent. The child who is regarded as the parent's sexual intimate is obviously endangered. In less extreme cases, the child is often asked to bear the kind of reciprocal role which he or she is either incapable of or which will almost certainly lead to developmental difficulties down the road. Certainly there will be intimate moments between father and child, but these should best be seen within the broader responsibilities of nurturing relations.

These three ideals are not so problematic as to be morally impermissible. They have greater problems than is true of the nurturant ideal, but they don't necessarily violate any duties of parents or rights of children. Rather the nurturant father ideal is proposed as in many respects superior to these other ideals, given the contemporary situation of many men. But the other ideals may themselves also have merits, especially within the context of very different social circumstances than those with which we are familiar.

III. Why Shouldn't Fathers Nurture?

Various reasons have been given for thinking that fathers should not conceive of themselves as nurturers. We consider the following positions. First, there are those who point to the biological differences between men and women, arguing that since men don't have wombs or breasts they are not constituted to be nurturers, and it would be harmful to the physical development of their children for men to try to nurture young children the way that women do. Second, there are psychological arguments indicating that women bond more easily with young children, and that it would be harmful to the psychological development of small children for men to play a major role in early childrearing. Third, there are positions which combine physical and psychological arguments together. In all three cases, we will provide counterarguments and counterexamples to these positions.

It has seemed most obvious that the role of fathers should be different from that of mothers when a child is a newborn. Fathers cannot give birth and they cannot breast-feed their newborns. They have not experienced the tremendous change in hormones which occurs to a woman during the late stages of pregnancy, changes which increase the so-called maternal instinct.[22] Since men have neither the physical organs which are uniquely suited for childrearing, nor the hormonal/instinctual drives to care for children, it is thought that they would be ill-advised to conceive of themselves as nurturers.

Nonetheless, increasingly fathers are taking a more active role in the birthing process. A nationwide group supporting natural childbirth refers to fathers as "coaches." This terminology is quite revealing. Of course there is the vaguely sexist connotation that the men are "in charge" of the birthing process, mothers being the mere team players. But beyond this, the role assigned to fathers is one of helping and even directing, rather than merely passively sitting in the waiting room, with cigars at the ready.

There is no reason to think that men can't bottle-feed as well as women, and little reason to think that birthing and breast-feeding *must* place the woman at the center of the infant's life in ways which push men off center. Fathers who assist at birth and who bottle-feed their infants would seem to have just as strong a potential to care for these infants as would mothers. The old thesis that women are instinctually better caregivers has met with strong opposition from most scientific quarters. One book on motherhood puts the point this way:[23]

> there are now no operative biological constraints that confine motherhood to one sex and make women of necessity more capable caregivers . . . nothing but tradition sends men out to work and keeps women at home.

It is interesting, though, that even this author devotes only a few pages to fatherhood, employing the term motherhood to cover the roles that are assumed by both female and male caregivers.

Aside from the physical argument, some have made a psychological argument in support of giving mothers priority over fathers in terms of nurturance. Breast-feeding is often characterized as the ultimate bonding process between women and newborns. Freud held that:[24]

> The libido there follows the paths of narcissistic needs and attaches itself to the objects which ensure the satisfaction of those needs. In this way the mother, who satisfies the child's hunger, becomes its first love-object and certainly also its first protection against all the undefined dangers which threaten it in the external world—its first protection against anxiety, we may say.

Freudian theory has made great use of the claim that both male and female children initially form their first attachments with their mothers, and then experience separation at weaning. Nancy Chodorow, quoting Edith Jacobson, talks of a "primitive, first, visual mother-image" that occurs in the feeding process, and which becomes the focus of all "libidinal stimulation and gratification" as well as the center of all memories of both positive and negative feelings of infancy.[25]

While breast-feeding may be important for many children, it is by no means a necessity since many children are not breast-fed. Many American children raised in the 1950's were bottle-fed and virtually all adopted infants, then and now, do not form their first attachments to their female parents through breast-feeding. The Freudian theorists who put so much emphasis on breast-feeding are really only addressing a portion of the infants in Western culture. Similarly the Freudian emphasis on penis envy and the oedipal complex have been recently discredited for the unjustified way that Freud and his followers attempted to generalize from an impoverished sample of cases.[26]

In 1956, Bruno Bettelheim provided one of the stronger versions of the view which we oppose by combining elements from biology and psychology. He argued that a father[27]

> undergoes no physiological and emotional changes comparable to the mother's, [and] has no comparable feelings of contributing intimately and directly to the baby's welfare. . . . When he tries to find greater fulfillment of his fatherhood by doing more for the child along the lines only mothers used to follow, the result is that he finds less rather than more fulfillment, not only for his fatherhood, but also for his manhood. . . . the relationship between father and child never was and cannot now be built principally around child-caring experiences. It is built around a man's function in society: moral, economic, political.

And Allan Bloom quite recently made a similar point when he said that the contemporary problems in the American family are traceable to the fact that men are trying to be child caretakers and women are trying to find achievement outside the home.[28]

In response to Bettelheim it is perhaps enough to refer to our own experiences, since all that is necessary to refute so absolutist a statement is one counterexample. It is simply not true that we experienced only frustration and loss of manliness when we nurtured our children. And in any event we find it odd indeed to think that men could establish much of a relationship at all with their children based solely on their economic or political functions. Perhaps when one's children are adults, such a basis for relationship will work, but with young children, to say nothing of infants and newborns, economics and politics are simply not a part of their conscious lives.

It is striking that Bettelheim seems to accept as given that the contemporary western social roles of men are the primary roles with which all fathers must identify. This is an example of the tendency in much of the literature about fatherhood to generalize from the basis of one narrow cultural perspective. There is, though, a lesson that can be learned from Bettelheim, although not one he intended. If men do not alter their self-conceptions and patterns of behavior, and if they instead just increase the time they spend with their children, problems will likely develop. They will indeed feel frustrated. And there will be more time to encourage their sons to be aggressive junior warriors and their daughters to be demure or submissive. Perhaps it would be better for *these* fathers to stay out of the child-raising domain.

Bloom's contemporary version of Bettelheim's argument is equally suspicious, although perhaps more subtle. The American family so idealized by conservative commentators like Bloom was very short-lived, lasting for perhaps a decade and a half for the members of one class in one society. And many of the women who were locked into the role of mother in those years express much regret for their lost life opportunities. Working class women and men never had the luxury so completely to separate the public and private spheres. But surely Bloom has picked the wrong target even if he is correct about the breakup of the family structure. So-called problem children in contemporary society do not result from those families where men want to nurture but rather from families where neither partner wants to, or is able to, nurture. It is hard to imagine that anyone would seriously maintain that having two nurturing parents is worse than having only one. Bloom seems to be able to envision only two alternatives, either one real nurturer, "the mom," or two inadequate ones; he fails to allow that two could nurture equally well. We conclude that none of these arguments give us any reason to think that there are insurmountable obstacles to our ideal of fathers as nurturers. In the next section, we will conclude by further discussing some of these difficulties as well as the positive advantages of this ideal of nurturance.

IV. Burdens and Benefits for the Nurturing Father

For those fathers who have a serious commitment to nurturance, even in the most egalitarian family settings, they often find that they are not as good at the mundane, day-to-day matters as their female partners. Men are socialized to be task-oriented and yet child-rearing involves a continuous, ephemeral process which involves endless repetition of tasks which are so seemingly simple as to be boring. If a task is completed, it typically has to be done again the next day—laundry, for example. Frustration and impatience are common feelings of men, although this is also true of many women, who are intimately involved in raising small children. (Perhaps this has given rise to views such as those of Bettelheim.) Part of the difficulty may be that men are not raised to know "how" to take care of children or to place value in the virtue of constancy. Yet another part of the problem also may be that men lack sensitivity to the needs of others, especially children who cannot yet express their needs straightforwardly.[29] Men who find it easy to remember to schedule regular maintenance appointments for their cars find it difficult to remember to schedule regular check-ups for their kids.

Regardless of the difficulties, there are compensating benefits for fathers, although some of them are hard to see at the time. Consider an example. You awaken out of a deep sleep, just a little light coming through the windows. Your four-year-old son is crying in the bathroom. He has diarrhea and has soiled his pajamas. You try to comfort him. He's feeling guilty and very unhappy. You put one arm around him, telling him it's OK. "These things just happen." With more hugs he begins to quiet down. He says with surprise, "it just came out, Dad." You say, yes, that sometimes happens when you're sick, "It's called diarrhea." He tries the word out a few times. You finish cleaning him up. You put him back in bed, and pat him for a while, more than he needs for he's already asleep. You feel like a father, even as you realize that you will be dead on your feet at work the next day. But as tired as you felt at the time, these images will come back to you often, with a warm sense of accomplishment.

For both of us, we were struck by the simplicity of our own child-care successes. In the early months, we both found that we could indeed calm our seemingly inconsolable newborns. If we paid attention to the child, and did the obvious things like changing diapers, feeding, and cuddling, and did not let ourselves get impatient, our kids could be comforted by the hugs and attention of their fathers. We could be the nurturers, although it was very good to have our female partners there to act as coaches, to turn the birth class language on its head. And here the sense of accomplishment was palpable and surely more than compensated for the burdens of fatherhood which Bettelheim discussed.

Fathers of newborn infants need to be wary of the patterns that get established early. The lack of socialization to comfort and cuddle and nurse should not be allowed to push men away from newborns and young children, for it will later be hard to get back into the middle of the child-rearing enterprise. The model of the adoptive parent should give all fathers cause for hope—most women who adopt learn to parent newborn children as a form of on-the-job training, where hormones have very little to do with it. Most men can also learn to deal with the psychological needs of the newborn child quite effectively. Even though men bring different skills to the parenting role, it is important that in the first year of life men not abdicate in favor of their somewhat more at ease female partners. Virginia Held has written:[30]

Taking care of small children for a few years of one's life is an incredibly interesting and satisfying kind of work. . . . I hardly expect that fathers would be so foolish as to let mothers get more than their fair share of the best work of young adulthood and let grandmothers get more than their fair share of the best work of late middle age. If fathers *would* be that foolish, they would still be entitled to equality, and mothers would have an obligation to help them realize it.

Fathers should also be resistant to the separate spheres approach, even in the face of the frustrations of child caretaking, because of the many positive benefits they can provide to *others* by their involvement in early child-raising. First, there are obvious benefits to the family from having two caregivers, who can alternate tasks, and so on. But these accrue to lesbian parents as well. A second major benefit concerns the development of the children. They no longer have to deal with a parent who is both there and not there, a person obviously of great importance in the family, but yet without much identity for the kids. Larry's father was around so little when he was growing up that he was left with no image of what males in a household were supposed to do. Thirdly, mothers will benefit from having partners who are more than just "helpers," hopefully sharing equally in the burdens of parenthood.

As fathers begin to see themselves as nurturers, their disciplinary roles will take on a different, more positive aspect for themselves and their children. In the recent past, when men disciplined their children they were able to retreat to office or backyard after punishment had been inflicted, thereby effectively avoiding the aftermath of punishment. As fathers take on greater shares in all aspects of the parenting process, they will have to contend with the child both before and after discipline is called for. This will make the disciplining task both more challenging and more beneficial for both child and father. Fathers cannot any longer be like the hooded executioners of the Middle Ages who evaded community displeasure for their acts. Fathers will have to face their own feelings of regret or shame for having inappropriately punished as well as the need to rebuild trust and a positive sense of self-worth in the child. And the trusting relationship that develops will have strongly positive payoffs for the future relationship between father and older child. In addition, their work in the family will be something about which they can feel a sense of accomplishment.

Men are generally socialized in Western culture to be competent in the public world, but not in the private world. While these categories are definitely not as clear-cut and mutually exclusive as was previously thought, there is a sense in which boys are brought up to prefer to be, and to become, competent in the sandlot baseball diamonds, the newspaper routes and the great outdoors generally rather than the confines of the home. Girls are often brought up to prefer to be, and to become, competent in the skills and tasks associated with the home. Yet, clearly child-raising should not typecast our children in this way, even though it has done so for those who are already adults. Many of the difficulties women experience today in the so-called "man's world of the (paid) workplace" are traceable to these differential, and disproportionately disabling, socializations. A recent study of Mary and Elizabeth Tudor, daughters of Henry VIII, reveals that some girls have been able to reverse the typical socialization, just as Elizabeth did, in the face of even greater social pressures than exist today. But most girls follow the path of Mary Tudor, feeling that they need to rely on a male to handle their public affairs. In Mary's case this clearly worked to her detriment.[31]

In this time of transition, nurturing fathers could use their socialized *public* skills to provide positive socialization especially for their girl children. Due to their socialization, men are better able to teach kids how to fend for themselves, especially how to assert themselves into a sometimes hostile world or sandbox. Given the differential socializations already experienced by adults today, fathers will be somewhat better at such roles than mothers. And by this we do not mean merely teaching girls to throw a ball "properly" (that is, not like a girl).[32] Rather, we have in mind taking children on regular outings to the playground or museum or just to the corner store and talking to one's children about strategies for coping with disparate problems, especially with male strangers, that can be encountered along the way.

But such limited roles for fathers are only the tip of the iceberg of what men can offer to the child-raising enterprise. Giving our children a broader, more expansive view of what men and women are capable of is perhaps the most important long-range developmental benefit of having a nurturing father. Daughters can hope to be mothers *and* firefighters, and sons can hope to be fathers *and* day-care teachers when they grow up. And if we are right about the benefits to future generations of children from having two nurturers rather than one, it can never be too early to start socializing boys, due to role modeling, to begin to identify themselves as nurturers. It is not easy to counteract the influences of television, as well as the influences of other children and their parents.

Now looking back, we have a greater confidence in the ability of men to overcome their role requirements. This is quite apparent in the nurturing care Bob's father (and grandfather) gave to his mentally retarded sister, the youngest in the family. Here in an unusual situation that fell outside normal circumstances they could display a care not expected from them in their "normal" roles. This greater display of nurturance by men as they grow older is apparently quite common.[33] But it was not a primary element as we grew up; for the most part our fathers were off working to provide for us, while our mothers actually delivered the goods.

We have tried to indicate that the burdens will be outweighed by the benefits that accrue to male nurturers and their families from adapting their socialization to cope with the needs of their children. But there is a further, social benefit. When men identify themselves as caregivers of their children, this will end, we hope, the noxious definition of certain issues as "women's issues," where humane parental leave policies, day care support, and the like remain defined as those of a "special interest," instead of the concern for the next generation of our society.

Fatherhood needs to be reconceptualized so that it takes account of the way that fathers have traditionally nurtured their children, and the ways that today's fathers can extend that nurturance so that it becomes the dominant characteristic of their role as fathers. We have argued for an ideal characterization of fatherhood in terms of nurturance which corresponds to the experiences many contemporary fathers are having or at least would aspire to. The ideal of fatherhood can be defined by reference to that dimension of nurturance which involves *caring* and *rearing toward maturity*, involving nourishment, but also humane discipline and creative education into the public domain. We hope this very preliminary analysis of nurturance in fatherhood will inspire as much work on the changing roles for men in our culture as has been spawned for the changing roles of women by recent feminist literature.[34]

Notes

1. *The Letters of Sigmund Freud, 1873–1939*, edited by Ernst Freud, translated by Tania Stern and James Stern, London: Hogarth, 1961, p. 237.

2. Mike W. Martin, in his chapter "Parents and Children" in *Everyday Morality*, Belmont, CA: Wadsworth, 1989, provides a good survey of such discussions. He concludes, without elaborating, by saying "Love is the aim and ideal of parent-child relationships. It is itself an ideal, not a duty" (p. 250). Our essay is an attempt to sketch the specific form of that love.

3. Some feminists have questioned the use of the term parenting to describe what fathers do, preferring instead to say that fathers *mother*. See Sara Ruddick, "Thinking about Fathers," in *Conflicts In Feminism*, edited by Marianne Hirsch and Evelyn Fox Keller, NY: Routledge, Chapman and Hall, 1990; and Sara Rae Peterson, "Against Parenting" in *Mothering*, edited by Joyce Trebilcot, Totowa, NJ: Rowman and Allanheld, 1983. Throughout this paper we give reasons for preferring to say that mothers and fathers *nurture*.

4. For some of the best in this literature see Angela Baron McBride, *The Growth and Development of Mothers*, NY: Harper and Row, 1973, especially chapter 8; and Joyce Trebilcot, editor, *Mothering*, op. cit.

5. Robert Filmer, *Patriarcha and Other Political Works*, edited by Peter Laslett, Oxford: Basil Blackwell Publishers, 1949, p. 57.

6. Ibid.

7. John Locke, *Two Treatises of Government*, edited by Peter Laslett, NY: Mentor Books, 1965, paragraph 62, p. 222.

8. Ibid., paragraph 52, p. 214.

9. Jean-Jacques Rousseau, *The First and Second Discourses*, edited and translated by Victor Gourevitch, NY: Harper and Row, 1986, Part II, paragraph 40, p. 188.

10. Ibid., paragraph 42, p. 190.

11. Jean-Jacques Rousseau, *Emile*, translated by Allan Bloom, NY: Basic Books, 1979, p. 48.

12. See Penny Weiss and Anne Harper, "Rousseau's Political Defense of the Sex-roled Family," *Hypatia*, vol. 5, no. 3 (Fall 1990) pp. 99–102.

13. See Arthur Schopenhauer, "On Women" in *Schopenhauer Selections*, NY: Charles Scribner's Sons, 1928, p. 435–446.

14. See *The Oxford English Dictionary*, p. 608.

15. Nel Noddings, *Caring*, Berkeley: University of California Press, 1984, p. 2.

16. Calvin Trillin, "Generation Rap," *Eleven Magazine* (the magazine of WTTW, Chicago), February 1990, p. 6.

17. Diane Ehrensaft, *Parenting Together: Men, Women, and Sharing the Care of their Children*, NY: Free Press, 1987, p. 138.

18. Ibid.

19. Ibid., p. 35.

20. Ibid., p. 126.

21. R. LaRossa and M.M. LaRossa, *Transition to Parenthood*, Beverly Hills, CA: Sage, 1981, cited in Alice S. Rossi, "Gender and Parenthood," *American Sociological Review*, volume 49, 1984, p. 7

22. For a critical discussion of this claim, see Caroline Whitbeck's essay "The Maternal Instinct," *The Philosophical Forum*, vol. 6, nos. 2–3, Winter-Spring 1974–1975.

23. Rudolph Schaffer, *Mothering*, Cambridge: Harvard University Press, 1977, p. 104.

24. Sigmund Freud, *The Future of an Illusion*, translated by W.D. Robson-Scott, NY: Anchor Books, [1927] 1964, p. 34.

25. Nancy Chodorow, *The Reproduction of Mothering: Psychoanalysis and the Sociology of Gender*, Berkeley: The University of California Press, 1978, p. 65.

26. See David Willbern's essay "Father and Daughter in Freudian Theory," in *Daughters and Fathers*, edited by Lynda E. Boose and Betty S. Flowers, Baltimore: The Johns Hopkins University Press, 1989.

27. Bruno Bettelheim, "Fathers Shouldn't Try to be Mothers," reprinted in *Feminist Frameworks*, edited by Allison Jagger and Paula Rothenberg, NY: McGraw-Hill, 1984, p. 308.

28. See Allan Bloom, *The Closing of the American Mind*, NY: Simon and Schuster, 1987, cited and discussed in Susan Moller Okin, *Justice, Gender and the Family*, New York: Basic Books, 1989, pp. 33–40, especially p. 35.

29. See our essay, "Male Friendship and Intimacy," reprinted from *Hypatia* in this volume.

30. Virginia Held, "The Equal Obligations of Mothers and Fathers," in *Having Children,* edited by Onora O'Neill and William Ruddick, New York: Oxford University Press, 1979, p. 238.

31. Leah S. Marcus, "Erasing the Stigma of Daughterhood: Mary I, Elizabeth I and Henry VIII," in *Daughters and Fathers*, op. cit.

32. See Iris Young's provocative essay, "Throwing Like a Girl: A Phenomenology of Feminine Body Comportment, Motility and Spatiality," in *Throwing Like a Girl and Other Essays in Feminist Philosophy and Social Theory*, Bloomington: Indiana University Press, 1990, pp. 141–169.

33. See Rossi, op. cit., p. 9: "It has been noted in a variety of studies that with age, men become less assertive, more tender and nurturant. . . ."

34. We are grateful for comments and suggestions supplied by Penny Weiss, Marilyn Friedman, Loretta Kensinger and the participants in the Women's Studies Symposium held at Purdue University in April of 1991.

PART FOUR

Men Relating to Men

6

Male Friendship and Intimacy

Robert A. Strikwerda and Larry May

Life is so very different when you have a good friend. I've
seen people without special friends, close friends. Other
men, especially. For some reason men don't often make
and keep friends. This is a real tragedy, I think, because in
a way, without a tight male friend, you never really are able
to see yourself. That is because part of shaping ourselves is
done by others; and a lot of our shaping comes from that
one close friend who is something like us.
    —Mr. Hal[1]

The "tradition" in the West has made comradeship between men the
paradigm of friendship. Friendships in their purest form have been
thought to exist more often among men than among women. Vera
Brittain summarizes:

> From the days of Homer the friendships of men have enjoyed glory and
> acclamation, but the friendships of women, despite Ruth and Naomi,
> have usually been not merely unsung, but mocked, belittled. . . .[2]

For the most part the characteristics of loyalty, fellow feeling, and
concern for the other's interests have been stressed much more heavily
than intimacy in male friendships. Moreover, the presence of these
characteristics has been thought to make male friendship superior to
female friendship.

    In contrast, recent studies of Americans indicate that men tend not
to have same-sex friendships that are as satisfying to them as same-
sex friendships are to women.[3] And men are beginning to wonder why
this is so. Daniel Levinson writes that in "our interviews, friendship
was largely noticeable by its absence. As a tentative generalization, we

would say that close friendship with a man or a woman is rarely experienced by American men."[4] In 1985, after a ten-year study of 5,000 American men and women, Michael McGill stated:

> To say that men have no intimate friends seems on the surface too harsh. . . . But the data indicate that it is not far from the truth. . . . Their relationships with other men are superficial, even shallow.[5]

This recognition of a connection between the absence of intimacy in friendships among men and dissatisfaction with these friendships is our starting point. What we provide here is an exploration of the *concept* of intimacy, especially in adult male relationships. We begin with an examination of comradeship, one form of male friendship, and use this to help develop, in the second section, an account of the nature and value of intimacy in friendship. We follow this with an account of obstacles to intimacy. In our fourth section, we suggest how our view parallels certain Aristotelian themes. In the final section, we focus on the process of developing intimacy among men, discussing some moments in that process and resources that men can employ in the attainment of intimacy, even if in a fashion different from that typical of women.

In developing our account of intimacy, we draw heavily on our own experiences, supplementing them with conceptual analysis, the accounts of others, and sociological and psychological research. This is not a survey of the literature. Our primary intent is the philosophic one of building a more adequate account of what intimacy can be in the context of male friendships. Our own experiences, from which this paper originated, are admittedly limited. Both of us are male, heterosexual, white, North American, and middle class. And both of us consider ourselves feminists, and we have tried to reassess male experience from a feminist perspective. Our experiences may not be typical, although our conversations and research lead us to think that our experiences are far from unique.

We believe that our topic deserves attention by feminist philosophers, whether male or female. Much feminist writing has focused on a reassessment of female experience in order to counter oppression against women. The social practice of men failing to develop and express their feelings does have the consequence that men in general are more able to oppress than would be true otherwise.[6] Phenomenologically, however, men simply do not see themselves as oppressors in this way. It does not seem to us that most men *intentionally* oppress women by failing to disclose their feelings; rather, many men are not even aware that they could be acting otherwise. Nonetheless, they do increasingly see themselves as lacking in intimate relationships. Thus we try to provide a positive sense of what male friendship could be like in a less oppressive society.[7] It is our hope that if men do become more intimate and caring with each other, they will also become so with the women and children in their lives, thus making it less likely that oppression will continue at its present level.

I. Comradeship and Male Bonding

Male friendships often resemble the relationships between very young children who engage in "parallel play." These children want to be close to each other in the sandbox, for example, but they just move the sand around without sharing or helping and *usually* without hurting each other. They don't really interact *with* each other; they merely play side-by-side—hence the term parallel play.

Here is a rather common adult example of parallel play. Two men sit in a bar, each sipping his third beer. Every few minutes one speaks, more by way of a speech (about last night's baseball game or the new beer on tap); the other nods in agreement but waits a while before speaking himself, and then often on a different topic altogether. The men are not concerned by the lack of conversation; indeed, they might tell you that they know each other so well that they don't need to have lengthy conversations, adding that it is the peace and quiet of one another's company that they each prize most highly. When they depart for home, they clasp hands or perhaps merely salute one another.[8]

Such companionship is enjoyable; at least, we have enjoyed it. Our point is not to criticize such relationships. Not every friendship needs to be intimate. However, it seems to us that if *all* of one's friendships display such a lack of intimacy, then one's life will be impoverished and unsatisfying. Such friendships are not in themselves impoverished, but a steady diet of them may lead one either to nutritional deficiency or to hunger for something more. Similarly, if men are open to intimacy only with female friends or partners, they cut themselves off from deeply rewarding relationships with other men, as well as help perpetuate a debilitating gender pattern in which women do the emotional work for men.

Some traditional male experiences have led to a form of friendship that may pass for intimacy—what we call comradeship. The sharing of certain kinds of experiences—such as those of teenage boys in a summer resort community, of soldiers in the trenches, or of sailors on long sea voyages—provides the occasion for mutual self-disclosure among males. In these situations, one is in a period of some stress, whether puberty or physical danger, with plenty of time and not enough activity to fill it. In war, men are forced to be with one another, and they report that in this situation they often reflect on aspects of their lives they normally would block. Soldiers not only fight shoulder to shoulder, but they sit for long hours in cramped quarters wondering if their lives will end in the next barrage of gunfire. Such occasions can bring men to talk about deeply personal matters in their lives and hence to form bonds with one another that may last long after the common experiences have ended.[9]

Loyalty clearly plays a significant role in comradeship. In *The Warriors*, J. Glenn Gray provides a phenomenological account of the experiences of comradeship that develop in combat settings.

> Near the front it was impossible to ignore, consciously or unconsciously, the stark fact that out there were men who would gladly kill you, if and when they got the chance. As a consequence, an individual was dependent on others . . . [and] in turn he was of interest only as a center of force, a wielder of weapons, a means of security and survival. This confraternity of danger and exposure is unequaled in forging links among people of unlike desire and temperament. . . .[10]

In combat situations, some men recognize that they are exposed and vulnerable in ways men normally do not acknowledge. From the position of mutual vulnerability, they come to seek out others on whom they can depend, rather than withdraw into their own self-contained egos.

Interestingly, in wartime situations comrades come to see each other in abstract rather than highly personal terms. As Gray points out, "comrades are loyal to each other spontaneously, and without any need for reasons."[11] But, as Gray also notes, this loyalty is fragile since it is not necessarily connected to "spontaneous liking and the feeling of belonging."[12] Indeed, the bonding that epitomizes comradeship is strictly non-particularistic. "Men are true comrades only when each is ready to give up his life for the other, without reflection and without thought of personal loss."[13]

This lack of reflection in comradeship has had terrible, destructive consequences, both in wartime and in so-called peacetime. The high rate of involvement of fraternities in college rapes is a case in point. Mary Daly explores this idea in *Gyn/Ecology*, building in part on Gray's phenomenological account. Accepting his distinction between comradeship and male friendship, she contrasts these with sisterhood and female friendship. Whereas for women sisterhood has a potential to become friendship, she sees comradeship as not leading to true friendship for men.[14] Our contention is that it is possible to expand the forms of friendship that occur, such that it will no longer be true, as Daly claims, that "male bonding/comradeship *requires* the stunting of individuality."[15]

Comrades are not necessarily intimate friends, for they are often bound to one another as generalized others, not in terms of who each one is as a unique member of the human race. Somewhat paradoxically, comrades are loyal to each other not out of concern for the particularity of the individual other, but out of an almost impartial respect for people of a certain type or in a certain situation: fellow soldiers, compatriots, coworkers, etc. Thus there can be a wide diversity of backgrounds and personality types among comrades in combat, without the reciprocal willingness to sacrifice one's life for the other varying as a result. Comradeship is a deontological regard for a generalized other and, in this sense, is quite different from intimate friendships, which are based on a regard for a particularized other and where consequences and contexts matter quite a bit.

In intimate friendship, the psychic boundary that normally encloses the male self, allowing for the characteristically self-confident, competent, single-minded pursuit of one's public roles, is temporarily opened to allow a new focus to develop, one that includes the man and another person. It is not the formation of a new boundary as typical in comradeship, but an expansion of one's concentration of attention from self to include the other. This new concentration may look similar to our stereotyped notion of male bonding. What often passes for intimate male bonding is really the deep loyalty of comradeship, which is based on so little information about the person to whom one is loyal that it is quite fragile and likely to change as new people come to instantiate the type to whom the comrade is loyal. In contrast, because intimate bonding is based on particular characteristics of the other, it will not generally break apart unless the people themselves change significantly.

Perhaps the following analogy is apropos. Just as some anthropologists describe the typical American marriage pattern as "serial monogamy" (just one spouse at a time), so for many men having friends is "serial best-friendship." As Stanley Bing puts it, a bit facetiously, "I don't miss my formerly essential friends, because I have been able to re-create over and over again the same satisfying infantile relationship with any number of adult males within lunching distance. Every one of these guys is precious, and every one can be replaced."[16] Similarly, we have friends who are "workfriends" or "next-door friends" or "racketball partners," involving more or less constricted friendships, limited in time, place, or social situation. Thus these friendships are likely to change when the situation does. As in marriages, "divorces" and "remarriages" occur in friendships, but perhaps it is time to reconsider what intimacy in a relationship is when one is marrying for the fifth time or, as Bing would put it, "re-creating one's fifth set of essential friends."

II. The Nature and Value of Intimacy

Intimacy paradigmatically occurs in a reciprocal relationship between two or more people. Knowing oneself intimately seems to us a derivative notion, though we will suggest self-knowledge does have an essential role to play in enabling reciprocal intimacy. Although there is a substantial knowledge element involved in intimacy, there is also a degree of what one might call understanding. It is not simply knowledge of facts about the person, or an ability to predict behavior, but also an understanding of why something is the way it is, of priorities and relations. As one might expect from its etymological roots (as the superlative form of *interior*—"innermost"), intimacy typically involves a sense of a deep or profound relationship. Finally, intimacy includes an element of warmth in two dimensions, that of caring receptivity and that of being comfortable, as in "an intimate club."

Intimacy in a friendship involves a mutual relation; one cannot really be an intimate friend without a reciprocity of intimacy from another. Indeed, the reciprocal enrichment and enjoyment that typically flow from intimate relationships may constitute the chief value of such relationships. Consider the friendships that might start with one co-worker asking another, "Wanna get some lunch?" Having once learned something about the other person and liking him, one typically acts to further the relationship, not just with a directly work-related suggestion, but with something that is optional. If one finds another person interesting but that person is not willing to make time for lunch or a beer, the relationship is unlikely to get off the ground. He has not given a sign of the mutuality of interest and respect that grounds intimate friendship. Nor is there a place for the simple enjoyment of each other's company or conversation.

Genuine intimacy involves a deep or intense mutual knowledge that allows the participants to grow in both self-understanding and understanding of others. That knowledge includes understanding the defining personal characteristics of an individual, conjoined with enjoyment of and loyalty to that person. Whereas one can speak of certain kinds of friends—for example, sports buddies—that one doesn't know very well, one wouldn't say this about an intimate friend. One might say, after some unexpected event, "I guess I didn't know my friend very well, but he's still my friend," but it would be quite odd to say, "I don't know him very well, but we're still intimate friends."

Even if mutual knowledge is linked to strongly positive emotional feelings for one another, these are not enough to constitute intimate friendship. It is possible for two people to know a great deal about each other and feel positively toward each other without that counting as intimate friendship. The relationship of counselor and counselee, especially when they both like each other, may involve knowledge and positive feelings without being an intimate friendship. The constrained nature and the distinctly different roles of the two people make it something other than an intimate friendship, at least until some other dimensions are added to their relationship.

Perhaps the most significant step in friendship is the achievement of a mutual trust based on some form of shared experience. To attain this trust, people usually need time in each other's company. Over time, that common experience leads to self-disclosure as a sign of trust. This trust engenders a corresponding loyalty and a further relaxation to heighten each other's enjoyment of shared activities.

As we saw in the examination of comradeship, to be intimate with another person one cannot be loyal to that person as a mere abstract other. Intimacy is not mere "fellow feeling" or mutual respect, although intimacy shares much in common with each of these concepts. Intimacy involves the kind of self-revelatory disclosures that go beyond what is necessary to generate sympathy or respect. Indeed, self-disclosure by itself often makes sympathy and respect more difficult. That is why one wants a sign of trustworthiness before one becomes intimate friends with another. When these elements of knowledge, positive feelings, trust, and reciprocity coalesce, then self-disclosure is a form of mutual enclosure in which two selves create a new, inclusive focus of attention, what Aristotle terms a complete friendship.

III. Obstacles to Intimacy in Male Friendships

As we have noted, many male friendships lack the dimension of mutual self-disclosure. The women we know report forming friendships through self-revealing discussion, whereas the men we know report that they typically form friendships based on common activities, such as work or participation in some sport, with self-revelation being at best tangential to the activity. On one level, it is certainly easier to engage in self-disclosure through discussion than by other, less-straightforward means, since one is able to disclose one's feelings with the least ambiguity by simply saying how one feels. But that presupposes capacities that many men currently lack. It is not a logical necessity that self-disclosure occur by means of discussion. Insofar as what we are is created by what we do as much as the reverse, action can be as vital a form of disclosure as speech.[17]

However, if one cannot accompany another person in the various aspects of the other's life, full disclosure through action is virtually impossible, and thus disclosure via speech becomes a practical necessity. Actions cannot easily disclose the past or project into the future without words to set the context. When one shares a past with another and shares a variety of activities—working at the same place, shopping at the same stores, attending the same church or synagogue—one can expect to disclose oneself gradually through action. The increasing diversity and mobility of North American life means that the route to intimacy through a shared past linked with shared present activities is not open to many of us. Thus, self-disclosure through speech is the only realistic possibility we have found.

The difficulties are not simply social or logistical. In order to be able to engage in self-disclosure, persons must be able to gain access to the feelings they are trying to disclose to their friends. And in order to gain this access, they must in some sense be aware of having certain feelings and be able to conceptualize them. Yet males in contemporary Western culture are encouraged not to show their feelings; indeed, from the dispassionate reasoner model of the philosopher to the Clint Eastwood image of manhood, males are encouraged not to let their feelings interfere at all with the conduct of their lives.[18] The culturally ingrained habit of hiding, rejecting, and denying legitimacy to one's feelings makes it much harder for these males, for us, to gain access to feelings and impedes the disclosure of these feelings to intimate friends.[19] We need others to help understand ourselves, as G. H. Mead has stressed, yet without some degree of self-awareness or self-intimacy we can only with great difficulty communicate what is most important about ourselves.

Larry had a revealing experience several years ago. Right before setting out for his grandfather's funeral, several friends remarked that he was keeping remarkably cool in the face of what must have been very emotionally difficult times. In reflecting on this on the way to the funeral, he discovered, much to his own amazement, that he simply had no feelings about the death of his grandfather. It was not that he and his grandfather had been distant or enemies; indeed, they had once been fairly close. But over the years, he had let the thought of his grandfather become less and less important until there simply were no positive or negative feelings attached to him. While there were no feelings here, except indifference, to disclose to his friends, the very lack of emotions could have been, but was not at that time, a basis for self-disclosure and self-realization.

It is our experience that most males we know have fewer and/or less complex emotional responses to situations than do most females. It is also true that men have been socialized to display callousness in those situations where their feelings might otherwise manifest themselves. Callousness is a lack of emotional response, or a diminished emotional responsiveness, to certain stimuli. Culturally ingrained callousness may lead to a lack of feeling, just as the metaphor suggests: the finger that has a callus will not feel as much pain as the finger without one. Callousness in men is produced by, among other ways, habitual association of a negative emotional response with images of people who are not considered (good or real) men. Negative psychological association stifles emotional feeling, just as the encrusting of nerve endings deadens sensory feeling. Over time, callousness may lead to the elimination of a certain kind of emotional response.[20] In our culture, men may disclose fewer feelings than do women simply because they have been socialized to be less aware of the few feelings they do have. They may thus be content with comradeship as we have described it as their paradigm of friendship. This socialization helps many men avoid dealing with the emotional consequences for others of their acts, at least for the short term.

At the very least, many men, ourselves included, report that they have been bewildered by the task of understanding their own feelings. For men, feelings simply seem inchoate in ways that generally do not seem to be true for women. A number of years ago Bob was almost entirely stymied when he tried to role-play the part of a woman friend in a variation of a common male-female interaction. He could recall how she had acted in the past but could not place himself in her position. He tried and failed, whereas she could play the male much better. He could not imaginatively experience how she might have felt and acted. This seems to be a much more typically male incapacity.[21] And this limits reciprocity and may also help explain why males report fewer intimate relationships than women do.

In order to have strongly positive emotional feelings for another person, as well as sustained mutual self-disclosure, it is important to be able both to have such feelings and to express them. To express such feelings, one must be able to trust another person. Yet sociological studies indicate that the dominant model is one of competition rather than trust between men.[22] Competition creates bonds between teammates but it also makes men reluctant to reveal things about themselves that would make them vulnerable, and hence cause them to risk being taken advantage of. Completing this paper took longer than anticipated because Bob's inability to admit that he simply works more slowly than Larry made it difficult to maintain their work schedule. Instead of working cooperatively, albeit differently, Bob slipped into seeing Larry more as a competitor and less as a partner. And this took some time to acknowledge. To have the openness to allow the mutual expressions of positive feelings toward one another, the people involved cannot be worrying about becoming more vulnerable than the other.

Men in American culture are clearly stymied in pursuing intimacy with other males because of fears involving their sexuality, especially culturally inbred homophobia. As teenagers, we learned not to display feelings toward other boys on pain of being ridiculed as "queers"; Bob and his brother were called "homos" for putting their arms around each other. The taboo against males touching, except in the firm public handshake, continues these teenage prohibitions. Such restrictions and taboos dampen the expression of deep feelings among males in much of American culture. And yet, in sports contexts for instance, there are clearly accepted exceptions to these taboos, such as the pat on the backside of a teammate. Perhaps here manliness is somehow assured. Homophobia is not an insurmountable obstacle to male intimacy, but it certainly does contribute to the difficulties that men have in expressing their deeply held feelings.

We see a complex of interacting factors—including homophobia, competitiveness, callousness, taboos against the expression of feelings, and social and cultural patterns—that culminate in many men in our society not being as well suited for intimacy as women are. The lack of socialization either to seek out the personal, defining characteristics of another person or to seek this information about oneself is significant. We don't ask! Rather, males best relate with one another on the basis of shared experiences, such as sports or work, rather than shared details of one another's personal life.

IV. Aristotle Revisited

·At first, we thought we were sketching a relatively novel philosophical account of friendship. Indeed, compared to much that has been written on friendship, that is probably true. But a reading of Aristotle reveals a number of places where our account parallels his. He describes three species of friendship: friendship based on utility, friendship based on pleasure, and what he calls a complete friendship. In the first two cases, friendship is based not on a love of the friend's character but on the usefulness or pleasure provided by the friend. Aristotle says that "the beloved is loved not in so far as he is who he is, but in so far as he provides some good or pleasure" (1156a15).[23]

As we have suggested, much of male friendship is based *not* on a thoroughgoing knowledge of the other but on the surface characteristics and social activities that friends share. Male friends are those one can "do things" with, whose temperament and responses coincide with one's own in such a way that one can participate in various activities with them without having to explain or to negotiate troubling compromises. Two male friends both have the same attitude toward playing tennis, for example; both take it seriously, but not too seriously. Or a friend at work enjoys your cynical sniping at the higher administration, and you willingly go on your friend's excursions to various new restaurants for lunch. But such friendships can be fragile. If this friend gets promoted into an administrative position or your financial situation changes so that restaurant lunches are too much of a drain on monetary resources, the friendship is likely to wither away.

This scenario exemplifies an Aristotelian friendship based on pleasure, not an intimate friendship.

Aristotle describes friendship among the young as typically based on pleasure: "They pursue above all what is pleasant for themselves and what is near at hand. But as they grow up what they find pleasant changes too. Hence they are quick to become friends, and quick to stop; for their friendship shifts with what they find pleasant, and the change in such pleasure is quick" (1156ab). As men grow older their pleasures may stop changing, and thus friendships last longer; the quality of the friendships, however, does not necessarily deepen. Our notion of American male friendship as serial best-friendship seems apt here. But this was not Aristotle's vision of complete adult male friendship in Athenian Greece, and it need not be our view of the future of contemporary adult male friendship either.[24]

Aristotle emphasizes that complete friendship takes time to develop, but he means more than simply time spent together. A genuine knowledge of the other is required, and this both comes from and helps sustain shared activities, or "living together":

> . . . as the proverb says, they cannot know each other before they have shared the traditional [peck of] salt, and they cannot accept each other or be friends until each appears lovable to the other and gains the other's confidence. (1156b)

Cooper claims that in the *Magna Moralia* Aristotle argues that "self-knowledge depends upon knowledge of others."[25] In that book Aristotle writes, reminding one of G. H. Mead: ". . . as when we wish to see our own face, we do so by looking into the mirror, in the same way when we wish to know ourselves we can obtain that knowledge by looking at our friend. For the friend is . . . a second self."[26]

There is a noteworthy difference in translations of another Greek proverb mentioned by Aristotle in the *Nicomachean Ethics*. W. D. Ross translates it as "Out of sight, out of mind,"[27] whereas Terence Irwin translates it as "Lack of conversation has dissolved many a friendship" (1156b8). The latter translation seems to us to capture more fully Aristotle's accompanying discussion: that physical distance does not necessarily "dissolve the friendship unconditionally" but merely requires a suspension of friendship until it can become active again. We might say, analogously, that the current failure of contemporary American males to have self-disclosing conversations has not destroyed the *potential* for intimacy. It is likely true, however, that just as a *long* absence due to distance can dissolve a friendship, so a *sustained* lack of self-disclosure can allow those necessary capacities to become so atrophied that intimate friendship may become impossible.

We differ from Aristotle in explicitly focusing on men. We place a greater emphasis on the psychological aspects of friendship. And we recognize that few friends today can emulate Aristotle's aristocratic Athenian friends, with their substantial leisure time—"Some friends drink together, others play dice, . . . or do philosophy. They spend their days together on whichever pursuit in life they like most" (1172a). We share with Aristotle the recognition that complete friendship is not just shared activities, parallel play; it also involves the "sharing of conversation and thought, not [just] sharing the same pasture, as in the case of grazing animals" (1170b).

V. Resources for Greater Male Intimacy

Supposing we want greater intimacy in our friendships, how can we move toward it? What are the obstacles one might face, and what resources might one draw on in this process? Here we are interested in the situation of the man who recognizes the inadequacy of typical contemporary American models for men, who does not aspire to be, for example, a hypermasculine warrior or laconic cowboy, but who also recognizes that intimacy does not come easily for him. This question has no simple answer for us; at the same time, we do not agree with Montaigne that "so many circumstances are needed to build [male friendship] up that it is something if fate achieves it once in three centuries."[28]

We do not think there is any good reason to hold that men are by nature less caring than women. Indeed, at most, the biological, sociological, and psychological evidence suggests that being female correlates more frequently with being caring, and that this is best explained in terms of socialized rather than natural differences between men and women.[29] While there are many reasons why men are in fact less likely to have intimate same-sex friendships than women are, there are also good reasons to think that it is both feasible and desirable for many men to change their attitudes so that being male and expressing intimacy correlate more frequently in the future.

Certainly, male friendships will continue to be constrained by the varieties of socially oppressive practices—sexism, heterosexism, racism, classism, and more. Nonetheless we believe that intimacy for men does not require their prior elimination, only their recognition and a serious effort to reduce their efficacy. For example, efforts to restructure work relations to make them less hierarchical and competitive could free some space for friendships to grow more easily. Given the male proclivity to emphasize shared activity over sharing disclosures, men can begin by doing things together. For us, friendship began with helping each other move into new homes, going with our families on political marches, talking about our children on jaunts with them to the library on Saturday mornings, and especially discussing philosophy and academic politics over lunch.[30]

For many men it is difficult to pursue the personal information about one another that would allow for intimate bonding. Yet they may openly describe their employment or financial problems to one another and may attempt to gain such information about those associates who seem to be in financial trouble—at least, as long as these can be presented as problems in the public realm. And this information is just as likely to display vulnerability as is more deeply personal information. Indeed, since males are generally socialized to view the public world as much more important than the private, one would think that it would be easier for men to reveal information about their private selves, since less is risked.

Unfortunately it is not easy to transfer these public skills into the realm of the personal. What is more consistent with the complexity of the phenomena we have been examining is to emphasize that intimate bonds can be as strong and as enjoyable as comradeship bonds and certainly can lead to greater personal support and growth. In wartime situations, those comrades who spend the time to find out who their comrades really are will often find that they are more rather than less motivated to sacrifice their lives for their fellow soldiers. It is almost impossible to care deeply for a person who is merely a generalized other. Gray recognized this in his account of wartime comrades, observing that "loyalty is rarely reliable with great masses of men unless it has some cement" in the feelings of liking or love.[31] And this can occur only out of sentiment for who the person is as a particular individual.

The fact that some men have developed intimacy in relationships that began as comradeships lends hope. Only if men were somehow blocked from realizing the value of intimacy would there be cause for despair. There are emotional resources that males have available to them that could, but normally do not, lead them to form intimate friendships. Among these are the ability to find common ground with those one meets for the first time, the ability to be constructively critical without adversely affecting the future of a relationship, and the ability to form longlasting bonds of loyalty with other males. Indeed, there are several types of feeling that men are generally socialized to express more readily than do women. Just as men already feel entitled to express anger, rage, and hostility, there is no reason to think that other feelings will be permanently blocked. Surely, though, what is most in need of change here is the current lack of attention on the part of most males in Western culture toward an understanding of their own feelings.

How can men learn to become intimate with each other? Not

quickly, but most likely through a process of learning while doing things together and talking about themselves. Indeed, achieving intimacy is a process, as opposed to an event to make happen or a goal to be achieved. The situation seems similar to the hedonistic paradox that those who directly seek happiness are often least likely to achieve that goal, since happiness often comes in the seeking of other things. Recently, Bob drew back from a new friend because that friend's personal disclosures made Bob quite uncomfortable; fortunately, because they continued to work together a greater *mutual* openness developed. We have not participated in the workshops or "gatherings" of the so-called Men's Movement, and so we hesitate to comment on it. If these do allow many men moments of intimacy with selves and others, they are still very different from the building of an intimate friendship.

In our own interactions, it seems that we have gotten to know each other best—achieved greater intimacy—in those conversations where we relaxed our boundaries and simply talked. We felt the tug of hesitations, inhibitions each of us has to confront one by one. Should I mention this, should I criticize or let it pass, should I ask about that, can I admit to this? Opportunities are lost, disclosure prevented. And men—we—need to develop a greater ability and inclination to reflect, both as individuals and as friends. This requires us to approach our relationships as more than "undigested interactions,"[32] as things upon which we are already reflecting, and make that more explicit. Instead of just swapping stories about our childhoods, we grew by asking ourselves questions such as, "Why did Bob react to his father in one way when disciplined and Larry to his father in a different fashion?" and, "Why did we not mention our mothers in this respect?" Here the beginnings of intimacy can enable more intimacy.

This process will not teach us to become caring, but how to develop and express our caring. We do not want to be interpreted as claiming that many men do not care about one another. Men do care, often very deeply, but at the same time in a stunted and inchoate fashion. The narrowness of our relations hinders the realization and expression of care. A friend's brother dies unexpectedly and we realize that we have little idea of what sort of relationship the two had. We don't know what to say. Perhaps they were intense rivals, drifting apart as one gained more success than the other. Perhaps not. We don't know.

Men can, however, come to know each other. We can learn to form together the intimate friendships that many women have. And just like women's friendships, eventually intimate male friendships can benefit us all.[33]

Notes

1. Alice Walker, *The Temple of My Familiar* (New York: Harcourt, Brace, Jovanovich, 1989), p. 114.

2. Vera Brittain, *Testament of Friendship: The Story of Winifred Holtby* (London: Macmillan, 1947). This passage is quoted by Blanche Cook in "Female Support Networks and Political Activism: Lillian Wald, Crystal Eastman, and Emma Goldman," *Chrysalis*, vol. 3 (1977), p. 44, who also perceptively discusses the scholarly disregard of female friendships.

3. See the summary of this research in Chapter 13 of Letty Cottin Pogrebin's *Among Friends* (New York: McGraw-Hill, 1987). See also Drury Sherrod, "The Influence of Gender on Same-Sex Friendships," in *Close Relationships*, edited by Clyde Hendrick (Newbury Park, CA: Sage Publishing Co., 1989); and Barry McCarthy, "Adult Friendships," in *Person to Person*, edited by George Graham and Hugh LaFollette (Philadelphia: Temple University Press, 1989).

4. Cited in Pogrebin, ibid., p. 253.

5. Ibid.

6. Jack W. Sattel, "The Inexpressive Male: Tragedy or Sexual Politics?" *Social Problems*, vol. 23/4 (1976), pp. 469–77.

7. See Sandra Harding's paper "After the End of 'Philosophy'," delivered at the 1989 Matchette conference at Purdue University. An earlier version of this paper is called "Who Knows? Identities and Feminist Epistemologies," in *Critical Issues in Feminist Inquiry*, edited by Ellen Messer Davidow and Joan Hartman, forthcoming.

8. Gerry Philipsen, in "Speaking 'like a man' in Teamsterville: Cultural Patterns of Role Enactment in an Urban Neighborhood," *Quarterly Journal of Speech*, vol. 61 (1975), pp. 13–22, insightfully examines how situational expectations govern male speech in one American community.

9. For a cautionary note on the durability of these relationships, see Roger Little, "Friendships in the Military Community," in *Friendship*, volume 2 of *Research in the Interweave of Social Roles*, edited by Helena Znaniecka Lopata and David Maines (Greenwich, CT: JAI Press, 1981).

10. J. Glenn Gray, *The Warriors* (New York: Harper Torchbooks, 1959), pp. 26–27 (p. 24 of this volume).

11. Ibid., p. 40 (p. 30 of this volume).

12. Ibid. (p. 30 of this volume).

13. Ibid., p. 46 (p. 33 of this volume).

14. Mary Daly, *Gyn/Ecology* (Boston: Beacon Press, 1978), p. 269.

15. Ibid., p. 279, emphasis added.

16. Stanley Bing, "No Man is an Isthmus," *Esquire*, August 1989, p. 53.

17. See Sherrod, op. cit., for a discussion of this question.

18. Judith Mayne explores some of the often overlooked complexities of Clint Eastwood movies in her essay "Walking the Tightrope of Feminism and Male Desire," in *Men and Feminism*, edited by Alice Jardine and Paul Smith (New York: Methuen, 1987).

19. See Susan Pollack and Carol Gilligan, "Images of Violence in Thematic

Apperception Test Stories," *Journal of Personality and Social Psychology*, vol. 42 (1982), pp. 159–67.

20. See Larry May's essay "Insensitivity and Moral Responsibility," *Journal of Value Inquiry*, vol. 26 (1992), pp. 7–22.

21. Lillian B. Rubin, *Intimate Strangers: Men and Women Together* (New York: Harper and Row, 1983), pp. 69–70.

22. See, for example, *Beyond Patriarchy*, edited by Michael Kaufman (Toronto: Oxford University Press, 1987).

23. This and other quotations from Aristotle, unless otherwise cited, are taken from *Nicomachean Ethics*, translated by Terence Irwin (Indianapolis: Hackett Publishing Co., 1985).

24. See Pat Easterling, "Friendship and the Greeks," in *The Dialectics of Friendship*, edited by Roy Porter and Sylvana Tomaselli (London: Routledge, 1989).

25. See John M. Cooper, "Friendship and the Good in Aristotle," *Philosophical Review*, vol. 86/3 (1977), pp. 290–315.

26. Aristotle, *Magna Moralia* 1213a translated by George Stock in vol. 9 of *The Works of Aristotle* (Oxford: Oxford University Press, 1925).

27. Aristotle, *Nicomachean Ethics*, translated by W. D. Ross in *The Basic Works of Aristotle*, edited by Richard McKeon (New York: Random House, 1941).

28. Michel de Montaigne, "On Friendship," *Essays*, translated by J. M. Cohen (Baltimore: Penguin Books, 1958), p. 92.

29. For supporting arguments for this point see, for example, Richard Lee and Richard Daly, "Man's Domination and Woman's Oppression: The Question of Origins," and Carmen Schifellite, "Beyond Tarzan and Jane Genes: Toward a Critique of Biological Determinism," in *Beyond Patriarchy*, op. cit.; and John Dupre, "Global versus Local Perspectives on Sexual Difference," in *Theoretical Perspectives on Sexual Difference*, edited by Deborah Rhode (New Haven, CT: Yale University Press, 1990).

30. For one result see Larry May and Robert Strikwerda, "Fatherhood and Nurturance," *Journal of Social Philosophy*, vol. 22/2 (1991), pp. 28–39.

31. Gray, op. cit., p. 40 (p. 30 of this volume).

32. This phrase was borrowed from Steve Duck and Kris Pond, "Friends, Romans, Countrymen: Rhetoric and Reality in Personal Relationships," in *Close Relationships*, op. cit.

33. We have benefited from the comments of Marilyn Friedman, Penny Weiss, Clark Rountree, and those who attended our presentation of an earlier version of this paper in the Purdue University Women's Studies Program Spring 1990 "Brown Bag Lecture Series." We also thank the referees and editor at *Hypatia* for valuable comments on the penultimate version of this paper.

7

Gender Treachery: Homophobia, Masculinity, and Threatened Identities[1]

Patrick D. Hopkins

One of my first critical insights into the pervasive structure of sex and gender categories occurred to me during my senior year of high school. The seating arrangement in my American Government class was typical—the "brains" up front and at the edge, the "jocks" at the back and in the center. Every day before and after class, the male jocks bandied insults back and forth. Typically, this "good-natured" fun included name-calling. Name-calling, like most pop-cultural phenomena, circulates in fads, with various names waxing and waning in popularity. During the time I was taking this class, the most popular insult/name was used over and over again, *ad nauseam*. What was the insult?

It was simply, "girl."

Suggestively, "girl" was the insult of choice among the male jocks. If a male student was annoying, they called him "girl." If he made a mistake during some athletic event, he was called "girl." Sometimes "girl" was used to challenge boys to do their masculine best ("don't let us down, girl"). Eventually, after its explicitly derogatory use, "girl" came to be used among the male jocks as merely a term of greeting ("hey, girl").

But the blatantly sexist use of the word "girl" as an insult was not the only thing that struck me as interesting in this case. There was something different about this school, which in retrospect leads to my

111

insight. My high school was a conservative Christian institution; no profanity (of a defined type) was allowed. Using "bad" words was considered sinful, was against the rules, and was formally punished. There was, therefore, a regulated lack of access to the more commonly used insults available in secular schools. "Faggot," "queer," "homo," or "cocksucker" were not available for use unless one was willing to risk being overheard by school staff, and thus risk being punished. However, it is important to note that, for the most part, these words were not restricted because of any sense of hurtfulness to a particular group or because they expressed prejudice. They were restricted merely because they were "dirty" words, "filthy" words, gutter-language words, like "shit" or "asshole." "Girl" was not a dirty word, and so presented no risk. It was used flagrantly in the presence of staff members, and even used by staff members themselves.[2]

In a curious twist, the very restriction of discursive access to these more common profanities (in the name of morality and decency) reveals a deeper structure of all these significations. "Girl," as an allowable, non-profane substitute for "faggot," "homo," and "cocksucker," mirrors and thus reveals a common essence of these insults. It signifies "not-male," and as related to the male speaker, "not-me."

"Girl," like these other terms, signifies a failure of masculinity, a failure of living up to a gendered standard of behavior, and a gendered standard of identity. Whether it was the case that a "failure of masculinity" actually occurred (as in fumbling the football) or whether it was only the "good-natured" intimation that it would occur (challenging future masculine functioning), the use of such terms demonstrates that to levy a successful insult, it was enough for these young men to claim that their target was insufficiently male; he was inadequately masculine, inadequately gendered.[3]

This story can, of course, be subjected to countless analyses, countless interpretations. For my purposes here, however, I want to present this story as an illustration of how important gender is to the concept of one's self. For these young males, being a man was not merely another contingent feature of their personhood. They did not conceive of themselves as people who were also male. They were, or wanted to be, *Men*. "Person" could only be a less descriptive, more generic way of talking about humans in the abstract. But there are no abstract humans; there are no "persons," rigorously speaking. There are only men and women. Or so we believe.

In what follows, I use this insight into gendered identity to make a preliminary exploration of the relationships between masculinity and homophobia. I find that one way to read homophobia and heterosexism in men is in terms of homosexuality's threat to masculinity, which in light of the connection between gender and personal identity translates into a threat to what constitutes a man's sense of self. To form a genuine challenge to homophobia, therefore, will not result from or result in merely increased social tolerance, but will be situated in a fundamental challenge to traditional concepts of masculinity itself.

What It Means To Be (A) Gendered Me

Categories of gender, in different ways, produce a multiplicity of other categories in a society. They affect—if not determine—labor, reproduction-associated responsibilities, childrearing roles, distributions of political power, economic status, sexual practices, uses of language, application of certain cognitive skills, possession of personality traits, spirituality and religious beliefs, and more. In fact, all members of a given society have their material and psychological statuses heavily determined by their identification as a particular gender. However, not only individuals' physical, economic, and sexual situations are determined by gender categories, but also their own sense of personal identity—their personhood. I use "personhood" here as a metaphor for describing individuals' beliefs about how they fit into a society, how they fit into a world, who and what they think they *are*.[4] Personhood is critically linked (or perhaps worse, uncritically linked) to the influence of the gender categories under which an individual develops.

Individuals' sense of personhood, their sense-of-self, is largely a result of their construction as members of particular social groups within society-at-large: religions, ethnicities, regional affinities, cultural heritages, classes, races, political parties, family lineages, etc. Some of the most pervasive, powerful, and hidden of these identity-constructing "groups" are the genders; pervasive because no individual escapes being gendered, powerful because so much else depends on gender, and hidden because gender is uncritically presented as a natural, biological given, about which much can be discovered but little can (or should) be altered. In most cultures, though not all, sex/gender identity, and thus much of personal identity, is regulated by a binary system—man and woman.[5] Men and women are constructed from the socially raw material of newborn human bodies—a process that masquerades as natural rather than constructive.[6] To a very large extent, what it means to be a member of society, and thus what it means to be a person, *is* what it means to be a girl or a boy, a man or a woman. There is no such thing as a sexually or gender undifferentiated person.[7]

Identity is fundamentally relational. What it means to have a particular identity depends on what it means not to have some other identity, and by the kinds of relationships one has to other possible and actual identities. To have personhood, sense-of-self, regulated by a binary sex/gender system means that the one identity must be different from the other identity; a situation requiring that there be identifiable, performative, behavioral, and psychological characteristics that allow for clear differentiation. Binary identities demand criteria for differentiation.

For a "man" to qualify as a man, he must possess a certain (or worse, uncertain) number of demonstrable characteristics that make it clear that he is not a woman, and a woman must possess characteristics demonstrating she is not a man. These characteristics are, of course, culturally relative, and even intraculturally dynamic, but in late twentieth-century U.S. culture the cluster of behaviors and qualities that situate men in relation to women include the by now well-known litany: (hetero)sexual prowess, sexual conquest of women, heading a nuclear family, siring children, physical and material competition with other men, independence, behavioral autonomy, rationality, strict emotional control, aggressiveness, obsession with success and status, a certain way of walking, a certain way of talking, having buddies rather than intimate friends, etc.[8]

Because personal identity (and all its concomitant social, political, religious, psychological, biological, and economic relations) is so heavily gendered, any threat to sex/gender categories is derivatively (though primarily non-consciously) interpreted as a threat to personal identity—a threat to what it means to *be* and especially what it means to *be me*. A threat to manhood (masculinity) is a threat to personhood (personal identity). Not surprisingly then, a threat to established gender categories, like most other serious threats, is often met with grave resistance, for challenging the regulatory operations of a gender system means to destabilize fundamental social, political, and personal categories (a profoundly anxiety-producing state), and society is always prejudiced toward the protection of established categories. Inertia is a force in culture as well as in physics.

There are many different threats to gendered identity, but I think they can all be generally grouped together under the rubric of "gender treachery."[9] A gender traitor can be thought of as anyone who violates the "rules" of gender identity/gender performance, i.e., someone who rejects or appears to reject the criteria by which the genders are differentiated.[10] At its most obvious, gender treachery occurs as homosexuality, bisexuality, cross-dressing, and feminist activism. Any of these traitorous activities may result in a serious reaction from those individuals and groups whose concept of personal and political identity is most deeply and thoroughly sexed by traditional binary categories.[11] However, homosexuality is particularly effective in producing the extreme (though not uncommon) reaction of homophobia—a response that is often manifested in acts of physical, economic, and verbal assault against perceived gender traitors, queers.[12] Homosexuals, intentionally or not, directly challenge assumptions concerning the relational aspects of the binary categories of sex/gender, and as such threaten individual identities. Since the homophobic reaction can be lethal and so theoretically suggestive, it deserves serious attention.

Homophobia/Heterosexism

Theorists debate the value of using the term "homophobia." For some, the "phobia" suffix codes anti-gay and anti-lesbian activity as appertaining to psychiatric discourse—the realm of irrationality, uncontrollable fear, a realm where moral responsibility or political critique seems inapplicable due to the clinical nature of the phobia.[13] We do not punish people for being claustrophobic; we do not accuse agoraphobics of ignorance or intolerance; why should we treat homophobics any differently?

Other terms have been used to describe the aggregation of prejudices against gays and lesbians, including homoerotophobia, homosexism, homonegativism, anti-homosexualism, anti-homosexuality, and homohatred.[14] "Heterosexism" has become the terminology of choice for some theorists, emphasizing similarities to racism and sexism. "Heterosexism" characterizes a political situation in which heterosexuality is presented and perceived as natural, moral, practical, and superior to any non-heterosexual option. As such, heterosexuals are *justly* accorded the privileges granted them—political power, sexual freedom, religious sanction, moral status, cultural validation, psychiatric and juridical non-interference, occupational and tax privilege, freedom to have or adopt children and raise families, civil rights protection, recourse against unfair hiring practices, public representation in media and entertainment industries, etc.

For many of us, however, "heterosexism," though accurate and useful, does not possess the rhetorical and emotional impact that "homophobia" does. "Heterosexism" is appropriate for describing why all television couples are straight, why marriage and joint tax returns are reserved for heterosexuals, why openly lesbian or gay candidates face inordinate difficulty in being elected to office, or why only heterosexuals can adopt children or be foster parents. But "heterosexism," though perhaps still technically accurate, does not seem strong enough to describe the scene of ten Texas teenage boys beating a gay man with nail-studded boards and stabbing him to death.[15] The blood pooling up on the ground beneath that dying body is evidence for something more than the protection of heterosexual privilege. It is evidence for a radical kind of evil.

It is neither my goal nor my desire here to set out specific definitions of homophobia. Though I will use the term primarily with reference to physical violence and strong verbal, economic, and juridical abuse against gays, I do not claim to establish a clear boundary between homophobia and heterosexism. No stable boundary could be set, nor would it be particularly useful to try to do so—they are not discrete. "Homophobia" and "heterosexism" are political words, political tools; they are ours to use as specific situations present specific needs.

However, for my purposes here, heterosexism—loosely characterized as valorizing and privileging heterosexuality (morally, economically, religiously, politically)—can be seen as the necessary precursor to homophobia. Heterosexism is the backdrop of the binary division into heterosexual and homosexual (parasitic on the man/woman binary), with, as usual, the first term of the binary good and second term bad. Heterosexism constructs the field of concepts and behaviors so that some heterosexists' hierarchical view of this binary will be reactionary, for a variety of reasons, thus becoming homophobic (read: violent/abusive/coercive). In the same way that a person doesn't have to be a member of a white supremacist organization to be racist, a person doesn't have to be homophobic to be heterosexist. This is not to say that heterosexism is not as bad as homophobia, but rather that though heterosexism presents less of an obvious, direct, personal physical threat to gays, it nonetheless situates the political arena such that homophobia can and is bound to exist. Heterosexism is culpable for the production of homophobia. Heterosexists are politically culpable for the production of homophobics.

But even when we choose to use the term "homophobia" for cases of brutality, fanatic claims, petitions for fascistic laws, or arbitrarily firing gay employees, this does not mean that we must always characterize homophobia as an irrational, psychiatric/clinical response. Such a characterization would be grossly inadequate. "Homophobia" has evolved as primarily a political term, not as a psychiatric one, and does not parallel claustrophobia or agoraphobia, for the political field is not the same.

Religious and political rhetorics of moral turpitude and moral danger do not attach to closed-in spaces or wide-open spaces in the way they attach to same-sex eroticism. In other words, the fear and abhorrence of homosexuals is often taught as a moral and practical virtue and political oppression is massed against gays and lesbians. As a result, oppositional strategies to homophobia must be located in political discourse, not just psychiatric or pop-psychiatric discourse. Homophobia is supported and subsidized by cultural and governmental institutions in ways that demand the need for a variety of analyses. Though homophobia may often seem irrational or semi-psychotic in appearance, it must not be dismissed as simply an obsessive individual psychological aberration. Homophobia is a product of institutional heterosexism and gendered identity.

How do people explain homophobia? And especially, though not exclusively, how do people in queer communities explain homophobia? Being the victims of it, what do they see in it? Why is it that some men react so strongly and so virulently to the mere presence of gay men?

The Repression Hypothesis

One of the most common explanations of homophobia among gay men is that of repressed homosexuality. Men who constantly make anti-gay slurs, tell anti-gay jokes, use anti-gay language, obsess about the dire political and moral impact of homosexuality on the family and country, or even who are known to attack gays physically are often thought to be repressing their own sexual attraction toward men. As a result of their terror in coming to grips with their own sexuality, they overcompensate, metastasizing into toxic, hypermasculine, ultra-butch homophobes who seem to spend far more time worrying about homosexuality than openly gay men do.

This kind of repressed-homosexual explanation was aptly demonstrated by one of my straight undergraduate ethics professors. While teaching a section on sexual ethics, my professor and the entire class read a series in the college newspaper by our Young Republican student editor about how "the homosexuals" were taking over the country and converting all the children. Finally, after yet another repetition of the "but they can't have babies and they're unnatural" columns, my exasperated professor wrote a response to the paper, and after a lengthy list of counterarguments, ended by saying simply, "Methinks thou doth protest too much."

His intimation was clear. He believed that the Young Republican's arguments were more for his benefit than for his readers'. As the typical response goes among gays who hear men constantly ranting about the perils of homosexuality and the virtues of heterosexuality— "He's not trying to convince us. He's trying to convince himself."

I think for many men this theory of repression is accurate. It is not unusual for openly gay men to talk about their days in the closet and report that they were assertively heterosexist/homophobic—and that yes, they were desperately trying to convince themselves that they were really heterosexual. Sadly enough, many of these repressed homosexuals manage to maintain their repression at great cost to themselves and often at great cost to others. Some marry and live a lie, unfulfilled emotionally and sexually, deceiving their wives and children, sometimes having furtive, sexual affairs with other men. They manage psychologically to compartmentalize their erotic orientation and same-sex sexual experiences so radically that they live two separate, tortuous lives. Some repressives become anti-gay activists and spend their lives trying to force gays and lesbians back into the closet, working against gay civil rights and protections.[16] Horrifyingly, some others undergo an even worse schism in their personalities, resulting in a bizarre, malignant, and persistent internalized war between homophobia and homophilia. This war can culminate in what John Money calls the exorcist syndrome, in which the repressive picks up, seduces, or even rapes a gay man, and then beats him or kills him in order to exorcise the repressive's "homosexual guilt."[17]

But while the repressive hypothesis is certainly accurate for some men, it is not accurate for all. I have no doubt that there are indubitably heterosexual men who hate and assault gays. To some extent, the explanation of repressed homosexuality may be wish fulfillment on the part of some gays. Forced by necessity of survival to be secretive and cryptic themselves, many gay men find it eminently reasonable to suspect any man of potential homosexual desire, and in fact, want such to be the case. It is reasonable, if optimistic, to hope that there are really more of you than there seem to be. And in light of the fact that many openly gay men report that they used to be homophobic themselves, the repression theory seems to be both empirically sound as well as emotionally attractive. There is also a certain sense of self-empowerment resulting from the repression hypothesis—out gays may see themselves as morally, cognitively, and emotionally superior to the men who continue to repress their sexuality. But homophobia is not so simple. What about those homophobes who clearly are not repressing their own homosexuality? What explanation fits them?

The Irrationality/Ignorance Hypothesis

Another explanation, one in perfect keeping with the roots of the word, is that homophobia is an irrational fear, based in ignorance and resulting from social training.[18] This explanation is also popular among liberal heterosexuals as well as liberal lesbians and gays. The stereotype of this kind of cultural/developmental homophobia is that of a little boy who grows up in a poorly educated, very conservative family, often in a rural area, who hears his parents and other relatives talk about the fags on TV or the homo child molester they caught in the next county and how he ought to be "strung up and shot." As the little boy grows, he models his parents' behavior, identifying with their emotions and desiring to emulate them. Although the boy has no idea of what a "fag" or "homo" is, he nevertheless learns the appropriate cues for application of those terms to situations and individuals, and the emotions associated with that application. He begins to use them himself, often as a general-use insult (like young children calling each other "nigger" even when they do not know what it means). He learns that certain kinds of behaviors elicit being called a fag and that he can achieve a degree of peer approval when he uses those terms. So he stands on the playground at recess and calls the boy who takes piano lessons a homo; his friends laugh. He asks the girls who are jumping rope with another boy why they are playing with a faggot; his friends laugh. Simultaneously, of course, the boy is learning all the other dictums of traditional heteromasculinity—girls are weak, boys are strong, girls play stupid games, boys play real games, girls that want to play football are weird, boys that do not want to play football are faggots. Eventually the boy learns the more complete definition of "faggot," "homo," "queer." Homos aren't just sissies who act like girls; they aren't just weak. They like to "do things" with other boys. Sick things. Perverted things.

A little knowledge is a very dangerous thing and the boy becomes a full-fledged homophobe who thinks boys who play the piano and do not like football want to touch him "down there." He learns that grown-up homos like to grab young boys and "do bad things to them." He learns that just as one can become a tougher, stronger, more masculine man by killing deer and by "slaughtering" the guys on the opposing football team, one can become more masculine, or prove one's masculinity, by verbally abusing or beating up queers.

Though this scenario may seem hyperbolic, it certainly does occur. I have seen it happen myself. The lesson that gets learned is that of the recurring conflict of essence and performance.

Essence: You (the little boy) have a natural, core, normal, good, essential identity; you are a *boy*, a *young man*, male, not-a-girl. This is just what you are. You were born this way. Little girls will like you. You have buddies. You're lucky. You are our *son*. It's natural and obvious that you will grow up and get married and be a *daddy*.

Performance: But even though you just *are* a little *boy*, even though it's perfectly natural, you must make sure you do not act (how? why?) like a girl. You must always make sure that you exhibit the right behavior for a boy (but isn't it natural?). Don't ever act like not-a-boy! Don't betray that which you are naturally, comfortably, normally. Don't not-be what you are. Perform like a man.

The stage is set. The child knows that he is a he and that being a he is a good, normal, natural thing. Being a he requires no effort. You just are a boy. But at the same time, there is lingering on the horizon the possibility, amorphous and not always spoken, that you might do something which violates what you are. It might be quiet—"Now put those down, son. Boys don't play with dolls." It might be loud—"What the hell are you doing playing with dolls like some sissy??!!" The little boy internalizes the expectations of masculinity.

This kind of explanation of homophobia, though useful and accurate for many purposes, tends to characterize homophobia as learned but completely irrational, unfounded, arbitrary, ignorant, counterproductive, and dysfunctional. However, such a simple analysis excludes much of the experience of the homophobe. It is not actually the case that the poor mindless homophobe simply veers through life distorting reality and obsessing over nothing, frothing at the mouth and seeing faggots behind every corner and homosexual conspiracies in every liberal platform, ruining his own life as well as others. In fact, homophobia is not dysfunctional in the way that agoraphobia is. Homophobia has functional characteristics.[19]

For example, in the story given above, the boy does not simply "catch" the obsessive, dysfunctional view of the world that his parents have. He learns that certain kinds of behaviors elicit rewarding emotions not only from his parents directly, but also from within himself when away from his parents. When the little boy plays with toy soldiers and pretends to slaughter communists or Indians, his parents smile, encourage him, and even play with him sometimes. If he plays house with his little sister, he is always the daddy and she is always the mommy and he pretends to get home from work and she pretends to have supper fixed for him—a game in which roles are correctly modeled and are thus emotionally rewarding—"I'm just like my daddy."

However, the emotional (and sometimes corporal) punishments function the same way. If the boy is caught playing with dolls, or pretending to be the mommy, he may be told that he is doing something wrong, or be punished, or may simply detect a sense of worry, disapproval, or distaste from his parents. Homophobic tendencies will be carried along with all the other traits of conservative masculinity. He will be "just like his daddy" when he calls some effeminate boy a sissy—an emotionally rewarding experience. He will receive approval from his peers when he pushes the class homo around—he will be tough and formidable in their eyes. And perhaps most importantly, he will be clearly and unambiguously performing the masculine role he perceives (correctly in context) to be so valued—an advantage in power, safety, admiration, and self-esteem. It is also in no small sense that homophobia can be functional in keeping other heterosexuals in line. The potential to accuse another boy of being a faggot, to threaten ostracism or physical assault, is a significant power.[20]

Thus, it is not the case that homophobia is somehow obviously dysfunctional on an individual or group level.[21] Homophobic activity carries with it certain rewards and a certain power to influence. In the case of the repressed homosexual, it externalizes the intra-psychic conflict and reaffirms a man's appearance of heterosexuality and thus his sense of stability, safety, and self. In the case of childhood modeling, homophobic activity wins approval from peers and authority figures, protects one from becoming the target of other homophobes, and reaffirms one's place in a larger context of gender appropriate behavior—protecting one's personal identity.

The Political Response Hypothesis

The recognition that there are rational, functional aspects of homophobia (in a heteropatriarchal context) leads to a third explanation of homophobia that reverses the second. This theory says that queers are a genuine political threat to heterosexuals and really do intend to eliminate heterosexual privilege. Homophobia, therefore, is a rational political response.[22] Radical feminist lesbians and certain radical gay men directly challenge the hetero-male-dominated structure of society, rejecting patriarchal rule, conventional morality, and patriarchal modes of power distribution. All of the primary institutional sites of power that have maintained patriarchal domination—the state, the church, the family, the medical profession, the corporation—are being challenged from without by queers who do not want merely to be accepted, or tolerated, or left alone, but who want to dismantle heteropatriarchal society and build something different in its place. In response to liberal heterosexuals who promote the irrationalist theory of homophobia, supporters of this theory might say that many of the so-called "ignorant" and "false" stereotypes of queers are in fact correct, but they are not bad stereotypes; they are good and should be praised, should be revered, should replace heterosexual values. Yes, lesbians do hate men. Yes, fags do want to destroy the nuclear family. Yes, dykes do want to convert children. Yes, homos are promiscuous.

The impetus for this theory of homophobia comes from lesbians and gays who view their sexuality as primarily a political identity, having chosen to reject heterosexuality and become lesbian or gay as a political act of resistance. They have chosen this identification because they want to fight, destroy, or separate from hetero-male-dominated society. According to this theory, homophobia is a perfectly rational, reasonable reaction to the presence of queers, because queers pose a genuine threat to the status of heterosexual privilege. It is only logical that heterosexuals would fight back, because if they do not fight back, their privilege, their power, and their dominance will be stripped away all the sooner.

There are people who seem, at least partially, to confirm this theory. It has been interesting to see that over the past ten years or so, it has become common for neo-conservative activist organizations to use the word "family" in their names. Among many gay, lesbian, and feminists activists, any organization with "Family" as part of its name is automatically suspected to be anti-gay, anti-lesbian, anti-feminist.[23] The frequency of the word "family" as an identification tag is seen as signifying a belief in the moral superiority of the traditional, heterosexual, nuclear family. This suggests that some "pro-family" activists trace and justify their anti-homosexual activism to the belief that lesbians and gays are threatening to destroy The Family and thus to destroy heterosexual morality.

It is also true that over the past twenty years or so, lesbian and gay thought has become radicalized in a variety of ways. Lesbians and gays have moved away from merely the hope of demedicalization and decriminalization to the hope of building cultures, ethics, practices, and politics of their own, hopes that include the destruction of hetero-sexist, or even heterosexual, society. There are some radical, separatist lesbians and separatist gays who view most human behavior in terms of rational, political aims, and for them homophobia is a predictable political response to their own oppositional politics. Nineteen ninety-two Republican presidential candidate Pat Buchanan was not simply being hyperbolic when he gravely predicted that the 1990's would be the decade of the radical homosexual. One of his campaign ads, featuring a film clip of near-nude, dancing, gay leathermen, formed the background for an attack on the grant policies of the National Endowment for the Arts. Such ads demonstrate that his homophobia is partially directed against queer-specific political and sexual challenges to his conservative Christian morality.

However, the political response hypothesis, like the others, accounts only for some homophobes, and I think, relatively few. This hypothesis suffers from too great a dose of modernist political rationalism. Like many traditional models of political activity, it overrationalizes the subjects involved. It assumes that members of the oppressor class interpret the world in political terms similar to that of members of an oppositional movement. Thus, the characterization of a homophobe is that of a rational individual with immoral goals who recognizes that the particular oppositional group of gays and lesbians is a genuine political threat to his or her power and privilege, and as such must take an active stand against that insurgent group. One of the best tactics for resisting the insurgents is terror—on individual levels with violence, on institutional levels with oppressive laws, and on sociocultural levels with boogeyfag propaganda.[24]

While this model has merit and may be partially accurate in accounting for some homophobia, it endows homophobes (and homosexuals) with a hyperrationality that does not seem to be in evidence. Most homophobes, even those who openly admit their involvement in physical and verbal attacks on gays and lesbians, do not consider their activity to be political. Most of them, in fact, do not perceive any obvious threat from the people they attack. Gary Comstock claims that perpetrators of anti-queer violence typically list the "recreational, adventuresome aspect of pursuing, preying upon, and scaring lesbians and gay men" as the first and foremost reason for their behavior. Only secondarily and less often do they list things like the "wrongness of homosexuality" as a reason for their activity. But even this "wrongness" is not listed as an explanation or political justification for their behavior as much as a background assumption that functions as cultural permission.[25]

A recent television news program interviewed a perpetrator of anti-gay violence and, like Comstock's interviewee, he had little or no explanation for why he was doing what he was doing except that it was fun. When asked how he could have fun hurting people, he said that he had never really thought of queers as real people. I think this suggests that interpreting all, or even most, homophobic violence as conscious political activity ignores that much of the "reasoning" behind homophobia, when there is any active reasoning at all, relies on a very abstract and loosely integrated background of heterosexist assumptions. Many homophobes view gays and lesbians as politically, morally, and economically insignificant. For those who have never had any personal interaction (positive or negative) with openly gay or lesbian folk, lesbian/gay people may be such an abstract other that they do not enter into one's political and moral consideration any more than people who kick dogs for fun consider the political and moral significance of dogs, except perhaps in terms of legal consequences.

Performing Gender and Gender Treachery

All three explanations of homophobia have one thing in common. They reside on a field of unequal, binary, sexual and gender differentiation. Behind all homophobia, regardless of its development, expression, or motivation, is the background of heterosexism. Behind all heterosexism is the background of gendered identities.

The gender category of men constructs its members around at least two conflicting characterizations of the essence of manhood. First, your masculinity (being-a-man) is natural and healthy and innate. But second, you must stay masculine—do not ever let your masculinity falter. So, although being a man is seen as a natural and automatic state of affairs for a certain anatomical makeup, masculinity is so valued, so valorized, so prized, and its loss such a terrible thing, that one must always guard against losing it. Paradoxically, then, the "naturalness" of being a man, of being masculine, is constantly guarding against the danger of losing itself. Unaware, the "naturalness," the "rightness," of masculinity exposes its own uncertainties in its incessant self-monitoring—a self-monitoring often accomplished by monitoring others. In fact, although the stable performance of masculinity is presented as an *outcome* of being a man, what arises in looking at heterosexism/homophobia is that being a man, or continuing to be a man, is the *outcome* of performing masculinity. But of course, not just anybody can make the performance. Anatomy is seen as prior even as the performance is required to validate the anatomy. Thus the performance produces the man, but the performance is also limited to and compulsory for a "man."[26]

The insults of the male high school jocks are telling. Even though one is recognized as a man (or boy) prior to evidenced masculinity, evidence must also be forthcoming in order to merit that continued "unproblematic" status. Whether performative evidence is provided with ease or with difficulty, it is nonetheless a compulsory performance, as compulsory as the initial anatomically based gender assignment. But because (proof of) masculinity has to be maintained not merely by anatomical differentiation but by performance, the possibility of failure in the performance is always there. It is enough to insult, to challenge, to question personal identity, by implying that one is not being masculine enough.

The logic of masculinity is demanding—protect and maintain what you are intrinsically, or you could lose it, mutate, become something else. The insults of my student peers suggest that the "something else" is being a girl—a serious enough demotion in a patriarchal culture. But of course, this is metaphor. One does not actually become a girl; the power of prior anatomy is too spellbinding, even when the performance fails. The "something else" is a male without masculinity, a monster, a body without its essential spirit, a mutation with no specifiable identity.[27]

So one mutation, which is so offensive it becomes the template of all mutations, occurs when a man finds that his erotic orientation is toward other men.[28] If he acts on that erotic orientation, he violates a tenet of masculinity, he fails at masculinity, and most importantly, appears to reject standards by which real men are defined as selves, as subjects. In a binary gender system, however, to be unmasculine means to be feminine; that is the only other possibility. But even as a cultural transformation into the feminine is attempted, it appears to be seriously problematic; it is not without resistance that the unmasculine male is shunted off to the realm of the feminine, for though femininity is devalued as the repository of the unmasculine, its presence as a discernible nonmasculine essence/performance is required to maintain the boundary of masculinity, and "feminine essences" do not easily coincide with "male" bodies.

The male body, which is supposed to house masculine essence from the first time it is identified as male, is out of place in the realm of unmasculine. That body is a manifestation of confusion, a reminder of rejection, an arrogant affront to all that is good and true about men, real men, normal men, natural men. How could this "man" give up his natural power, his natural strength, his real self? Why is he rejecting what he should be, what I am?

If the male is neither masculine, nor feminine enough, what is he? He becomes a homosexual, a member of that relatively new species of creature, originally delineated by psychiatry, which does not simply engage in unmasculine behavior, but which has an essential, unmasculine essence; no positive essence of his own, mind you, but rather a negative essence, an absence of legitimate essence, and thus the absence of legitimate personhood.[29] But what is the response to a creature with an illegitimate essence, to a creature with the husk of a man but with the extremely present absence of masculinity? That depends entirely on the situatedness of the responder in the distribution of gender identities and personal identities.

The repressive sees and fears becoming *that,* and must distance himself from *that* by any means necessary, often overcompensating, revealing his repression through his obsession, sometimes through active malignancy—assaulting or killing or merely registering disgust at that which he hates embodied in that which he desires.[30]

The ignorant will dismiss *those* as not really human, creatures so unidentified that they do not merit the response given to genuine identities (whether positive or negative—even enemies have genuine, if hated, identities). *It* can be killed, can be beaten, can be played with, can be dismissed.

The heterosupremacist reactionary will raise the warning—*They* are dangerous! *They* are getting out of hand! *They* are here! *They* are threatening your homes, your churches, your families, your children! And in some sense the threat may be real; *they* really do reject many of the beliefs upon which the heterosupremacists' political and personal identities are maintained.

Fortunately, the logic of masculinity, like any other logic, is neither universal nor irresistibly stable. Not every individual classified as a male in this culture will be adequately represented in my sketchy characterization of masculine personhood. My characterization is not to be interpreted so much as an empirically accurate description of all men in this society as it is a description of the mythology of masculinity that informs all constructions of men, the masculine, the "self" in Western culture, and that which could threaten them. I do not claim that all heterosexual males are homophobic (although I do think that the vast majority of heterosexual males are heterosexist). While I describe three homophobic reactions to the identity threat represented by gay men (repression, abusive ignorant bigotry, political reactionism), these in no way exhaust the variety of male reactions.

Some men, though they hate and are sickened by gays, lack the bravado to do anything more about their hate than make private slurs. Others, particularly liberals, are tolerantly heterosexist; they have no "real" problem with gays provided they are discreet and replicate the model of conventional heterosexual morality and family. And then there is the rare, genuinely subversive heterosexual man, a kind of gender traitor himself, whose identity is not coextensive with his assignment as a man. Although comfortable with himself, he wouldn't mind being gay, or mind being a woman—those are not the categories by which he defines, or wants to define, his personhood.

Do not, however, take this as a disclaimer to the effect that homophobia is the exception, the out-of-nowhere, the unusual case. Heterosexism may be the father of homophobia, modeling in public what is done more blatantly in hiding, but hidden does not mean rare. Do not think that homophobes, even violent ones, are few and far between—occasional atavistics "suffering" from paleolithic conceptions of sex roles. Even though many instances of anti-gay/anti-lesbian crime go unreported due to fear of outing, lack of proof, fear of retaliation, or police hostility, evidence is accumulating that such crime is widespread and that violent attack is higher among gays and lesbians than for the population at large. In a recent Philadelphia study, 24 percent of gay men and 10 percent of lesbians *responding* said that they had been physically attacked—a victimization rate twice as high for lesbians and four times as high for gay men than for women and men in the urban population at large.[31] Economic threat and verbal assault are, of course, even more common.

The gender demographics of physical homophobic attack suggest something about the correlation between masculinity and homophobia. Consider the findings in a recent study on violence against lesbians and gays by Gary Comstock: 1) 94 percent of all attackers were male; 2) 99 percent of perpetrators who attacked gay men were male, while 83 percent of those who attacked lesbians were male; 3) while 15 percent of attacks on lesbians were made by women, only 1 percent of attacks on gay men were made by women.[32]

Homophobic violence seems to be predominantly a male activity. What is the relationship between homophobia and masculinity? Is the man who attacks gay men affirming or reaffirming, consciously or subconsciously, his own masculinity/heterosexuality and thus his own sense of self? How is masculinity implicated in homophobia?

I have suggested in this essay that one reading of homophobia is that queers pose a threat to (compulsory) masculinity and as such, pose a threat to men whose personhood is coextensive with their identity as men. Certainly, homophobia could not exist without the background assumptions of (heterosexist) masculine identity. There could be no fear or hatred of gays and lesbians if there were no concept of a proper gender identity and a proper sexual orientation. Masculinity assumes, essentializes, naturalizes, and privileges heterosexuality. A violation of heterosexuality can be seen as treachery against masculinity, which can register as an affront or threat to a man's core sense of self, a threat to his (male) identity. In this sense, homophobia requires masculinity (and femininity); it is necessarily parasitic on traditional categories of sex/gender identity. Homophobia is the malignant "correction" to a destabilizing deviation. Without gendered standards of identity, there could be nothing from which to deviate, and thus nothing to "correct."

If this reading is accurate, homophobia is not just a social prejudice (on the xenophobic/minoritarian model) that can be eliminated by education or tolerance training.[33] It will not be eliminated just by persuading people to be "more accepting." While these approaches may be helpful, they do not get at the basis of homophobia—binary gender systems and heterosexism. The only way to ensure that heterosexism and its virulent manifestation homophobia are genuinely eliminated is to eliminate the binary itself—challenge the assumption that one must be sexed or gendered to be a person. Eliminate the binary and it would be impossible to have heterosexism or homophobia, because hetero and homo would have no meaning. This does not mean humans would have to be "fused" into some androgynous entity ("androgyny" has no meaning without the binary). It means simply that identities would no longer be distributed according to anatomically based "sexes."

While this hope may seem utopian and may have theoretical problems of its own, it nonetheless suggests an approach to studies of masculinity that may be incommensurable with other approaches. When using the model of masculinity (and femininity) as a social construct that has no intrinsic interpretation, there seems to be little use in trying to reconstruct masculinity into more "positive" forms, at least as long as masculinity is somehow viewed as an intrinsically appropriate feature of certain bodies. To make masculinity "positive" could easily devolve into retracing the boundaries of appropriate behavior without challenging the compulsory nature of that behavior. Delving into mythology and folklore (along the lines of some of the men's movement models) to "rediscover" some archetypal masculine image upon which to base new male identities is not so much wrong or sexist as it is arbitrary. Discovering what it means, or should mean, to be a "real man" is an exercise in uselessness. A "real man" is nothing. A "real man" could be anything. This is not to say that searching through mythohistory for useful metaphors for living today is not useful. I believe that it is.[34] But such a search will never get anyone closer to being a "real man" or even to being just a "man." There is no such thing. Nor should there be.

For some of us who have been embattled our entire lives because our desires/performances/identities were "immorally" or "illegally" or "illegitimately" cross-coded with our anatomies, we fear the flight into "rediscovering" masculinity will be a repetition of what has gone before. Gendered epistemologies will only reproduce gendered identities. I personally do not want to be a "real man," or even an "unreal man." I want to be unmanned altogether. I want to evaluate courses of behavior and desire open to me on their pragmatic consequences, not on their appropriateness to my "sex." I want to delve into the wisdom of mythology, but without the prior restrictions of anatomy.

I want to betray gender.

Notes

1. I want to thank Larry May for his encouragement and editing suggestions throughout the writing of this paper. I also want to make it clear that although I think some of this essay is applicable to hatred and violence directed against lesbians (sometimes called lesbophobia), for the purposes of a volume specifically on masculinity I have deliberately (though not exclusively) focused on males and hatred and violence directed against gay males. Even with this focus, however, I am indebted to work on homophobia by lesbian researchers and theorists. In a future, more comprehensive project I will explore the oppression and marginalization of a wider variety of gender traitors.

2. Although the scope of this essay prevents a lengthy discussion, it should be pointed out that many male teachers and coaches call their students and team members "girls": to be playful, to be insulting, or to shame them into playing more roughly.

3. It should also be pointed out that gay men often use the word "girl" to refer to each other. In these cases, however, signifying a lack of masculinity is not registering insult. Often, it is expressing a sentiment of community—a community formed by the shared rejection of compulsory heterosexuality and compulsory forms of masculinity.

4. I deliberately sidestep the philosophical debate over the existence of a "self" in this discussion. While I am quite skeptical of the existence of any stable, core self, I do not think the argument in this paper turns on the answer to that problem. "Self" could simply be interpreted as a metaphor for social situatedness. In any case, I do not mean to suggest that subverting gender is a way to purify an essential human "self."

5. For work on Native American societies that do not operate with a simple gender binary, see Walter L. Williams, *The Spirit and the Flesh: Sexual Diversity in American Indian Culture* (Boston: Beacon Press, 1986) and Will Roscoe (ed.), *Living The Spirit: A Gay American Indian Anthology* (New York: St. Martin's Press, 1988).

6. For works on the social construction of gender and sexuality see: Judith Butler, *Gender Trouble: Feminism and the Subversion of Identity* (New York: Routledge, 1990); Michel Foucault, *Herculine Barbin: Being the Recently Discovered Memoirs of a Nineteenth Century French Hermaphrodite* (New York: Pantheon, 1980); Michel Foucault, *The History of Sexuality: Volume I, An Introduction* (New York: Vintage Books, 1980); Montique Wittig, *The Straight Mind and Other Essays* (Boston: Beacon Press, 1992).

7. In the United States and many other countries, if a baby is born with anatomical genital features that do not easily lend themselves to a classification within the gender/sex system in place, they are surgically and hormonally altered to fit into the categories of male or female, girl or boy.

8. I am grateful to Bob Strikwerda for pointing out that none of these characteristics taken by itself is absolutely necessary to be perceived as masculine in contemporary U.S. culture (except perhaps heterosexuality). In fact, a man who possessed every characteristic would be seen as a parody.

9. I borrow the insightful term "gender treachery" from Margaret Atwood. In her brilliant dystopian novel, *The Handmaids' Tale* (Boston: Houghton Mifflin, 1986), set in a post-fundamentalist Christian takeover America, criminals are executed and hanged on a public wall with the name of their crime around their necks for citizens to see. Homosexuals bear the placard "gender traitor."

10. It doesn't matter if this rejection is "deliberate" or not in the sense of direct refusal. Any deviant behavior can be seen as treacherous unless perhaps the individual admits "guilt" and seeks a "cure" or "forgiveness."

11. Someone might ask: But why those people most *thoroughly* sexed rather than those most insecure in their sexuality? My point here is a broad one about the categories of gender. Even those people who are insecure in their sexuality will be laboring under the compulsory ideal of traditional binary gender identities.

12. "Queers"—the name itself bespeaks curiosity, treachery, radical unidentifiability, the uncategorized, perverse entities, infectious otherness.

13. See Gregory M. Herek, "On Heterosexual Masculinity: Some Psychical Consequences of the Social Construction of Gender and Sexuality," *American Behavioral Scientist*, vol. 29, no. 5, May/June 1986, 563–77.

14. For all these terms except "homohatred," see Gregory M. Herek, "Stigma, Prejudice, and Violence Against Lesbians and Gay Men," pp. 60–80, in J. C. Gonsiorek and J. D. Weinrich (eds.), *Homosexuality: Research Implications for Public Policy* (London: Sage Publications, Inc., 1991). For "homohatred," see Marshall Kirk and Hunter Madsen, *After the Ball: How America Will Conquer its Fear & Hatred of Gays in the 90's* (New York: Penguin Books, 1989).

15. See Jacob Smith Yang's article in *Gay Community News*, August 18–24, vol. 19, no. 6, 1991, p. 1. The brutal July 4 murder of Paul Broussard sparked an uproar in Houston's queer community over anti-gay violence and police indifference. To "quell the recent uproar," Houston police undertook an undercover operation in which officers posed as gay men in a well-known gay district. Although police were skeptical of gays' claims of the frequency of violence, within one hour of posing as gay men, undercover officers were sprayed with mace and attacked by punks wielding baseball bats.

16. See Kirk and Madsen, p. 127. They mention the case of Rose Mary Denman, a United Methodist minister who was a vocal opponent of the ordinations of gays and lesbians until she eventually acknowledged her own lesbianism. Upon announcing this, however, she was defrocked. Kirk and Madsen quote a *New York Times* article that states: "In retrospect, she attributed her previous vehement stand against ordaining homosexuals to the effects of denying her unacknowledged lesbian feelings."

17. See John Money, *Gay, Straight and In-Between: The Sexology of Erotic Orientation* (Oxford: Oxford University Press, 1988), pp. 109–110.

18. See Suzanne Pharr, *Homophobia: A Weapon of Sexism* (Little Rock, AR: Chardon Press, 1988) and also Kirk and Madsen, *After The Ball*. The stereotypical story is one I have elaborated on from Kirk and Madsen's book, chapter 2.

19. See Herek, "On Heterosexual Masculinity . . .", especially pp. 572–73.

20. One can think of the typical scene where one boy challenges another boy to do something dangerous or cruel by claiming that if he does not do so, he is afraid—a sissy. Similarly, boys who are friends/peers of homophobes may be expected to engage in cruel physical or verbal behavior in order to appear strong, reliable, and most importantly of all, not faggots themselves. They know what happens to faggots.

21. See Herek, *On Heterosexual Masculinity*, p. 573.

22. See Celia Kitzinger, *The Social Construction of Lesbianism* (London: Sage Publications, Inc., 1987).

23. For example, in my own area of the country we have Rev. Don Wildmon's American Family Association, headquartered in Tupelo, Mississippi—an ultraconservative media watchdog group dedicated to the elimination of any media image not in keeping with right-wing Christian morality. Also, in Memphis, Tennessee, there is FLARE (Family Life America for Responsible Education Under God, Inc.), a group lobbying for Christian prayer in public schools, the elimination of sex education programs, and the installation of a "Family Life Curriculum" in public schools that would stress sexual abstinence and teach that the only form of morally acceptable sexual activity is married, heterosexual sex.

24. I borrow the term "boogeyfag" from David G. Powell's excellent unpublished manuscript, *Deviations of a Queen: Episodic Gay Theory*. Powell deconstructs California Congressman Robert Dornan's claim that "The biggest mass murderers in history are gay."

25. Gary David Comstock, *Violence Against Lesbians and Gay Men* (New York: Columbia University Press, 1991), p. 172.

26. For this analysis of masculinity and performance, I owe much to insights garnered from Judith Butler's article "Imitation and Gender Insubordination," in Diana Fuss, *Inside/Out: Lesbian Theories, Gay Theories* (New York: Routledge, 1991).

27. I use the term "monster" here in a way similar to that of Donna Haraway in her essay "A Cyborg Manifesto: Science, Technology, and Socialist-Feminism in the Late Twentieth Century," reprinted in her book *Simians, Cyborgs, and Women: The Reinvention of Nature* (New York: Routledge, 1991). Haraway says: "Monsters have always defined the limits of community in Western imaginations. The Centaurs and Amazons of ancient Greece established the limits of the centred polis of the Greek male human by their disruption of marriage and boundary pollutions of the warrior with animality and woman" (p. 180). I loosely use "monster" in referring to homosexuality in the sense that the homosexual disrupts gender boundaries and must therefore be categorized into its own species so as to prevent destabilizing those boundaries.

28. Aquinas, for example, viewed the "vice of sodomy" as the second worst

"unnatural vice," worse even than rape—a view echoed in contemporary legal decisions such as Bowers v. Hardwick (106 S. Ct. 2841, 1986), which upheld the criminal status of homosexuality. See Arthur N. Gilbert, "Conceptions of Homosexuality and Sodomy in Western History," in Salvatore J. Licata and Robert P. Peterson (eds.), *The Gay Past: A Collection of Historical Essays* (New York: Harrington Park Press, 1985), pp. 57–68.

29. On the creation of homosexuality as a category, see Foucault, *The History of Sexuality*.

30. In this sense: The repressive hates the species "homosexual," but nonetheless desires the body "man." It is only an historically contingent construction that desiring a certain kind of body "makes" you a certain kind of person, "makes" you have a certain kind of "lifestyle." Unfortunately, it is also true that being a certain "kind" of person can carry with it serious dangers, as is the case for homosexuals.

31. See Comstock, p. 55.

32. See Comstock, p. 59.

33. This is not to say that gays and lesbians are not often treated as a minority; good arguments have been made that they are. See Richard D. Mohr, "Gay Studies as Moral Vision," *Educational Theory*, vol. 39, no. 2, 1989.

34. In fact, I very much enjoy studies in applied mythology, particularly the work of Joseph Campbell. However, I am extremely skeptical about any application of mythology that characterizes itself as returning us to some primal experience of masculinity that contemporary culture has somehow marred or diminished. There is always the specter of essentialism in such moves.

PART FIVE

Pornography and the Rape Culture

8

Why Do Men Enjoy Pornography?

Alan Soble

Under stress of hatred, of boredom, of sudden panic, great
gaps open. It is as if a man and a woman then heard each
other for the first time and knew, with sickening conviction,
that they share no common language, that their previous
understanding had been based on a trivial pidgin which had
left the heart of meaning untouched. Abruptly the wires are
down and the nervous pulse under the skin is laid bare in
mutual incomprehension.
　　　　　—George Steiner, 'After Babel'

Why do men enjoy pornography? I want to offer a partial explanation,
in Marxist terms, of why men in capitalism consume pornography and
why pornography has the characteristics it has. To accomplish this
goal we need to consider why male sexuality in capitalism elevates the
visual and downgrades the tactile, why it separates sex and affection,
and what effects it has on women and their sexuality.

In Byron's *Don Juan* (I, 194) Donna Julia utters these infamous
words:

> Man's love is of man's life a thing apart,
> 'Tis Woman's whole existence.

Of course, Byron could not have foreseen that the pattern he saw as
normal and unproblematic would eventually be the subject of political
economy and that Freud would make it the theme of one of his most
ambitious ventures in social psychology.[1] Byron could not have recognized the irony in his choice of the word "apart" (a-part, a part); but
in one stroke he captured the essence of atomistic bourgeois society
and the effect of its mode of production on male sexuality. Similarly,
there is a world of irony in his word "whole," which expresses the

effect that women's confinement to the spheres of reproduction and holistic service production has on their sexuality. The difference recognized by Byron is the leitmotif of this chapter.[2] . . .

Pornography in Capitalism: Consumerism

I begin with the observation that most pornography (with the exception, say, of the pornography collected at the Kinsey Institute for Sex Research) is consumed in order to experience sexual arousal, to gratify sexual curiosity, to generate sexual fantasies, or otherwise to satisfy sexual desires, with or without masturbation. Pornography is designed and produced with these consumer purposes in mind. It is a mass-produced commodity, vast quantities made possible primarily by a photographic technology that employs negatives and a publishing technology that can churn out inexpensive paperbacks. As a commodity, pornography represents the expansion of capital into another area of life. A useful idea, although not a new one, is that sexuality in capitalism has been commodified; the best examples are prostitution and the "circulation" and "exchange" of sexuality in promiscuity. But commodification applies as well to "normal" sexual relations. Pornography makes sexual arousal and pleasure into a commodity. Moreover, pornography replicates the commodification of sexual activity and women's bodies.[3]

When sexual feelings and sexual activity become commodified, they are governed by the same principles that control commodities in capitalism: the desire for sexual experiences is manipulated and encouraged, their availability is restricted to create scarcity, the cost of high-quality or esoteric activities increases inversely with supply, and the whole process is passed off as the inevitable result of natural law.[4] In short, the commodification of sexuality represents the imposition of a demand on consumers. Without further details, this account does not take us very far. It only repeats the Marxist idea that the desire for consumer goods in capitalism is as much the result of the needs of capitalist production, as mediated by the sales effort, as it is of an independently existing consumer need. Why has the imposition of demand in this case been so successful? Factors beyond the pornography industry must be invoked.[5]

The commodification of sexual experiences involves both its *actual* scarcity, created by cultural elements that perpetuate restrictive sexual standards (what I call the Victorian element), and its *perceived* scarcity, manufactured by cultural elements that perpetuate norms of health or morality defined in terms of sexual freedom (the liberal health and psychology industry). The Victorian element creates scarcity through its norms of premarital chastity, monogomous marriage, and especially the regulation of women's sexuality, and it relies on guilt and anxiety to establish conformity with these norms. The liberal health element creates the perception of scarcity, not only by bringing to attention the "irrational" restrictive norms of the Victorian element, but also by promising a world rich in sexual experience; the imagined wealth of this sexual utopia makes the actual scarcity appear worse than it is. The liberal health element, paradoxically, also uses guilt and anxiety to establish conformity with its norms (for example, some women feel anxiety if they are not clitoral *enough*, or do not masturbate, or do not have multiple orgasms); one feels guilty if one is not living up to "enlightened" norms of sexual health, rather than feeling guilty because one is too weak-willed to obey Victorian prohibitions.[6] The Victorian element and the liberal element are battling each other for social power. They are competitors in the business of selling another commodity—judgment-norms—and consumers are in the unenviable position of having to decide which corporation offers the best buy.

Persons who hear *both* that sex is wrong except in certain approved situations *and* that a mark of mental, physical, and social well-being is an active sex-life are torn between contradictory pronouncements. The consumption of pornography by men during the last twenty-five years is partially explainable as the result of the forces of liberal sexual health vanquishing the forces of Victorian sexual prohibition. Liberals recognized the connection between pornography and their sexual-freedom norms, and they fought for relaxation of legal controls on pornography; the liberalization of the law surely made the production and distribution of pornography possible (especially hard-core pornography), but it does not exactly explain why this pornography has been consumed. The liberal health industry, with its own set of products and services and its own style of generating institutional power, has been replacing the Victorian religion-theology industry as the supplier of sexual judgment-norms. This partially explains the consumption of pornography. It can also be seen as an attempt by men to escape the conflict between these opposing pronouncements. The use of pornography in masturbatory sexuality satisfies, in a convoluted way, both conservative prohibitions (no "real" sexual activity is engaged in; one is not literally unfaithful to one's wife) and liberal norms ("if it feels good, do it"). One of the attractive features of this explanation is that it does not appeal to a hydraulic model of sexuality; that is, the consumption of pornography is not the result of sexual energy spilling out of a container that tries valiantly but unsuccessfully to hold it. Both the avoidance of sexuality and the search for sexual experience result from the commodification of sexuality and the imposition of demands: desire to avoid sexual activity, created by the Victorians, and desire to engage in sexual activity, created by the competing liberals.[7]

Men's interest in pornography is also produced by the desensitization of the male body. In limiting the erotic range of smell, taste, and touch, the desensitization of the body makes the visual component of male sexuality a central source of sexual arousal and pleasure. Men's consumption of pornography has consisted mostly of photographic magazines, films, and videos. In leaving only the penis sensitive, desensitization provides what must appear to the consumer to be a natural link between visual pornography and genital masturbation. This causal connection between the mode of production, its effects on the laborer, and the consumption of pornography operates in tandem with other features of capitalist society. In particular, visual pornography allows the consumer to walk the line between the conservative prohibition and the liberal encouragement of sexual activity. Sexual pleasure induced by visual stimuli is not derived from genuine intimate contact, and therefore visual sexuality does not literally violate conservative prohibitions ("look, but don't touch"); at the same time, the consumer vicariously participates in a broader range of sexual activity and thereby satisfies the liberal pronouncement that he should feel free to enjoy whatever sexual experiences are available. That the use of pornography is not consistent with the *spirit* of either pronouncement is ignored by the rationalizing consumer. A common Victorian criticism of pornography is that the voyeurism encouraged by pornography undermines intimacy. The liberal, too, doubts the mental adjustment of those who derive too much pleasure from vicarious sexuality and not enough from "real" sexual activity. The use of pornography is the consumer's semi-rational response to being caught between these quite different standards.

The consumption of pornography can be partially understood in terms of men's visual sexuality, the genital primacy of the desensitized consumer, and the victory of liberal health professionals over religious and other conservatives (or as the consumer's response to the contradiction between the two), in addition to the commodity imposition carried out by the pornography industry. A full explanation, however, must make intelligible not just the consumption of pornography, but its *vast* consumption. I doubt that this consumption is only the result of mass production, marketing techniques, expanded visual sexuality, and penile hypersensitivity. Men must be terribly dissatisfied with their sexual lives, or they must believe that pornography adds something to their sexual lives, or they must be otherwise motivated by a sense that pornography is important. People whose wants have been created and manipulated do spend large amounts of money on items they admit are frivolous. But the consumption of pornography is not the consumption of hula-hoops, nor is it viewed that way by the men who use it. The fiery legal battles, the secrecy and persistence of male consumers, and the millions spent annually on pornography show that men take pornography seriously. We might almost say that men have found out, not merely that they enjoy it, but that they need it.

Pornography in Capitalism: Powerlessness

My explanation for the vast consumption of pornography appeals to both the boredom and the powerlessness yielded by capitalist work relations, the nature of labor, and the centralization of economics and politics. Pornography is a diversion, an escape from the dull, predictable world of work. Continued boredom also partially explains the quantity of pornography consumed. The sexual experience that involves visual stimuli, fantasies, and masturbation is intense (because of the hypersensitized penis), but it is short-lived and requires repetition. Visual stimuli arouse quickly but they need to be replaced with new stimuli, hence the quantity of pornography consumed and the attendant "throwaway" commodification of women's bodies. Powerlessness, however, is the more important factor. Being bored with one's wife or lover, or with life in general, is only a small part of the story. And the boredom is just a form of powerlessness or derived from it.

A common view holds that pornography causes men to have sexual thoughts, ideas, or fantasies that they otherwise would not have.[8] To a certain extent this is true; no one reading de Sade's *120 Days of Sodom* is likely to finish the book without a handful of new ideas. But probably closer to the truth is the view that pornography allows men a great deal of autonomy in constructing sexual images. Goldstein and Kant defend the idea that pornography merely causes men to have sexual ideas when they distinguish between erotic daydreaming and pornography:

> In our view erotic pictures, stories, and movies simply serve as a substitute for the self-generating daydreams of the pornography user. . . . The daydream comes apparently from some inner stimulation to one's imagination. In the case of erotica, the theme portrayed comes from someone else's imagination, is depicted in tangible form, and can be thought of as separate from one's own wishes and motivations.[9]

To be sure, there is a difference between sexual daydreaming and the fantasies men have when using pornography, but Goldstein and Kant's suggestion, that in the former case the ideas come from "inside" and in the latter they come from "outside," is an oversimplification. Some of the content of our sexual daydreams comes ultimately from "outside," and the ideas entertained by users of pornography are not merely imprints from the "outside," transferred, as it were, directly and without modification from the pornographic magazine into the mind. The crude view is succinctly put by George Steiner: "Sexual relations are . . . one of the citadels of privacy. . . . The new pornographers subvert this last, vital privacy; they do our imagining for us."[10] Curiously, a defender of pornography responds to Steiner by claiming that *this* "is exactly what all good writers have done since the birth of literature. The measure of their talent has . . . been their ability to *make* us see the world through their eyes."[11] But writers of good literature, even as they do show us another view of the world, do not make us—force us—to think anything, and they do not do our imagining for us.[12] One might want to insist that here we have a nice distinction between pornography and good literature: the former does our imagining for us; the latter does not.[13] For example, Joseph Slade claims that photographic and filmed pornography leave "nothing . . . to the imagination."[14] But Slade exposes the defect of this crude view when he later writes that "the cameraman cannot get inside the performers' minds."[15] He concludes from this that the consumers of pornography "do not know what" the performers are thinking. But it is in virtue of this feature of the camera that the consumer has freedom in actively filling in the thoughts, sensations, or feelings of the performers. The viewer can also add details or activities in his mind to those depicted.

To emphasize the causal determination of ideas by pornography is therefore one-sided. It overlooks the fact that pornography presents a partial picture of a fantasy world, that pornographic literature leaves gaps for the reader to fill in, and that pornographic films and especially photographs leave even larger gaps for the viewer to fill in.[16] The consumer of pornography uses the material not so much to learn of sexual variations but to obtain the visual and descriptive foundation upon which to build a fantasy. The brute facts provided by the photograph are transformed into a fantastic scenario, and the consumer creates a drama in which he is director, participant, or member of the audience at will. Pornography appeals to the user in virtue of this dramatic scenario; indeed, its partially undefined content, waiting to be expanded into a full script, explains why men consume it in vast quantities.

Pornography allows men to gain a sense of control. In his fantasy world the consumer of pornography is the boss: Mr. X shall screw Ms. Y in position P and at time t while she wears/disrobes/reveals/lubricates/laughs/exclaims/resists/seduces/pouts/farts in exactly the way the consumer wants. (This explanation also illuminates the appeal of prostitution: with a woman he has hired, a man can experience what he wants when he wants it.) Pornographic fantasies provide sexual experiences without the entanglements, mistakes, imperfections, hassles, and misunderstandings that interfere with pleasure and that accompany sex with a wife, lover, girlfriend, or stranger. Or, if there are to be complications, pornographic fantasy allows men to imagine the particular complications that they find arousing. Of course, no mode of sexual activity is ideal; all forms—masturbation with pornography, paying a prostitute, getting married, having sex with strange women—have their advantages and disadvantages. The vast consumption of pornography over the last twenty-five years implies that men perceive the relative benefits of masturbation with pornography as increasingly significant, enough to make that mode of sexuality a contender equal with the others.[17] And the pleasure of fantasized sexuality is not limited to the pleasure of wanting the fantasized activity to actually occur.[18] The pornographic sexual experience is not always a mere substitute for "real" sexual activity; it is often "an authentic, autonomous sexual activity."[19]

In a sense, the grab at control through fantasized arrangements is literally infantile,[20] especially if we understand maturity as a willingness to work out problems with the people one associates with. But the male user of pornography has decided, at least implicitly and for certain times or places, that maturity in this sense is not worth the loss of pleasure.[21] Men want these particular pleasures here and now, and in fantasy they have things exactly the way they want them.[22] We would be expecting far too much of people raised in an infantilizing society were we to complain about such regressions; we would be blaming the victims. The use of pornography is an attempt to recoup in the domain of sexual fantasy what is denied to men in production and politics; in this sense the use of pornography in capitalism provides substitute gratification. Pornographic fantasy gives men the opportunity, which they otherwise rarely have, to order the world and conduct its events according to their individual tastes. In the fantasy world permitted by pornography men can be safely selfish and totalitarian. The illusion of omnipotence is a relief from the estranged conditions of their lives and, with a little rationalization, can make existence in that real world, in which they have substantially less power, bearable. Men use pornography as compensation for their dire lack of power; pornography is therefore not so much an expression of male power as it is an expression of their lack of power.

The powerlessness for which pornographic fantasy compensates is not simply productive, political, and economic powerlessness. This powerlessness in capitalism can explain a tendency for people to fantasize, and it does contribute to pornographic fantasizing.[23] But if this general powerlessness were the only cause of fantasizing, we would expect not specifically sexual fantasies but Walter Mitty fantasies of astounding successes in business and politics. This kind of powerlessness explains the appeal of adventure stories and Dirty Harry movies, but it doesn't take us far enough in understanding pornography.[24] In addition, pornography compensates specifically for sexual powerlessness, the powerlessness of males in their sexual relationships with women.

In his discussion of the effects of industrialization in the early nineteenth century, Edward Shorter tells us about the

> shift toward powerlessness for men in the arena of real-world politics, whereby all the little people who had possessed some tiny stake—and feeble voice—in the governance of the traditional village community now became completely disenfranchised politically, until the advent of universal male voting toward the century's end. There has been no end of speculation, though little evidence, that the political powerlessness which men perceive is expressed in their resentment of women. If that is true, we might have further grounds for anticipating an increase in rapes in these factory-industrial regions.[25]

Supposing that the speculation contains some truth, I do not find altogether convincing the idea that an increase in rape, if understood as a *sexual* crime, is mostly due to men's *political* powerlessness. Political powerlessness should (*ceteris paribus*) lead to a political response. Therefore, to connect rape and men's powerlessness one must invoke at some point either sexual powerlessness or a reconception of rape. Shorter begins to provide the requisite sort of analysis when he discusses the increase in rape beginning in the 1960s in the Anglo-Saxon countries.[26] He suggests that rape became a political act directed at women, a response to the feminist-inspired challenge to male power. In this case the connection is made by reconceptualizing rape.

But in the case of pornography today, invoking men's sexual powerlessness is better than ignoring the sexual nature of men's interest in pornography. There are at least two sources of men's dissatisfaction in their relationships with women, dissatisfactions that can be dealt with by recouping a sense of power in the fantasy world made possible by pornography. First, men tend to be more interested in sex for its own sake than women, and they emphasize the sexual over the affectionate aspects of their relationships with women. Men who have this interest in sexual activity for its own sake to a certain extent lack control over their sexual lives and recoup this perceived loss of power in a fantasy world. There is some truth to the folk-wisdom that women can often find a sexual partner more easily than men, and that women decline an invitation to engage in sexual activity more readily than men. Pornography restores men's sense that they have control over their sexuality, by allowing them to populate their fantasy world with women who are equally interested in sex for its own sake.[27]

Second, women's accommodation to male sexuality has never been complete and is becoming less so. Earlier I explained some of women's alienation in terms of the requirements of male sexuality and the practices that socialize women or lead to their accommodation. But socialization is not omnipotent, and women can simply refuse to accommodate. Refusals to accommodate may even be entirely rational. To the extent that women refuse to fit the requirements of male sexuality, men experience frustration and powerlessness. Socialization is less effective as a mechanism for producing what men want, so they have less control over the sexuality of women. A decrease in the accommodation of women to male sexuality, which has resulted from an increase in feminist and quasi-feminist consciousness over the last twenty-five years, has contributed to male powerlessness, specifically sexual powerlessness.[28] Men whose sexual partners have not sufficiently accommodated to male sexuality, and who become sexually bored with partners over whom they have less control, turn to pornographic fantasy in which their sexual desires are satisfied by fully accommodating women.[29] If Shorter is right that rape has increased in response to the women's movement, rape can be construed as a counter-offensive, as backlash. But men who turn to pornography in response to the decreased accommodation of women are retreating, not attacking. The attempt to gain a sense of sexual control in the realm of fantasy is an admission of defeat, a resignation to the way the women's movement has changed the world.[30]

On the one hand, the use of pornography is an attempt to retain in the world of fantasy the prerogatives of masculinity that are being eroded. If sex has been, but is no longer, "a domain of activity where the individual male can conceive of himself as being plausibly efficacious,"[31] then the flight to pornography can be seen as an attempt to establish a new domain for sexual prowess under the *same* prevailing notion of masculinity. But, on the other hand, one can detect in the consumption of pornography a rejection of the prevailing notion of masculinity.[32] Masturbation violates the prevailing standards of masculinity: the real man screws real women, he does not jerk off. If the vast consumption of pornography implies that a good deal of masturbation is going on, then men are rejecting the prevailing standards of masculinity. The consumption of pornography suggests, therefore, that men are abandoning the idea that, to prove themselves, they need to seduce women. Furthermore, for men who are living alone, who are postponing or avoiding marriage, or who realize, from divorce statistics, that relationships are not the stabilizing and secure retreats from the world they once might have been, masturbation with pornography is a useful and pleasurable activity that complements the new, evolving masculine role. If pornography is used in these two ways—as adherence in the realm of fantasy to the old style of masculinity, and as embracing the trend toward a new style of masculinity—then we can again understand the consumption of pornography as a balancing act that attempts to satisfy the demands of competing pronouncements: the conservative pronouncement to be a man, and the liberal pronouncement to reject old-fashioned notions of manhood.

Notes

1. Sigmund Freud, "The Most Prevalent Form of Degradation in Erotic Life," in Phillip Rieff, editor, *Sexuality and the Psychology of Love* (New York: Collier, 1963), pp. 58–60.

2. My thesis, that the sexuality of men is atomistic and that of women holistic, is of course a generalization; there are complications, exceptions, and recent changes in the pattern, some of which I discuss later. Carol Gilligan's *In a Different Voice* (Cambridge, MA: Harvard University Press, 1982) has found a parallel difference between men and women's conceptions of self and approaches to morality. For men, separateness from others (atomism) is the significant feature, while for women it is interdependence and connection (holism).

3. For the former, see Douglas Stewart, "Pornography, Obscenity, and Capitalism," *Antioch Review*, vol. 35, Fall 1977, p. 395. For the latter, see (one of many examples) Peter Michelson, *The Aesthetics of Pornography* (New York: Herder and Herder, 1971), p. 217.

4. See Richard Lichtman, "Marx and Freud, Part 3: Marx's Theory of Human Nature," *Socialist Revolution*, vol. 7/6, 1977, p. 57.

5. In her explanation of the consumption of romances by women, Janice Radway takes a different slant. She wants to make sure we understand that this consumption is not only a function of the needs of women, but "equally a function of . . . production, distribution, advertising, and marketing techniques." *Reading the Romance* (Chapel Hill: University of North Carolina Press, 1984), p. 20.

6. Using the terminology of "Jehovanist" and "Naturalist," Murray Davis (*Smut: Erotic Reality/Obscene Ideology*, Chicago: University of Chicago Press, 1983, p. 194) makes a similar point: "Naturalists have managed to replace the old 'sin' of giving into sexual desire with the new 'sickness' of not having enough sexual desire to give into."

7. Rather than speaking about the manipulation of women's sexuality by these competing social forces, Christine Pickard reasserts a repression model in bemoaning Victorian influences on women: "The fact that so many women 'fell by the wayside' bears testimony to the presence of strong sexual urges that could not always be submerged despite strong forces inducing her to do so." ("A Perspective on Female Responses to Sexual Material," in Yaffe and Nelson, editors, *The Influence of Pornography on Behavior*, London: Academic Press, 1982, pp. 91–117, at p. 98.) Why not say that the fact that so many women "stayed the course" bears testimony to the absence of strong sexual urges that could not always be created despite the strong liberal forces inducing them to do so?

8. For example, Diana Russell, "Pornography and Violence: What Does

the New Research Say?'' in Lederer, editor, *Take Back the Night* (New York: Morrow, 1980), pp. 218–38.

9. Michael Goldstein and Harold Kant, *Pornography and Sexual Deviance* (Berkeley: University of California Press, 1973), pp. 135–36.

10. George Steiner, "Night Words," in David Holbrook, editor, *The Case Against Pornography* (LaSalle: Open Court, 1973), pp. 227–36, at pp. 234–35.

11. Kenneth Tynan, "Dirty Books Can Stay," in Douglas Hughes, editor, *Perspectives on Pornography* (New York: St. Martin's, 1970), pp. 109–21, at p. 119 (italics added).

12. "The good writer creates character by a cunning combination of the said and the unsaid," (Felix Pollack, "Pornography: A Trip Around the Halfworld," in Hughes, ibid., pp. 170–96, at p. 194). Pollack defends pornography by arguing that it, too, allows the active participation of the user. See also Gore Vidal, "On Pornography," *The New York Review of Books*, March 31, May 12, 1966, p. 6.

13. See Davis, *Smut*, op. cit., pp. 136–37.

14. Joseph Slade, "Pornographic Theaters Off Times Square," in Ray Rist, editor, *The Pornography Controversy* (New Brunswick, NJ: Transaction Books, 1975), pp. 119–39, at p. 129.

15. Ibid., p. 130.

16. See Susan Sontag, *On Photography* (New York: Farrar, Straus and Giroux, 1973), pp. 106–109.

17. Leslie Farber's reading of Masters and Johnson concludes that the perfect orgasm is "wholly subject to its owner's will, wholly indifferent to human contingency or context. Clearly, this perfect orgasm is the orgasm achieved on one's own," through masturbation (*Lying, Despair, Jealousy, Envy, Sex, Suicide, Drugs, and the Good Life*, New York: Basic Books, 1976, p. 140.) If the perfect orgasm is the one achieved in masturbation, then the important question is not "why do men consume so much pornography?" but rather "why do men ever bother with sex with prostitutes, wives, girlfriends, strangers?" Davis remarks, "Considering the obstacles, one wonders how two people ever manage to copulate at all," (*Smut*, op. cit., p. 20) and he answers: "Plainly, human beings must possess something sexually arousing that animal species, natural phenomena, and technological products lack. That something else is a social self" (p. 106). But one need not wax so metaphysical to explain why masturbation with pornography does not replace other modes of sexuality altogether. Pornography cannot reproduce certain sexual sensations that can be experienced only with another person. Indeed, the ability of pornography to provide satisfaction is reduced if a person cannot use the material to conjure up fantasies based on memories of "real" sexual activity.

18. See Susan Feagin, "Some Pleasures of Imagination," *Journal of Aesthetics and Art Criticism*, vol. 43/1, 1984, p. 51.

19. Susan Barrowclough, review of "Not a Love Story," *Screen*, vol. 23/5, 1982, p. 33.

20. Ann Snitow discusses pornography as satisfying the desire to reexperience the omnipotence of childhood, in "Mass Market Romance: Pornography for Women is Different," *Radical History Review*, vol. 20, 1979, pp. 153–54.

21. Nancy Hartsock argues that men enjoy pornography because it allows them to avoid the dangers of intimacy with women, that men's "fear" of

146

Part Five, Chapter Eight

intimacy drives them to reassert control through pornography (*Money, Sex and Power*, New York: Longman, 1983, pp. 169–70, 176, 252). But this thesis rules out altogether that for some men masturbation with pornography is a sexual activity in its own right with its own advantages. Hartsock also magnifies men's perceptions of relationships when she says they "fear" intimacy. We should not forget that "a woman without a man is like a fish without a bicycle" works both ways.

22. Molly Haskell makes the same point about women's fantasies ("Rape Fantasy," *Ms.*, November 1976, p. 85).

23. Lawrence Rosenfield explains the consumption of pornography in capitalism *entirely* as a function of political powerlessness and the powerlessness derived from noncollectivized labor ("Politics and Pornography," *Quarterly Journal of Speech*, vol. 59, 1973, especially pp. 414–19).

24. Geoffrey Gorer argues that pornography is best understood by including it with "the literature of fear, the ghost story, the horror story, the thriller," and for example, "books of wine connoisseurship," all of which invoke physical responses (*The Danger of Equality*, New York: Weybright and Talley, 1966, pp. 222–24).

25. Edward Shorter, "On Writing the History of Rape," *Signs*, vol. 3/2, 1977, p. 479.

26. Ibid., p. 481.

27. David Chute agrees that pornography is "a symptom of impotence rather than power," but he insists that pornography is largely consumed by young, shy, and unattractive men; hence, he believes that pornography is an expression only of *their* powerlessness to entice partners." ("Dirty Pillow Talk," *The Boston Phoenix*, September 23, 1980, p. 5). But consumption by these men does not explain the billions of dollars spent on pornography. Sexually active men also consume pornography, and the explanation I offer applies to them as well. Note that the President's Commission found that most patrons of adult book stores and movie theaters were white, middle-aged, middle-class men (*Report on the Commission on Obscenity and Pornography*, New York: Bantam, 1970, pp. 25–26, 157–63).

28. Consciousness-raising groups, feminist psychotherapy, and the media (e.g., *Ms.*) undoubtedly undermine socialization and encourage refusals to accommodate.

29. Heidi Hartmann ("The Family as the Locus of Gender, Class, and Political Struggle," *Signs*, vol. 6, 1981, pp. 377ff) argues against the view that the power of men over women in the home has recently been weakened. But she shows only that men have retained power over women's domestic labor, not their sexuality.

30. I think Michele Barrett and Mary McIntosh get it backward when they write (*The Anti-Social Family*, London: NLB, 1982, p. 76) "Men would not be willing to pay prostitutes if it were not for the fact that their heterosexual desires have been indulged and accorded legitimacy and women's constructed as weak and receptive, in the interests of a male-dominated marriage system. The same applies to pornography." On my account it is precisely because men's sexuality has *not* been "indulged" by not fully accommodating women that they find both prostitution and pornography inviting. (I can imagine Woody Allen's reply: men do not use pornography because there are not

enough good women lovers; rather, men sleep with women because they cannot get enough good pornography.)

31. John Gagnon and William Simon, *Sexual Conduct: The Social Sources of Human Sexuality* (Chicago: Aldine, 1973), p. 272.

32. Barbara Ehrenreich (*The Hearts of Men: American Dreams and the Flight from Commitment*, Garden City, NY: Anchor Press, 1983, pp. 125–26) argues that men's "revolt" against the male sex role can be perceived in male-submissive sadomasochistic pornography. I extend her insight by suggesting that all pornography can be understood this way.

9

Pornography and the Alienation of Male Sexuality

Harry Brod

This paper is intended as a contribution to an ongoing discussion. It aims to augment, not refute or replace, what numerous commentators have said about pornography's role in the social construction of sexuality. I have several principal aims in this paper. My primary focus is to examine pornography's model of male sexuality. Furthermore, in the discussion of pornography's role in the social construction of sexuality, I wish to place more emphasis than is common on the social construction of pornography. As I hope to show, these are related questions. One reason I focus on the image of male sexuality in pornography is that I believe this aspect of the topic has been relatively neglected. In making this my topic here, I do not mean to suggest that this is the most essential part of the picture. Indeed, I am clear it is not. It seems clear enough to me that the main focus of discussion about the effects of pornography is and should be the harmful effects of pornography on women, its principal victims. Yet, there is much of significance which needs to be said about pornography's representation, or perhaps I should more accurately say misrepresentation, of male sexuality. My focus shall be on what is usually conceived of as "normal" male sexuality, which for my purposes I take to be consen-

An earlier version of this paper was presented at the Philosophers for Social Responsibility National Workshop on Pornography, Eastern Division Meetings of the American Philosophical Association, New York, December 1987. I am grateful to members of the audience, and to Roger Gottlieb, Lenore Langsdorf, Maria Papacostaki, and Ricky Sherover-Marcuse for helpful comments.

sual, non-violent heterosexuality, as these terms are conventionally understood. I am aware of analyses which argue that this statement assumes distinctions which are at least highly problematic, if not outright false, which argue that this "normal" sexuality is itself coercive, both as compulsory heterosexuality and as containing implicit or explicit coercion and violence. My purpose is not to take issue with these analyses, but simply to present an analysis of neglected aspects of the links between mainstream male sexuality and pornography. I would argue that the aspect of the relation between male sexuality and pornography usually discussed, pornography's incitement to greater extremes of violence against women, presupposes such a connection with the more accepted mainstream. Without such a link, pornography's messages would be rejected by rather than assimilated into male culture. My intention is to supply this usually missing link.

My analysis proceeds from both feminist and Marxist theory. These are often taken to be theories which speak from the point of view of the oppressed, in advocacy for their interests. That they indeed are, but they are also more than that. For each claims not simply to speak for the oppressed in a partisan way, but also to speak a truth about the social whole, a truth perhaps spoken in the name of the oppressed, but a truth objectively valid for the whole. That is to say, Marxism is a theory which analyzes the ruling class as well as the proletariat, and feminism is a theory which analyzes men as well as women. It is not simply that Marxism is concerned with class, and feminism with gender, both being united by common concerns having to do with power. Just as Marxism understands class as power, rather than simply understanding class differences as differences of income, lifestyle, or opportunities, so the distinctive contribution of feminism is its understanding of gender as power, rather than simply as sex role differentiation. Neither class nor gender should be reified into being understood as fixed entities, which then differentially distribute power and its rewards. Rather, they are categories continually constituted in ongoing contestations over power. The violence endemic to both systems cannot be understood as externalized manifestations of some natural inner biological or psychological drives existing prior to the social order, but must be seen as emerging in and from the relations of power which constitute social structures. Just as capitalist exploitation is caused not by capitalists' excess greed but rather by the structural imperatives under which capitalism functions, so men's violence is not the manifestation of some inner male essence, but rather evidence of the bitterness and depth of the struggles through which genders are forged.[1]

For my purposes here, to identify this as a socialist feminist analysis is not, in the first instance, to proclaim allegiance to any particular set of doctrinal propositions, though I am confident that those I subscribe to would be included in any roundup of the usual suspects, but rather to articulate a methodological commitment to make questions of power central to questions of gender, and to understand gendered power in relation to economic power, and as historically, materially structured.[2] If one can understand the most intimate aspects of the lives of the dominant group in these terms, areas which would usually be taken to be the farthest afield from where one might expect these categories to be applicable, then I believe one has gone a long way toward validating claims of the power of socialist feminist theory to comprehend the totality of our social world. This is my intention here. I consider the analysis of male sexuality I shall be presenting part of a wider socialist feminist analysis of patriarchal capitalist masculinity, an analysis I have begun to develop elsewhere.[3]

As shall be abundantly clear, I do not take a "sexual liberationist" perspective on pornography. I am aware that many individuals, particularly various sexual minorities, make this claim on pornography's behalf. I do not minimize nor negate their personal experiences. In the context of our society's severe sexual repressiveness, pornography may indeed have a liberating function for certain individuals. But I do not believe an attitude of approval for pornography follows from this. Numerous drugs and devices which have greatly helped individual women have also been medical and social catastrophes—the one does not negate the other.

I shall be claiming that pornography has a negative impact on men's own sexuality. This is a claim that an aspect of an oppressive system, patriarchy, operates, at least in part, to the disadvantage of the group it privileges, men. This claim does not deny that the overall effect of the system is to operate in men's advantage, nor does it deny that the same aspect of the system under consideration, that is, male sexuality and pornography under patriarchy, might not also contribute to the expansion and maintenance of male power even as it also works to men's disadvantage. Indeed, I shall be arguing precisely for such complementarity. I am simply highlighting one of the "contradictions" in the system. My reasons for doing so are in the first instance simply analytic: to, as I said, bring to the fore relatively neglected aspects of the issue. Further, I also have political motivations for emphasizing this perspective. I view raising consciousness of the prices of male power as part of a strategy through which one could at least potentially mobilize men against pornography's destructive effects on both women and men.

It will aid the following discussion if I ask readers to call to mind a classic text in which it is argued that, among many other things, a system of domination also damages the dominant group, and prevents them from realizing their full humanity. The argument is that the dominant group is "alienated" in specific and identifiable ways. The text I have in mind is Marx's "Economic and Philosophic Manuscripts of 1844." Just as capitalists as well as workers are alienated under capitalism according to Marxist theory (in a certain restricted sense, even more so), so men, I shall argue, and in particular male modes of sexuality, are also alienated under patriarchy. In the interests of keeping this paper a manageable length, I shall here assume rather than articulate a working familiarity with Marx's concept of alienation, the process whereby one becomes a stranger to oneself and one's own powers come to be powers over and against one. Since later in the paper I make use of some of Marx's more economistic concepts, I should however simply note that I see more continuity than rupture between Marx's earlier, more philosophical writings and his later, more economic ones.[4] While much of this paper presents an analysis of men's consciousness, I should make clear that while alienation may register in one's consciousness (as I argue it does), I follow Marx in viewing alienation not primarily as a psychological state dependent on the individual's sensibilities or consciousness but as a condition inevitably caused by living within a system of alienation. I should also note that I consider what follows an appropriation, not a systematic interpretation, of some of Marx's concepts.

Alienated pornographic male sexuality can be understood as having two dimensions, what I call the objectification of the body and the loss of subjectivity. I shall consider each in greater detail, describing various aspects of pornographic male sexuality under each heading in a way which I hope brings out how they may be conceptualized in Marx's terms. Rather than then redoing the analysis in Marx's terms, I shall then simply cite Marx briefly to indicate the contours of such a translation.

1. Objectification of the Body

In terms of both its manifest image of and its effects on male sexuality, that is, in both intrinsic and consequentialist terms, pornography restricts male sensuality in favor of a genital, performance oriented male sexuality. Men become sexual acrobats endowed with oversized and overused organs which are, as the chapter title of a fine book on male sexuality describes, "The Fantasy Model of Sex: Two Feet Long, Hard as Steel, and Can Go All Night."[5] To speak non-euphemistically, using penile performance as an index of male strength and potency directly contradicts biological facts. There is no muscle tissue in the penis. Its erection when aroused results simply from increased blood flow to the area. All social mythology aside, the male erection is physiologically nothing more than localized high blood pressure. Yet this particular form of hypertension has attained mythic significance. Not only does this focusing of sexual attention on one organ increase male performance anxieties, but it also desensitizes other areas of the body from becoming what might otherwise be sources of pleasure. A colleague once told me that her favorite line in a lecture on male sexuality I used to give in a course I regularly taught was my declaration that the basic male sex organ is not the penis, but the skin.

The predominant image of women in pornography presents women as always sexually ready, willing, able, and eager. The necessary corollary to pornography's myth of female perpetual availability is its myth of male perpetual readiness. Just as the former fuels male misogyny when real-life women fail to perform to pornographic standards, so do men's failures to similarly perform fuel male insecurities. Furthermore, I would argue that this diminishes pleasure. Relating to one's body as a performance machine produces a split consciousness wherein part of one's attention is watching the machine, looking for flaws in its performance, even while one is supposedly immersed in the midst of sensual pleasure. This produces a self-distancing self-consciousness which mechanizes sex and reduces pleasure. (This is a problem perpetuated by numerous sexual self-help manuals, which treat sex as a matter of individual technique for fine-tuning the machine rather than as human interaction. I would add that men's sexual partners are also affected by this, as they can often intuit when they are being subjected to rote manipulation.)

2. Loss of Subjectivity

In the terms of discourse of what it understands to be "free" sex, pornographic sex comes "free" of the demands of emotional intimacy or commitment. It is commonly said as a generalization that women tend to connect sex with emotional intimacy more than men do. Without romantically blurring female sexuality into soft focus, if what is meant is how each gender consciously thinks or speaks of sex, I think this view is fair enough. But I find it takes what men say about sex, that it doesn't mean as much or the same thing to them, too much at face value. I would argue that men do feel similar needs for intimacy, but are trained to deny them, and are encouraged further to see physical affection and intimacy primarily if not exclusively in sexual terms. This leads to the familiar syndrome wherein, as one man put it:

> Although what most men want is physical affection, what they end up thinking they want is to be laid by a Playboy bunny.[6]

This puts a strain on male sexuality. Looking to sex to fulfill what are really non-sexual needs, men end up disappointed and frustrated.

Sometimes they feel an unfilled void, and blame it on their or their partner's inadequate sexual performance. At other times they feel a discomfitting urgency or neediness to their sexuality, leading in some cases to what are increasingly recognized as sexual addiction disorders (therapists are here not talking about the traditional "perversions," but behaviors such as what is coming to be called a "Don Juan Syndrome," an obsessive pursuit of sexual "conquests"). A confession that sex is vastly overrated often lies beneath male sexual bravado. I would argue that sex seems overrated because men look to sex for the fulfillment of nonsexual emotional needs, a quest doomed to failure. Part of the reason for this failure is the priority of quantity over quality of sex which comes with sexuality's commodification. As human needs become subservient to market desires, the ground is laid for an increasing multiplication of desires to be exploited and filled by marketable commodities.[7]

For the most part the female in pornography is not one the man has yet to "conquer," but one already presented to him for the "taking." The female is primarily there as sex object, not sexual subject. Or, if she is not completely objectified, since men do want to be desired themselves, hers is at least a subjugated subjectivity. But one needs another independent subject, not an object or a captured subjectivity, if one either wants one's own prowess validated, or if one simply desires human interaction. Men functioning in the pornographic mode of male sexuality, in which men dominate women, are denied satisfaction of these human desires.[8] Denied recognition in the sexual interaction itself, they look to gain this recognition in wider social recognition of their "conquest."

To the pornographic mind, then, women become trophies awarded to the victor. For women to serve this purpose of achieving male social validation, a woman "conquered" by one must be a woman deemed desirable by others. Hence pornography both produces and reproduces uniform standards of female beauty. Male desires and tastes must be channeled into a single mode, with allowance for minor variations which obscure the fundamentally monolithic nature of the mold. Men's own subjectivity becomes masked to them, as historically and culturally specific and varying standards of beauty are made to appear natural and given. The ease with which men reach quick agreement on what makes a woman "attractive," evidenced in such things as the "1–10" rating scale of male banter and the reports of a computer program's success in predicting which of the contestants would be crowned "Miss America," demonstrates how deeply such standards have been internalized, and consequently the extent to which men are dominated by desires not authentically their own.

Lest anyone think that the analysis above is simply a philosopher's ruminations, too far removed from the actual experiences of most men, let me just offer one recent instantiation, from among many known to me, and even more, I am sure, I do not know. The following is from the *New York Times Magazine*'s "About Men" weekly column. In an article titled "Couch Dancing," the author describes his reactions to being taken to a place, a sort of cocktail bar, where women "clad only in the skimpiest of bikini underpants" would "dance" for a small group of men for a few minutes for about 25 or 30 dollars, men who "sat immobile, drinks in hand, glassy-eyed, tapping their feet to the disco music that throbbed through the room."

> Men are supposed to like this kind of thing, and there is a quite natural part of each of us that does. But there is another part of us—of me, at least—that is not grateful for the traditional male sexual programming, not proud of the results. By a certain age, most modern men have been so surfeited with images of unattainably beautiful women in preposterous contexts that we risk losing the capacity to respond to the ordinarily beautiful women we love in our bedrooms. There have been too many times when I have guiltily resorted to impersonal fantasy because the genuine love I felt for a woman wasn't enough to convert feeling into performance. And in those sorry, secret moments, I have resented deeply my lifelong indoctrination into the esthetic of the centerfold.[9]

3. Alienation and Crisis

I believe that all of the above can be translated without great difficulty into a conceptual framework paralleling Marx's analysis of the alienation experienced by capitalists. The essential points are captured in two sentences from Marx's manuscripts:

> 1. *All* the physical and intellectual senses have been replaced by the simple alienation of *all* these senses; the sense of *having*.[10]
> 2. The wealthy man is at the same time one who *needs* a complex of human manifestations of life, and whose own self-realization exists as an inner necessity, a need.[11]

Both sentences speak to a loss of human interaction and self-realization. The first articulates how desires for conquest and control prevent input from the world. The second presents an alternative conception wherein wealth is measured by abilities for self-expression, rather than possession. Here Marx expresses his conceptualization of the state of alienation as a loss of sensuous fulfillment, poorly replaced by a pride of possession, and a lack of self-consciousness and hence actualization of one's own real desires and abilities. One could recast the preceding analysis of pornographic male sexuality through these categories. In Marx's own analysis, these are more properly conceived of as the results of alienation, rather than the process of alienation itself. This process is at its basis a process of inversion, a reversal of the subject-object relationship, in which one's active powers become estranged from one, and return to dominate one as an external force. It is this aspect which I believe is most useful in understanding the alienation of male sexuality of which pornography is part and parcel. How is it that men's power turns against them, so that pornography, in and by which men dominate women, comes to dominate men themselves?

To answer this question I shall find it useful to have recourse to two other concepts central to Marxism, the concept of "crisis" in the system and the concept of "imperialism."[12] Marx's conception of the economic crisis of capitalism is often misunderstood as a prophecy of a cataclysmic doomsday scenario for the death of capitalism. Under this interpretation, some look for a single event, perhaps like a stock market crash, to precipitate capitalism's demise. But such events are for Marx at most triggering events, particular crises, which can shake the system, if at all, only because of the far more important underlying structural general crisis of capitalism. This general crisis is increasingly capitalism's ordinary state, not an extraordinary occurrence. It is manifest in the ongoing fiscal crisis of the state as well as recurring crises of legitimacy, and results from basic contradictory tensions within capitalism. One way of expressing these tensions is to see them as a conflict between the classic laissez-faire capitalist market mode, wherein capitalists are free to run their own affairs as individuals, and the increasing inability of the capitalist class to run an increasingly complex system without centralized management. The result of this tension is that the state increasingly becomes a managerial committee for the capitalist class, and is increasingly called upon to perform functions previously left to individuals. As entrepreneurial and laissez-faire capitalism give way to corporate capitalism and the welfare state, the power of capitalism becomes increasingly depersonalized, increasingly reft from the hands of individual capitalists and collectivized, so that capitalists themselves come more and more under the domination of impersonal market forces no longer under their direct control.

To move now to the relevance of the above, there is currently a good deal of talk about a perceived crisis of masculinity, in which men are said to be confused by contradictory imperatives given them in the wake of the women's movement. Though the male ego feels uniquely beleaguered today, in fact such talk regularly surfaces in our culture—the 1890's in the United States, for example, was another period in which the air was full of a "crisis of masculinity" caused by the rise of the "New Woman" and other factors.[13] Now, I wish to put forward the hypothesis that these particular "crises" of masculinity are but surface manifestations of a much deeper and broader phenomenon which I call the "general crisis of patriarchy," paralleling Marx's general crisis of capitalism. Taking a very broad view, this crisis results from the increasing depersonalization of patriarchal power which occurs with the development of patriarchy from its pre-capitalist phase, where power really was often directly exercised by individual patriarchs, to its late capitalist phase where men collectively exercise power over women, but are themselves as individuals increasingly under the domination of those same patriarchal powers.[14] I would stress that the sense of there being a "crisis" of masculinity arises not from the decrease or increase in patriarchal power as such. Patriarchal imperatives for men to retain power over women remain in force throughout. But there is a shift in the mode of that power's exercise, and the sense of crisis results from the simultaneous promulgation throughout society of two conflicting modes of patriarchal power, the earlier more personal form and the later more institutional form. The crisis results from the incompatibility of the two conflicting ideals of masculinity embraced by the different forms of patriarchy, the increasing conflicts between behavioral and attitudinal norms in the political/economic and the personal/familial spheres.

4. From Patriarchy to Fratriarchy

To engage for a moment in even broader speculation than that which I have so far permitted myself, I believe that much of the culture, law, and philosophy of the nineteenth century in particular can be re-interpreted as marking a decisive turn in this transition. I believe the passing of personal patriarchal power and its transformation into institutional patriarchal power in this period of the interrelated consolidation of corporate capitalism is evidenced in such phenomena as the rise of what one scholar has termed "judicial patriarchy," the new social regulation of masculinity through the courts and social welfare agencies, which through new support laws, poor laws, desertion laws and other changes transformed what were previously personal obligations into legal duties, as well as in the "Death of God" phenomenon and its aftermath.[15] That is to say, I believe the loss of the personal exercise of patriarchal power and its diffusion through the institutions of society is strongly implicated in the death of God the Father and the secularization of culture in the nineteenth century, as well as the modern and postmodern problem of grounding authority and values.

I would like to tentatively and preliminarily propose a new concept to reflect this shift in the nature of patriarchy caused by the deindividualization and collectivization of male power. Rather than speak simply of advanced capitalist patriarchy, the rule of the *fathers*, I suggest we speak of fratriarchy, the rule of the *brothers*. For the moment, I propose this concept more as a metaphor than as a sharply defined analytical tool, much as the concept of patriarchy was used when first popularized. I believe this concept better captures what I would argue is one of the key issues in conceptualizing contemporary masculinities, the disjunction between the facts of public male power and the feelings of individual male powerlessness. As opposed to the patriarch, who embodied many levels and kinds of authority in his single person, the brothers stand in uneasy relationships with each other, engaged in sibling rivalry while trying to keep the power of the family of man as a whole intact. I note that one of the consequences of the shift from patriarchy to fratriarchy is that some people become nostalgic for the authority of the benevolent patriarch, who if he was doing his job right at least prevented one of the great dangers of fratriarchy, fratricide, the brothers' killing each other. Furthermore, fratriarchy is an intragenerational concept, whereas patriarchy is intergenerational. Patriarchy, as a father-to-son transmission of authority, more directly inculcates traditional historically grounded authority, whereas the dimension of temporal continuity is rendered more problematic in fratriarchy's brother-to-brother relationships. I believe this helps capture the problematic nature of modern historical consciousness as it emerged from the nineteenth century, what I would argue is the most significant single philosophical theme of that century. If taken in Freudian directions, the concept of fratriarchy also speaks to the brothers' collusion to repress awareness of the violence which lies at the foundations of society.

To return to the present discussion, the debate over whether pornography reflects men's power or powerlessness, as taken up recently by Alan Soble in his book *Pornography: Marxism, Feminism, and the Future of Sexuality,* can be resolved if one makes a distinction such as I have proposed between personal and institutional male power. Soble cites men's use of pornographic fantasy as compensation for their powerlessness in the real world to argue that "pornography is therefore not so much an expression of male power as it is an expression of their lack of power."[16] In contrast, I would argue that by differentiating levels of power one should more accurately say that pornography is both an expression of men's public power and an expression of their lack of personal power. The argument of this paper is that pornography's image of male sexuality works to the detriment of men personally even as its image of female sexuality enhances the powers of patriarchy. It expresses the power of alienated sexuality, or, as one could equally well say, the alienated power of sexuality.

With this understanding, one can reconcile the two dominant but otherwise irreconcilable images of the straight male consumer of pornography: on the one hand the powerful rapist, using pornography to consummate his sexual violence, and on the other hand the shy recluse, using it to consummate his masturbatory fantasies. Both images have their degree of validity, and I believe it is a distinctive virtue of the analysis presented here that one can understand not only the merits of each depiction, but their interconnection.

5. Embodiment and Erotica

In the more reductionist and determinist strains of Marxism, pornography as ideology would be relegated to the superstructure of capitalism. I would like to suggest another conceptualization: that pornography is not part of patriarchal capitalism's superstructure, but part of its infrastructure. Its commodification of the body and interpersonal relationships paves the way for the ever more penetrating ingression of capitalist market relations into the deepest reaches of the individual's psychological makeup. The feminist slogan that "The Personal is Political" emerges at a particular historical moment, and should be understood not simply as an imperative declaration that what has previously been seen solely as personal should now be viewed politically, but also as a response to the real increasing politicization of personal life.

This aspect can be illuminated through the Marxist concept of imperialism. The classical Marxist analysis of imperialism argues that it is primarily motivated by two factors: exploitation of natural resources and extension of the market. In this vein, pornography should be understood as imperialism of the body. The greater public proliferation of pornography, from the "soft-core" pornography of much commercial advertising to the greater availability of "hard-core" pornography, proclaims the greater colonization of the body by the market.[17] The increasing use of the male body as a sex symbol in contemporary culture is evidence of advanced capitalism's increasing use of new styles of masculinity to promote images of men as consumers as well as producers.[18] Today's debates over the "real" meaning of masculinity can be understood in large part as a struggle between those espousing the "new man" style of masculinity more suited to advanced corporate, consumerist patriarchal capitalism and those who wish to return to an idealized version of "traditional" masculinity suited to a more production-oriented, entrepreneurial patriarchal capitalism.[19]

In a more theoretical context, one can see that part of the reason the pornography debate has been so divisive, placing on different sides of the question people who usually find themselves allies, is that discussions between civil libertarians and feminists have often been at cross purposes. Here one can begin to relate political theory not to political practice, but to metaphysical theory. The classical civil liberties perspective on the issue remains deeply embedded in a male theoretical discourse on the meaning of sexuality. The connection between the domination of nature and the domination of women has been argued from many Marxist and feminist points of view.[20] The pivot of this connection is the masculine overlay of the mind-body dualism onto the male-female dichotomy. Within this framework, morality par excellence consists in the masculinized mind restraining the feminized body, with sexual desires seen as the crucial test for these powers of restraint. From this point of view, the question of the morality of pornography is primarily the quantitative question of how much sexual display is allowed, with full civil libertarians opting to uphold the extreme end of this continuum, arguing that no sexual expression should be repressed. But the crucial question, for at least the very important strain of feminist theory which rejects these dualisms which frame the debate for the malestream mainstream, is not *how much* sexuality is displayed but rather *how* sexuality is displayed. These theories speak not of mind-body dualism, but of mind/body wholism, where the body is seen not as the limitation or barrier for the expression of the free moral self, but rather as the most immediate and intimate vehicle for the expression of that self. The question of sexual morality here is not that of restraining or releasing sexual desires as they are forced on the spiritual self by the temptations of the body, but that of constructing spirited and liberating sexual relationships with and through one's own and others' bodies. Here sexual freedom is not the classical liberal freedom *from* external restraint, but the more radical freedom *to* construct authentically expressive sexualities.

I have argued throughout this paper that pornography is a vehicle for the imposition of socially constructed sexuality, not a means for the expression of autonomously self-determined sexuality. (I would add that in contrasting imposed and authentic sexualities I am not endorsing a sexual essentialism, but simply carving out a space for more personal freedom.) Pornography is inherently about commercialized sex, about the eroticization of power and the power of eroticization. One can look to the term's etymology for confirmation of this point. It comes from the classical Greek "*pornographos*, meaning 'writing (sketching) of harlots,' " sometimes women captured in war.[21] Any distinction between pornography and erotica remains problematic, and cannot be drawn with absolute precision. Yet I believe some such distinction can and must be made. I would place the two terms not in absolute opposition, but at two ends of a continuum, with gray areas of necessity remaining between them. The gradations along the continuum are marked not by the explicitness of the portrayal of sexuality or the body, nor by the assertiveness vs. passivity of persons, nor by any categorization of sexual acts or activities, but by the extent to which autonomous personhood is attributed to the person or persons portrayed. Erotica portrays sexual subjects, manifesting their personhood in and through their bodies. Pornography depicts sex objects, persons reduced to their bodies. While the erotic nude presents the more pristine sexual body before the social persona is adopted through donning one's clothing, the pornographic nude portrays a body whose clothing has been more or less forcibly removed, where the absence of that clothing remains the most forceful presence in the image. Society's objectification remains present, indeed emphasized, in pornography, in a way in which it does not in erotica. Erotica, as sexual art, expresses a self, whereas pornography, as sexual commodity, markets one. The latter "works" because the operation it performs on women's bodies resonates with the "pornographizing" the male gaze does to women in other areas of society.[22] These distinctions remain problematic, to say the least, in their application, and disagreement in particular cases will no doubt remain. Much more work needs to be done before one would with any reasonable confidence distinguish authentic from imposed, personal from commercial, sexuality. Yet I believe this is the crucial question, and I believe these concepts correctly indicate the proper categories of analysis. Assuming a full definition of freedom as including autonomy and self-determination, pornography is therefore incompatible with real freedom.

6. Conclusions

It has often been noted that while socialist feminism is currently a major component of the array of feminisms one finds in academic feminism and women's studies, it is far less influential on the playing fields of practical politics.[23] While an analysis of male sexuality may seem an unlikely source to further socialist feminism's practical political agenda, I hope this paper's demonstration of the interconnections between intimate personal experiences and large-scale historical and social structures, especially in what may have initially seemed unlikely places, may serve as a useful methodological model for other investigations.

In one sense, this paper hopes to further the development of socialist feminist theory via a return to Hegel, especially the Hegel of the *Phenomenology*. Not only is Hegel's master-servant dialectic the *sine qua non* for the use of the concept of alienation in this paper, but the inspiration for a mode of analysis, which is true to the experimental consciousness of social actors while at the same time delimiting that consciousness by showing its partiality and placing it in a broader context, is rooted in Hegel's *Phenomenology*. It is not a coincidence that the major wave of socialist feminist theory and practice in the late 60's and early 70's coincided with a wave of Marxist interest in Hegel, and that current signs of a new feminist interest in Hegel coincide with signs of the resurgence of radical politics in the United States.[24]

Analogous to the conception of socialist feminism I articulated in the Introduction to this paper, my conception of Hegelianism defines Hegelianism as method rather than doctrine.[25] In some sense, contemporary Marxism and feminism can already be said to be rooted in Hegel, in the case of Marxism through Marx himself, and in the case of feminism through Beauvoir's *The Second Sex*. A more explicitly Hegelian influenced socialist feminism would embody a theory and practice emphasizing the following themes: the dialectic between individual consciousness and social structure, a thoroughly historical epistemology, a non-dualistic metaphysics, an understanding of gender, class, and other differences as being constituted through interaction rather than consisting of isolated "roles," the priority of political over moralistic or economistic theory, a probing of the relations between state power and cultural hegemony, a program for reaching unity through difference rather than through sameness, a tolerance of if not preference for ambiguity and contradiction, and an orientation toward process over end product.[26]

I would like to conclude with some remarks on the practical import of this analysis. First of all, if the analysis of the relationship between pornography and consumerism and the argument about pornography leading to violence are correct, then a different conceptualization of the debate over the ethics of the feminist anti-pornography movement emerges. If one accepts, as I do, the idea that this movement is not against sex, but against sexual abuse, then the campaign against pornography is essentially not a call for censorship but a consumer campaign for product safety. The proper context for the debate over its practices is then not issues of free speech or civil liberties, but issues of business ethics. Or rather, this is the conclusion I reach remaining focused on pornography and male sexuality. But we should remember the broader context I alluded to at the beginning of this paper, the question of pornography's effects on women. In that context, women are not the consumers of pornography, but the consumed. Rather than invoking the consumer movement, perhaps we should then look to environmental protection as a model.[27] Following this line of reasoning, one could in principle then perhaps develop under the tort law of product liability an argument to accomplish much of the regulation of sexually explicit material some are now trying to achieve through legislative means, perhaps developing a new definition of "safe" sexual material.

Finally, for most of us most of our daily practice as academics consists of teaching rather than writing or reading in our fields. If one accepts the analysis I have presented, a central if not primary concern for us should therefore be how to integrate this analysis into our classrooms. I close by suggesting that we use this analysis and others like it from the emerging field of men's studies to demonstrate to the men in our classes the direct relevance of feminist analysis to their own lives, at the most intimate and personal levels, and that we look for ways to demonstrate to men that feminism can be personally empowering and liberating for them without glossing over, and in fact emphasizing, the corresponding truth that this will also require the surrender of male privilege.[28]

Notes

1. I am indebted for this formulation to Tim Carrigan, Bob Connell, and John Lee, "Toward a New Sociology of Masculinity," in Harry Brod, ed., *The Making of Masculinities: The New Men's Studies* (Boston: Allen & Unwin, 1987).

2. For the *locus classicus* of the redefinition of Marxism as method rather than doctrine, see Georg Lukács, *History and Class Consciousness: Studies in Marxist Dialectics*, trans. Rodney Livingstone (Cambridge, MA: MIT Press, 1972).

3. See my Introduction to Brod, *The Making of Masculinities*. For other recent books by men I consider to be engaged in essentially the same or a kindred project, see Jeff Hearn, *The Gender of Oppression: Men, Masculinity, and the Critique of Marxism* (New York: St. Martin's Press, 1987) and R. W. Connell, *Gender and Power* (Stanford, CA: Stanford University Press, 1987), particularly the concept of "hegemonic masculinity," also used in Carrigan, Connell, and Lee, "Toward A New Sociology of Masculinity." Needless to say, none of this work would be conceivable without the pioneering work of many women in women's studies.

4. For book-length treatments of Marx's concept of alienation, see István Mészáros, *Marx's Theory of Alienation* (New York: Harper & Row, 1972), and Bertell Ollman, *Alienation: Marx's Conception of Man in Capitalist Society* (Cambridge: Cambridge University Press, 1971).

5. Bernie Zilbergeld, *Male Sexuality: A Guide to Sexual Fulfillment* (Boston: Little, Brown and Company, 1978).

6. Michael Betzold, "How Pornography Shackles Men and Oppresses Women," in *For Men Against Sexism: A Book of Readings*, ed. Jon Snodgrass (Albion, CA: Times Change Press, 1977), p. 46.

7. I am grateful to Lenore Langsdorf and Paula Rothenberg for independently suggesting to me how this point would fit into my analysis.

8. See Jessica Benjamin, "The Bonds of Love: Rational Violence and Erotic Domination," *Feminist Studies* 6 (1980): 144–74.

9. Keith McWalter, "Couch Dancing," *New York Times Magazine*, December 6, 1987, p. 138.

10. Karl Marx, "Economic and Philosophic Manuscripts: Third Manuscript," in *Early Writings*, ed. and trans. T. B. Bottomore (New York: McGraw-Hill, 1964), pp. 159–60.

11. Marx., pp. 164–65.

12. An earlier version of portions of the following argument appears in my article "Eros Thanatized: Pornography and Male Sexuality" with a "1988

Postscript," forthcoming in Michael Kimmel, ed., *Men Confronting Pornography* (New York: Crown, 1989). The article originally appeared (without the postscript) in *Humanities in Society* 7 (1984) pp. 47–63.

13. See the essays by myself and Michael Kimmel in Brod, *The Making of Masculinities*.

14. Compare Carol Brown on the shift from private to public patriarchy: "Mothers, Fathers, and Children: From Private to Public Patriarchy" in Lydia Sargent, ed., *Women and Revolution* (Boston: South End Press, 1981).

15. According to Martha May in her paper " 'An Obligation on Every Man': Masculine Breadwinning and the Law in Nineteenth Century New York," presented at the American Historical Association, Chicago, Illinois, 1987, from which I learned of these changes, the term "judicial patriarchy" is taken from historian Michael Grossberg *Governing the Hearth: Law and the Family in Nineteenth Century America* (Chapel Hill: University of North Carolina Press, 1985) and "Crossing Boundaries: Nineteenth Century Domestic Relations Law and the Merger of Family and Legal History," *American Bar Foundation Research Journal* (1985): 799–847.

16. Alan Soble, *Pornography: Marxism, Feminism, and the Future of Sexuality* (New Haven: Yale University Press, 1986), p. 82. I agree with much of Soble's analysis of male sexuality in capitalism, and note the similarities between much of what he says about "dismemberment" and consumerism and my analysis here. (See p. 141 of this volume.)

17. See John D'Emilio and Estelle B. Freedman, *Intimate Matters: A History of Sexuality in America* (New York: Harper & Row, 1988).

18. See Barbara Ehrenreich, *The Hearts of Men: American Dreams and the Flight from Commitment* (New York: Anchor-Doubleday, 1983); and Wolfgang Fritz Haug, *Critique of Commodity Aesthetics: Appearance, Sexuality, and Advertising in Capitalist Society*, trans. Robert Bock (Minneapolis: University of Minnesota Press, 1986).

19. See my "Work Clothes and Leisure Suits: The Class Basis and Bias of the Men's Movement," originally in *Changing Men* 11 (1983) 10–12 and 38–40, reprint forthcoming in *Men's Lives: Readings in the Sociology of Men and Masculinity*, ed. Michael Kimmel and Michael Messner (New York: Macmillan, 1989).

20. This features prominently in the work of the Frankfurt school as well as contemporary ecofeminist theorists.

21. Rosemarie Tong, "Feminism, Pornography and Censorship," *Social Theory and Practice* 8 (1982): 1–17.

22. I learned to use "pornographize" as a verb in this way from Timothy Beneke's "Introduction" to his *Men on Rape* (New York: St. Martin's Press, 1982).

23. See the series of ten articles on "Socialist-Feminism Today" in *Socialist Review* 73–79 (1984–1985).

24. For the most recent feminist re-examinations of Hegel, see Heidi M. Raven, "Has Hegel Anything to Say to Feminists?", *The Owl of Minerva* 19 (1988) 149–68. Patricia Jagentowicz Mills, *Women, Nature, and Psyche* (New Haven: Yale University Press, 1987); and Susan M. Easton, "Hegel and Feminism," in David Lamb, ed., *Hegel and Modern Philosophy* (London: Croom Helm, 1987). Hegel enters contemporary radical legal thought primarily

through the Critical Legal Studies movement. Especially relevant here is the work of Drucilla Cornell, for example, "Taking Hegel Seriously: Reflections on Beyond Objectivism and Relativism," *Cardozo Law Review* 7 (1985): 139; "Convention and Critique," *Cardozo Law Review* 7 (1986): 679; "Two Lectures on the Normative Dimensions of Community in the Law," *Tennessee Law Review* 54 (1987); 327; "Toward a Modern/Postmodern Reconstruction of Ethics," *University of Pennsylvania Law Review* 133 (1985): 291. See also papers from the Conference on "Hegel and Legal Theory," March 1988 at the Cardozo Law School of Yeshiva University, New York City, forthcoming in a special issue of the *Cardozo Law Review*. For signs of radical resurgence in the United States, I would cite such phenomena as the Jackson candidacy and the 1988 National Student Convention. In a recent issue of *The Nation* (actually, the current issue as I write this) Jefferson Morley writes: "The most fundamental idea shared by popular movements East and West is the principle of 'civil society.' " Jefferson Morley, "On 'Civil Society,' " *The Nation*, May 7, 1988, p. 630.

25. I believe this is true to Hegel's own conception of Hegelianism, for Hegel put the Logic at the core of his system, and at the center of the Logic stands the transfiguration and transvaluation of form and content.

26. Much of the feminist critique of the philosophical mainstream echoes earlier critiques of the mainstream made in the name of "process thought." See *Feminism and Process Thought: The Harvard Divinity School/Claremont Center for Process Studies Symposium Papers*, ed. Sheila Greeve Davaney (Lewiston, NY: Edwin Mellen Press, 1981).

27. I am indebted to John Stoltenberg for this point.

28. I attempt to articulate this perspective principally in the following: *The Making of Masculinities*, Introduction and "The Case for Men's Studies"; *A Mensch Among Men: Explorations in Jewish Masculinity* (Freedom, CA: The Crossing Press, 1988), especially the Introduction; and "Why is This 'Men's Studies' Different From All Other Men's Studies?,' " *Journal of the National Association for Women Deans, Administrators, and Counselors* 49 (1986): pp. 44–49. See also generally the small men's movement magazines *Changing Men: Issues in Gender, Sex and Politics* (306 North Brooks St., Madison, WI 53715), *brother: The Newsletter of the National Organization for Changing Men* (1402 Greenfield Ave., #1, Los Angeles, CA 90025), and *Men's Studies Review* (Box 32, Harriman, TN 37748).

PART SIX

Empowerment and Social Movements

10

The Oppression Debate in Sexual Politics[1]

Kenneth Clatterbaugh

It is a fundamental claim of feminism that women are
oppressed.
—Marilyn Frye, *The Politics of Reality*

We identify the agents of our oppression as men.
—Redstockings Manifesto

The "Man Question" in Feminism

The "man question" in feminist theory is: "Where should men be
located in feminist theory and practice? This question encompasses
such issues as: "What are the roles of men in creating and maintaining
women's social condition?" "What are the roles of men in helping to
change women's social condition?" "What are the benefits and/or
costs to women and men of these roles?" Of course each of these
questions has a multitude of specific forms depending on the particular
feminist theory.

The "man question" in feminist theory immediately translates for
men into the "self question." How are men to think about themselves
in relationship to feminist theory and practice?" One does not face
this question only if one is a profeminist man. Antifeminist men and
even those who seek some neutral ground must decide to which of the
many conflicting feminist claims they should be opposed, be supportive, or be neutral.

I want to explore a particular version of the "self question," starting
with the fundamental belief that the condition of women in modern

169

society is best described as one of oppression. This version continues in holding that men collectively and individually cause and maintain women's oppression; men are the oppressors. In contrast to women, men are not oppressed but privileged beneficiaries of women's oppression. And, because they benefit from women's oppression, men are unreliable allies in the struggle to end women's oppression.

To use the language of "oppression" is to use strong language; to be oppressed is more serious than to be discriminated against, treated unfairly, unequally, or unjustly, although it may well include all of these. And, to be an oppressor is a more serious moral flaw than to be the perpetrator of discrimination or unequal treatment, although an oppressor may well be guilty of these injustices as well. The remedy for oppression is also more threatening to the status quo; oppression demands radical solutions (revolutions of liberation) while inequality typically requires only reform.

To illustrate the greater seriousness of the oppression description of the condition of women let me contrast this view with the view that women's condition in society is one of simple inequality to men. According to the inequality description, most of the principles of distributive justice for our society are good principles, if only they were applied fairly for both men and women. Men are not at fault for having what they have if women are given equal access to what men have. There is even in this version a way of admitting that women are not equal *and at the same time* blaming women for their condition, namely, if only women would not choose to stay at home, avoid math courses, or take career breaks for child rearing then women would gain greater equality to men. Through such allowances even conservative men can be made comfortable with an inequality account. Oppression descriptions are, on the other hand, much more painful to men; they suggest that what men have gained has come at the expense of women and that fine tuning the system may not help much. These differences probably account for the fact that there is far more literature by men challenging the oppression story, and correspondingly more literature by men accepting the inequality story.

What is of interest in this paper is the specific counterclaim that men are oppressed. This claim is critical to two of the major challenges to the oppression story. First, men have claimed that both men and women are oppressed by a social system that neither created.[2] Second, the more antifeminist challenge is that the story is reversed; it is men who are oppressed to a large extent by women who are not oppressed and who benefit from men's oppression.[3] It is frequently this rejoinder that launches the oppression debate in sexual politics. My contribution to this debate shall be as follows. First, I defend a theory of oppression that seems to me to meet some obvious criteria of adequacy for such a theory. Second, I use that theory to give content to the rejoinder claim that men are oppressed. Third, I argue that the rejoinder claim that men are oppressed is not well-grounded. The usual arguments for this conclusion fail. In this essay nothing I say assumes that women are oppressed, although I believe that that is the true condition of women. Also, I shall not explore whether even if men are oppressed that gets men off the hook of being the oppressors of women. In fact, I doubt that such a fact would make men less culpable.

Some Basic Assumptions

Most writers on oppression agree that oppression is social, systematic, and aimed at identifiable groups.[4] It is not a personal issue when one is oppressed, because oppression is not directed toward individuals. Individuals may be persecuted, but oppression typically falls on individuals *in virtue of their membership in a group.*[5] In fact, one of the aspects of oppression that makes it morally abhorrent is that it affects individuals regardless of their character, merit, or moral standing. Oppression issues blanket judgments, often grounded in stereotypes, through which individuals are treated as a type rather than as individuals. It matters not whether membership in the oppressed group is a matter of choice or a consequence of birth.

Oppression of a group is systematic; that is, it exists throughout a society, usually over a substantial period of time, and the institutions of society interlock and reinforce each other in ways that create and maintain the oppression.[6] For example, oppressed groups may be denied access to valuable resources of the society and in turn their lack of such resources may be used as evidence that they should continue to be denied access. Thus, the practice feeds the justification and the justification supports the practice.

Finally, oppression is only possible if there is a way of identifying the group to be oppressed.[7] There must be some set of common characteristics that are reasonably easily identified that mark out those and (almost) only those who are members of the target population. Where identification is difficult or impossible either the oppressive institutions fail or steps must be taken to ensure identification; ghettoization, wearing identification badges, or carrying passes may be examples of artificially introduced identification procedures. Where it is possible to hide, members of oppressed groups may go "underground" or "closet" themselves. Such practices, besides extracting a personal toll on the individuals, do not usually end oppression unless they result in the extinction of the oppressed group.

Apart from these three characteristics, however, there are few other points of agreement concerning the nature of social oppression.

Criteria for the Adequacy of a Theory of Social Oppression

The concept of oppression is widely used with various meanings. It can be applied to almost anything "bad" that happens to a social group; for example, if that group is demeaned, discriminated against, exploited, or alienated. In this essay I hope to give the concept a more specific content. In so doing I shall propose a set of criteria for the adequacy of a theory of social oppression. In offering these criteria I do not argue that they are complete nor do I deny that I am engaged in a prescriptive and constructive task by enumerating them. I do think the results justify the task by yielding a more precise and useful concept of oppression.

1. *Ascertainability*. It should be possible to determine when a group is socially oppressed and when a group is not socially oppressed. There is no presumption here that it is easy to determine whether a group is oppressed. A theory of oppression has ascertainability, for example, if one or both of the following is the case: in the social sciences it is possible to find instruments such as questionnaires or surveys that can measure oppression or in history it will be possible to identify conditions and documents that are widely accepted as evidence of oppression.

2. *Discriminability*. An adequate definition when applied should lead to the conclusion that some groups are socially oppressed and some are not socially oppressed. A theory that makes every actual and possible group oppressed is too weak; a theory that makes no actual or possible group oppressed is too strong.

3. *Preanalytic Conformity*. The theory of social oppression should fit with the sincere reflections of members of *paradigm* oppressed groups when they talk or write about their experiences. An adequate theory of oppression should be grounded in the actual world. Hypothetical cases are certainly relevant to testing theories of oppression, but the theory should be guided by the actual experiences of those who are oppressed. As with any notion that may bring with it certain entitlements, groups may claim oppression when they are not oppressed. The concept of oppression is subject to inflation; thus, it is important to have a set of paradigms to which we can refer when identifying what social conditions are oppressive.

4. *Historical Accuracy*. An adequate theory of social oppression should pick out obvious instances of oppression and exclude obvious instances of nonoppression. The criterion of historical accuracy lends support to the criterion of preanalytic conformity, although the former criterion looks to the words of members of oppressed groups, while historical accuracy looks to the words of those engaged in historical research. Ideally, there is overlap in the membership—some historians should also be members of oppressed groups. Both criteria make an

adequate theory useful as a way of understanding the actual world. While we may hope that one day the world may be free of oppression, this criterion assumes that there have been oppressed groups in the past and that there are oppressed groups in the present.

If a theory of oppression meets all of the above criteria I shall say that that theory is *applicable*. Applicability insures that a theory of social oppression will be useful in dealing with concrete questions, such as: "Is a particular social policy or program lessening, increasing, or not affecting the social oppression of a particular group?" "Has there been a decline in oppression of a group over the past 40 years?"

Theories of Oppression

Although the concept of oppression has received surprisingly little attention, there are three theories of social oppression that are most prevalent. I categorize these theories as follows:

A. Psychological Theories

Some philosophers have argued that oppression is (largely) an internal state. Thus, Judith Tormey states:

> [In oppression] one must be made . . . to have beliefs about oneself including beliefs about the proper social position one is to occupy that result in patterns of behavior which conform to an inferior or subsidiary social role, beliefs which, in effect keep one down.[8]

B. Inequality Theories

Perhaps the best statement of the inequality theory is found in *Oppression: A Socio-History of Black-White Relations in America:*

> Oppression can be defined as a situation in which one or more identifiable segments of the population in a social system systematically and successfully act over a prolonged period of time to prevent another identifiable segment or segments . . . from attaining access to the scarce and valued resources [wealth, power, prestige] of that system.[9]

C. Limitation Theories

These theories can take a number of different forms. Limitation theories are widely held by feminist social theorists. The basic idea is that when options are denied to individuals in virtue of membership in a group, the limitation constitutes oppression. Bell Hooks, Alison Jaggar, and Marilyn Frye all seem to defend such a theory:

Being oppressed means the absence of choices.[10]

Oppression is the imposition of unjust constraints on the freedom of individuals or groups.[11]

The experience of oppressed people is that the living of one's life is confined and shaped by forces and barriers which are not accidental or occasional and hence avoidable, but are systematically related to each other in such a way as to catch one between and among them and restrict or penalize motion in any direction. It is the experience of being caged in: all avenues, in every direction, are blocked or booby trapped.[12]

A General Critique of Theories of Oppression

Psychological theories of oppression typically do not offer a definition of oppression, because they generally recognize that internal states are produced by external oppressive social conditions. In fact, it would be the ultimate form of blaming the victim to hold that people are oppressed *simply* because they feel oppressed. If oppression were only a matter of feeling oppressed, the proper remedy for oppression would not be social revolution, but therapy to remove these feelings or, at least, to make them more endurable. An understanding of the psychology of oppression is vitally important for those who are oppressed or who work with the oppressed, but because psychological theories leave unanswered the nature of social oppression, I shall not consider such theories further in this paper.

There is a generalized argument that undermines most efforts to explicate the concept of oppression. It begins by asking: Are there social conditions in which the proposed oppressive conditions (inequality, limitation, etc.) obtain, but which fail to be oppressive? If there are, then we are justified in distinguishing oppressive inequality from simple inequality, oppressive limitation from simple limitation, and so forth. The distinction in each case forces us to ask again: "What is oppression?" "What is that extra condition that makes some inequities oppressive or that makes some limitations oppressive?"

Consider a hypothetical case of inequality. Suppose that within a society there are two groups of people who for religious reasons have a tradition of ethnic animosity. They each control a certain amount of wealth, political power, and prestige. But they systematically discriminate against each other so that they successfully deny to the other group any sharing of the wealth, political power, and prestige that they each control. Neither group needs to be oppressed by this systematic discrimination, although hostility between the two groups might be extreme. This is easy to see where both groups are relatively powerful and wealthy, even if the distribution of resources is not equal. (The Walloons and Flemish of Belgium might be an actual case in point.)

The point is that neither inequality or successful denial is sufficient for oppression.

One might object, at this point, that in the above cases the inequality is not absolute; even the less advantaged group still controls some resources and power. Maybe we should count inequality as oppressive only when there is *absolute* denial of wealth, power, and prestige to a target group. But surely, this amendment is too strong. Groups can be oppressed even when they are not absolutely denied power and wealth. To make absolute denial a condition may well result in there being no oppressed groups or far fewer than we normally recognize, thus violating the historical accuracy criterion. For example, we might have to eliminate Jews in Tsarist Russia, even though they are probably a paradigm example of an oppressed group.

Consider one more example that shows that successful, systematic denial of scarce and valued resources will not do as an account of oppression. Consider two identifiable groups in society. One lives at subsistence level, the other below subsistence level. The first group can survive *only by denial* to the sub-subsistence group the resources and social power that they control. Surely, one could not accuse the subsistence group of oppressing the less fortunate group or even of doing anything wrong if they successfully protect what they have. Here I am assuming that the subsistence-level group can genuinely continue to exist only by protecting what they have and that they do not take unnecessary measures to protect their resources.

Limitation theories encounter a similar set of objections. There are obvious cases of limitation that are not oppressive.[13] Many limitations occur simply through circumstances such as weather, bad luck, ignorance, or well-intentioned human mistakes. Therefore, trying to identify those patterns of limitation that are oppressive from those that are not shows the need for further conditions than simple limitation, unless we want to hold (in violation of discriminability) that everyone is oppressed. Thus, Jaggar tries to argue that only certain kinds of constraints constitute oppression, namely, *unjust* constraints.

But even unjust constraints hardly constitute oppressive limitations. Are well-known Hollywood personalities oppressed because they cannot travel freely in the city or eat at a favorite restaurant without a crush of admirers? Surely such constraint is unjust in that the personalities are denied freedom from interference that is generally available to others. The basic point is that privilege in a society, even the kind of privilege antithetical to oppression, is compatible with unjust constraint. The prince who would be king or the Nazi who would be ideologically pure are subjected to extreme constraints, which may even be enforced with violence; such constraints are certainly unjust. Still, it would be an unfortunate consequence of a theory of oppression

that privileged groups that are identifiable, and systematically constrained, become paradigm oppressed groups.

In part because she wants to rule out men as an oppressed group,
Frye, too, struggles to discover further conditions on the limitations
that constitute women's oppression. Frye argues therefore for a benefit
condition:

> The boundary that sets apart women's sphere is maintained and promoted
> by men generally for the benefit of men generally, and men do benefit
> from its existence, even the man who bumps into it and complains of the
> inconvenience. That barrier is protecting his classification and status as a
> male, as superior. . . .[14]

In the first place such specific restriction—women are oppressed by
their limitations because men benefit from them—is unavailable to me
since I do not assume in this explication of oppression that either men
or women are or are not oppressed. Second, even if generalized,
Frye's condition does not seem to work. Although it is usually the
case, it is not necessarily the case that the oppressor benefit from the
oppressed. One need only consider an incompetent oppressor whose
practices actually work to the short-term and/or long-term benefits of
the oppressed. For example, imagine a people who due to natural
catastrophe are dying and another group takes them in, saves their
lives but enslaves them. In enslaving them however the second group
out of laziness and lack of forethought turns over complete control of
their technological society to the slaves, ultimately putting themselves
completely at the mercy of the enslaved group. Still, the enslaved
group is oppressed, even if the short-term and long-term benefits
accrue to the enslaved.

In view of this critique we are left with a need to discover more
precisely what it is that makes a certain set of conditions oppressive.
We too readily encounter inequalities and unjust constraints that are
not oppressive. The search for such a feature need not be an *a priori*
project. We can discover such a feature when we examine the lives of
those who are members of groups that serve as paradigms of oppressed
populations. We can discover such a feature by comparing the lives of
those groups to the lives of others who may also suffer from social
harms such as discrimination, limitation, and inequality but are not
oppressed.

At this point it is relevant to mention Iris Young's insightful essay
"Five Faces of Oppression."[15] In this essay Young argues that because
the concept of oppression cannot be strictly defined and "there is no
attribute or set of attributes that all oppressed people have in common"
that oppression needs to be thought of as a cluster concept involving
"five disparate categories," namely, "exploitation, marginality, pow-

erlessness, cultural imperialism, and violence."[16] While I agree with Young that an *a priori* explication of oppression is impossible, I do not agree that there is not a common condition of being oppressed. Young's claim that "there is no attribute or set of attributes that all oppressed people have in common" is ambiguous. It is true that the mechanisms by which peoples are oppressed vary widely. Some groups are treated very violently, others marginalized, and some are both marginalized and treated violently. But to concede this truism is not to agree that there is no commonality among all oppressed groups; in fact I shall argue that there is a commonality, namely, systematic dehumanization within society and that only by thinking of these mechanisms as producing that dehumanization do we get a complete account of social oppression.

Our previous concern applies to Young's mechanisms as well. Not all exploitation, marginalization, powerlessness, cultural imperialism, and (legitimate) violence constitute oppression. For example, modern capitalism includes workers who are very privileged. They are exploited in that the value they produce far exceeds what they receive, but they enjoy high wages, job security, social prestige, and political importance. These workers have the kinds of power in society that is most antithetical to oppression. Marginalization is Young's term for systematic inequalities, which we have already shown is not sufficient to pick out oppressive conditions. Similarly, powerlessness may or may not be oppressive. Many children are powerless in that they lack authority or the ability to control much of their life. While I would not deny that many children are oppressed, it is not simply because of their powerlessness that oppression occurs. Cultural imperialism is a form of marginalization in which the experiences of one group are considered universal and the norm. Yet there could be good reasons for disregarding a group's experiences as a norm—the subculture may be violent and abusive in the extreme, for example. Violence, too, is frequently part of oppressive tactics. But violence against criminals, in self-defense, or in war need not be oppressive even though it is abundantly present and legitimate. In short, Young's excellent list of mechanisms demands completion. Even though Young does not propose a unitary concept of oppression, we are left wondering which exploitations, marginalities, etc., are oppressive and when.

Toward a Theory of Social Oppression

Rosa Parks once observed that she refused to give up her seat on the bus because she just wanted to be treated like a human being. Academic philosophers from Kant to Rawls have argued that everyone is entitled to equal respect as a human being. Similar themes have appealed to those who write about oppression. Leaving open what it means to treat someone as a human being, one suggestion is that it is oppressive to act in a systematically dehumanizing way toward an identifiable group of humans.

In *Pedagogy of the Oppressed,* Friere notes that "while both humanization and dehumanization are real alternatives, only the first is man's vocation. This vocation is constantly negated by . . . injustice, exploitation, oppression, and the violence of the oppressors."[17] Frye claims that women are not heard because they are excluded from the class of persons.[18] Daniel McGuire in setting out the criteria for those who are entitled to preferential treatment notes that one criterion is that prejudice against those who are so entitled has reached the level of depersonalization.[19] Sandra Lee Bartky notes that "psychological oppression is . . . separating of a person from some of the essential attributes of personhood."[20]

The common thread in each of these authors is the concept of *dehumanization* or *depersonalization*. The dehumanization theory that I shall develop holds that *oppression is the systematic dehumanization of an identifiable target human group*. To dehumanize a group is to deny that the members of that group possess the complete range of human abilities, needs, wants, and achievements that are valued at that time as important to being a human being. It also counts as dehumanizing to treat, overtly or covertly, a human group as if its members lack the abilities, needs, wants, or achievements of a more complete human being. It is not important whether the members of a group are conceived as *non*human or *defectively* human. Of course, groups that are oppressed under one standard need not be oppressed under another. In fact there are some dramatic changes in history where a group that was not oppressed in one century was oppressed in the next.[21]

Of course what constitutes a complete human being is a social construct, which is historically and culturally relative. It may not even be an accurate and complete account of what humans really are. I am not claiming that a group is oppressed just because the historical concept of a complete human being leaves out some abilities, needs, wants, and achievements that they in fact have. It is not a question of how well a group's perceived characteristics match their actual ones, but how well their perceived abilities, needs, wants, and achievements match what the broader society values as human.

A group is not oppressed if there are qualities included in being a human being that are denied of them and which they in fact lack. Thus, it is not oppressive to treat people who cannot walk as if they cannot walk, although it would be oppressive to deny that they have other human needs, for example, needs for privacy and dignity when they have such needs. Again, a group is not oppressed if there are qualities included in being a human that are denied of them and which society does *not* value as important to being human.

A social structure becomes oppressive under this definition, if it assumes, promotes, or treats the target population as if it is defective in any of the defining human abilities, needs, wants, or achievements. I use "social structure" in a very broad sense to include such items as social institutions, practices, policies, laws, humor, ideology, and work relations. Usually, when a group is oppressed in a society these social structures interlock and support each other. Thus, to take an example, if African-American children are denied access to education and therefore do not achieve in academic pursuits, the systems interlock when lack of achievement justifies continued denial of opportunity.

While this paper is not the place for a complete defense of the dehumanization theory of social oppression, we can make at least a preliminary argument that shows that it satisfies our criteria of adequacy. In most societies the valued traits of being human are not explicitly listed. But in societies that maintain oppressive structures there is a discernible trail of beliefs, stories, laws, and science that all point to the *defectiveness* of the target group. The availability of this trail in personal letters, diaries, policy statements, scientific papers, social myths, and law will vary with the society, but it makes dehumanization ascertainable and historically accurate.

African Americans who found themselves enslaved were stripped of their nationality, their locality of origin, their name, religion, familial connections, and most human rights.[22] Myths were created concerning their inability to feel pain, cold, heat, and most especially their sexuality and lack of intelligence.[23] Laws forbade them to run away, to fight back, to defy in gesture or word the orders of a white person. "By the early 1700s, they were no longer defined as legal persons but as chattel property—little more than 'beasts of burden'."[24]

The dehumanization, which began in slavery, continued well into the twentieth century. As late as 1933 there was a zero percent overlap between white and black traits as determined by whites and there was no question as to which set of traits were valued as most truly human; by 1982 that overlap had increased to only 22 percent.[25]

Usually the valued trait that is denied of an oppressed group will be a trait such as intelligence, which is seen as underlying other traits such as the ability to behave morally or to have aesthetic appreciation.[26] Thus, it can be argued that those who lack intelligence cannot benefit from having the rights of citizens or the responsibilities of commerce. "Moral judgment, like business judgment, social judgment, or any other kind of higher thought process, is a function of intelligence. Morality cannot flower and fruit if intelligence remains infantile."[27] Coupled with the idea that the intelligence of whole groups of individuals is impaired, this linking of traits can only lead to one conclusion, namely, that the social roles of individuals within these groups should be severely limited. Oppression is always systematic. Thus, Terman argued:

> Among laboring men and servant girls there are thousands like them. . . . The tests have told truth. These boys are ineducable beyond the merest rudiments of training. No amount of school instruction will ever make them intelligent voters or capable citizens. . . . They represent the level of intelligence which is very, very common among . . . negroes.[28]

These are the kinds of evidential trails that make the dehumanization theory ascertainable.

The dehumanization theory also discriminates among groups. Clearly there are those who are held up as more completely human, indeed as paradigm cases of human being. To this group is extended the full rights of citizenship and the responsibilities of business, government, morality, and politics. It is this group's standards of excellence that are embraced as the appropriate standards. And, it is this group's definitions that are used to determine the deficiencies of other groups (cultural imperialism). Thus, for example, Andrew Carnegie argues in *Triumphant Democracy* that "the defective classes" cannot be expected to overcome "their inherent lack of abilities."[29] Whereas people like himself, Anglo-Americans, are not defective in the above ways, in fact they exhibit the complements of these defects, namely, "genius," "ability," "concentration," "honesty," and even openmindedness.[30]

The dehumanization theory also fits well with the kind of preanalytic descriptions of oppression that are found among members of the oppressed. Frederick Douglass, for example, describes the appraisal of an estate on the death of a master:

> There was the intensified degredation of the spectacle. What an assemblage! Men and women, young and old, married and single; moral and thinking human beings, in open contempt of their humanity, leveled at a blow with horses, sheep, horned cattle, and swine. . . . all holding the same rank in the scale of social existence. . . .[31]

The connection between oppression as systematic dehumanization and the earlier theories of oppression is evident. If the oppressed are perceived as lacking some important human making traits, then there will be justifications for denying those groups equal access to resources and restricting their choices. The justification will either involve an argument similar to Terman's that they are incapable of benefiting from the resources or the choices, or that it would be positively dangerous for social stability to grant greater options. Slaves must not be taught to read; the colonized must be controlled by colonial government; the vote must be kept for the capable classes; and all must be inculcated to accept the authority of the oppressors through the mechanisms of oppression.

Are Men Oppressed?

When we turn to the issue of whether men can claim oppression, we must make it clear what we are asking. We are not concerned with the question of whether or not men fall into targeted groups. Men clearly have been and are oppressed as African Americans, as Jews, as colonials in French Algeria. The question here is whether men, as men, have a claim to be oppressed in twentieth-century America? It is the arguments toward this conclusion that I shall now address.

There are three primary arguments to the conclusion that men are oppressed as men. The first is what I call the "socialization argument"; it holds that because men are socialized just as women are socialized, and since that socialization is oppressive for women, it is also oppressive for men. The second argument, which I shall call the "reversal argument," finds that the oppression of men benefits women and that women help to maintain it. Women are viewed as unreliable allies in the struggle to end men's oppression. This argument is the mirror image of the oppression story that is used to describe the condition of women. The final argument is the "expendability argument." Men's lives are seen as expendable in a way that women's lives are not; the usual evidence for this claim is drawn from images in fictive film, the draft laws, casualties of war, and even domestic violence statistics.

A. The Socialization Argument

The first argument has its beginnings in the liberal profeminist men's movement.[32] According to liberal feminist analysis women are denied their full humanity by their restricted social role; profeminist men argued, similarly, that men, too were subjected to restricted social roles and thereby denied their full humanity.[33] If such restriction is oppressive to women, then it is also oppressive to men. Many liberal profeminist men do not hesitate to draw this conclusion. They speak of the "oppressive, dehumanizing sex roles" that afflict men or "the oppression we feel by being forced to conform to the narrow and lonely roles of men in this society.[34] The Berkeley Men's Center Manifesto declares that "we are oppressed by conditioning."[35] As long as women's subjugation to the feminine mystique was oppressive, men believed that they too were oppressed by the masculine mystique. This argument depends on the parallel between the social conditioning of women and that of men.

There are many grounds on which this argument may be criticized. It is not obvious that either masculinity or femininity is a unified role or that either is a role that cannot be readily altered to suit individual needs. In other words one or both of these roles, as normative, may be easily violated.[36] Masculinity and femininity, either or both, may not even qualify as social roles; the norms that guide them may be too vague.[37]

However, I wish to raise another concern. It is far from clear that the claim that "if the limitations of the feminine role are oppressive so are the limitations of the masculine role" is true or plausible. We have already noted that it does not seem to be plausible to view restriction (limitation) just by itself as oppressive. The reason is that members of privileged and dominant groups within society may be severely constrained in the social roles that they are allowed to play. Thus, if men are a privileged group within society and women are second-class citizens, they may both confront limitations, but for different reasons. Imagine a young boy who announces that he wants to be a nurse. While that occupation is less off limits today than it was a decade ago, it is easy to imagine that he will be told that the occupation is unworthy of him. Of course, he *could* be a nurse, if he tried, but doctors are more prestigious, better paid, and worthy of the challenge of being a man. A young girl who announces her intention to be a doctor may face a different set of objections. She is told that she *cannot* be a doctor; it requires abilities that she lacks, for example, a talent for science and mathematics, physical strength, or emotional toughness, and it may even cause her to miss her menstrual cycle. In fact Mary Roth Walsh tells a story very much like this one in her book *"Doctors Wanted: No Women Need Apply": Sexual Barriers in the Medical Profession, 1835–1975.*[38]

But the point is simple, to make the parallel one needs to show that the constraints put on men and women both derive from dehumanization as we have defined it. But if men are constrained because they are groomed for dominance and women are constrained because of a perceived lack of abilities, the former is not oppressive and the latter certainly is. And since there is a strong *prima facie* case that men are perceived as reservoirs of valued human traits, especially relative to women, it becomes incumbent on anyone using this argument to show that the source of constraint is the same in each case. The reason this argument has survived for the past twenty years is that those who offer it are satisfied to think of oppression only in terms of constraint. And, obviously, such a limited analysis does not get one to the conclusion that men too are oppressed.

B. The Reversal Argument

The 1980s saw a different kind of argument emerging. It abandoned the parallel and argued that the situations of men and women are sufficiently different that the oppression of men needs to be talked about in a new way. It has long been recognized within the writing about men that there are harms that come out of the masculine role. But it took a new argument to conclude from the harms of the masculine role to the conclusion that men are oppressed.

It was in *The Hazards of Being Male* that Herb Goldberg began to develop his case for men's oppression.[39] Goldberg and others were aware that masculinity, in most feminist analysis, was considered a dominating and privileged social role. This belief had also been held by the liberal and radical profeminist men who wrote on masculinity. Hence, Goldberg's first move is to argue that the feminist picture inverts reality. It is men who are underprivileged:

> By what perverse logic can the male continue to imagine himself "top dog"? Emotionally repressed, out of touch with his body, alienated and isolated from other men, terrorized by the fear of failure, afraid to ask for help, thrown out at a moment's notice . . . when all he knew was how to work. . . . The male has become an artist in the creation of many hidden ways of killing himself.[40]

Next, Goldberg tries to explain how it is that men and women are misinformed about male privilege. He suggests that masculinity is considered a privileged role because men are highly visible and socially successful; men are "the heroes, the studs, the providers, the warriors, the empire builders, the fearless ones."[41] The hidden nature of the male role makes the oppression of men different in kind from the oppression of women:

> Unlike some of the problems of women, the problems of men are not readily changed through legislation. The male has no apparent and clearly defined targets against which he can vent his rage. Yet he is oppressed by the cultural pressures that have denied him his feelings, by the mythology of the woman and the distorted and self-destructive way he sees and relates to her, by the urgency for him to "act like a man" . . . and by a generalized self-hate that causes him to feel comfortable only when he is functioning well in harness. . . .[42]

Finally, women, to their own advantage, play a significant role in keeping men in their oppressed situation by perpetuating the myth that men are "top dog" and that women are their victims. It is men who are the "oppressors," "abusers," chauvinists," and "sexist pigs," and who have the perks in society.[43] These myths make men feel guilt and self-hate; the result is male subservience and blame rather than change.[44] Goldberg seems to believe, further, that women have already escaped their oppression; now they have the choice to be "wife, mother, or business executive."[45] Thus, women are liberated, but women's liberation requires that men stay in harness; otherwise a woman would not have a choice of being a wife and mother (with a man to provide).

This reversal argument has been advanced by many writers since Goldberg's original formulation. Roy Schenk in *The Other Side of the Coin: Causes and Consequences of Men's Oppression* identifies women as "society's agents in the oppression of us men."[46] Because women believe themselves to be morally superior, a belief that is widespread in society and that gives them great power over men, men cannot even protest this arrangement and consequently are left feeling anger, rage, and guilt. Women gain from this arrangement, and men lose.[47]

Men Freeing Men: Exploding the Myth of the Traditional Male is a collection of writings that come out of the Free Men movement, of which Goldberg was a founder.[48] The authors in this book repeat this argument over and over in various formulations. Women have the real power but it benefits women to perpetuate the myth that men are the heavies and that men have the real power—they keep their options open and an income coming in.[49]

This reversal argument can be challenged at several levels. Even a cursory look at the situation of women in society makes it problematic as to whether women really have a choice to be wife, mother, or executive.[50] Further, feminists have long argued that women do not benefit when men are the provider. They do not benefit because they do not learn the skills to take care of themselves in divorce or death; they do not benefit because they are unable to fulfill many of their own desires to work; and they do not benefit by a system that puts control of salaries, wages, and work only in the hands of men; they do not benefit from dependency on men. These are elementary points in feminist theory, points that go back to Betty Friedan's *The Feminine Mystique*.

And, for all his efforts to illustrate the costs of masculinity, Goldberg has not shown that those costs are not the effects of privilege and dominance. It is not enough to say rhetorically: "how can the male continue to imagine himself 'top dog' " when he is subjected to a sufficiently long list of disorders. Profeminist male writers, whom Goldberg does not acknowledge, noted all of these harms in the early 1970s, yet they found them to be due to the competitive roles that dominant persons play in society.[51] It is a twist of logic to try to argue, as Goldberg does, that because there are costs in having power, one does not have power. Shorter life expectancy, access to drugs, fear of failure, and disorders due to competitive activities may well be the costs for men in a society that privileges men. By itself the need to be in control of life, women, and work produces many of the harms that are so frequently mentioned, especially in a world where control is rarely possible.[52] Until a sustained argument is made that shows that the afflictions of masculinity are *not* the result of trying to maintain power and advantage, there is no reason to allow the reversal argument to proceed. In its first premise this argument essentially begs the question; it assumes that the costs of masculinity are either due to oppression or that they constitute oppression simply because they are limiting.

In brief, if Goldberg is arguing directly from the costs of masculinity to the view that men are oppressed, then he begs the question and avoids the difficult issue as to whether these harms are in fact due to male dominance. If Goldberg is falling back on some generalized claim that men are oppressed because men do not control everything in their lives or that men are oppressed because men are constrained in their social roles, these arguments depend upon a seriously flawed theory of oppression, namely, oppression as limitation.

C. The Expendability Argument

The first two arguments really get to the conclusion that men are oppressed by using a notion of oppression by which everyone is oppressed, namely, oppression is limitation. The final argument that I now consider, at least, appears more compatible with the concept of oppression as dehumanization. The idea behind this argument is that violence against men is acceptable in our society (compared to violence against women or children). From this observation it is concluded that men's lives are valued less and therefore men are oppressed. The crucial premise of this argument is that violence against men is acceptable in our society. Usually this premise is defended by pointing out that only men are drafted, only men can serve in combat in a war, men are "killed" much more regularly in television and movies, and domestic violence against men is not treated as the serious social problem that domestic violence against women is.

> Asked about women in combat at her confirmation hearings, then–Supreme Court nominee Sandra Day O'Connor said she'd hate to see them come home in coffins. Why are men expendable in her eyes?[53]

> By *expecting* men to play life-threatening roles, we are less horrified when their lives are lost. By being less horrified, we can continue the assignment rather than look at our roles . . . *sponsoring* violence against men by turning to war films, murder mysteries, westerns, or TV movies in which men are killed routinely for our entertainment.[54]

> If . . . we turn to the only large nationally representative sample of spouse abuse . . . *we find that 12 percent of husbands were violent toward wives and 12 percent of wives were violent toward husbands. A ratio of 1 to 1.*[55]

Once again, however, there are a great many logical and factual questions that these arguments fail to address. The domestic violence studies that are used, over and over, are purely behavioristic; that is, they study how many times a spouse slammed a door, threw an object, threatened with a knife, etc. There is no effort to study the context in which these behaviors occurred.[56] On a strictly behavioristic analysis, if x threatens y and y reacts by pulling a knife on x to protect her/his life, y is judged to be domestically violent in this situation. When aggression is factored in, however, and defensive behavior excluded, men are overwhelmingly more violent.[57]

Those who offer the expendability argument never give a criterion for determining when a social practice is acceptable. Sometimes they even seem to slide from the fact that violence with men as victims is very widespread to the conclusion that it is acceptable or that men's lives are not valued.[58] Surely some things that are widespread are acceptable, but not everything that is widespread is acceptable.

Finally, we again face the same serious oversight in this argument that occurred in the previous two arguments. Is the fact that only men are drafted and used in combat the result of valuing men's lives less or the result of a patriarchal society that through its institutions holds that only men are capable of being soldiers; only men have the courage, strength, and military intelligence to defend their country. Women, on the other hand, are the property and the spoils of war that victors take along with the roads, homes, farms, and factories of the vanquished. The historical rhetoric suggests the second hypothesis far more than the first.[59] Add to this observation the fact that the military has provided a primary road of upward mobility for men through elaborate subsidizations in insurance, home loans, educational opportunities and monies, preferential hiring, and tax benefits.[60] The military experience is one in which most men do *not* serve and in which *very few* men become "expendable." One cannot help but doubt that the military experience oppresses men as *men* when further facts are indicated, namely, that the men who serve in the front lines, the "cannon fodder" are overwhelmingly African American, Hispanic, and poor. If there is a case to be made it is that the history of the military is deeply patriarchal with most benefits, honor, and glory going to white men.[61]

Conclusion

The arguments intended to show that men are oppressed have been offered almost exclusively by the men's rights perspective, even though the beginnings of this position are in the profeminist men's movement.[62] These arguments are widespread and have found favor among many men and even some feminist women. Typically the notion of oppression in these arguments is a limitation theory of oppression. But oppression is not limitation. I have argued, instead, that social oppression is a systematic dehumanization of an identifiable group. Thus, it is a serious failure of these arguments that they fail to show that men as men are systematically dehumanized.

It is not hard to imagine a possible world in which men are systematically dehumanized. Imagine that our world is suddenly controlled by humanoid aliens who establish a new hegemony over the traits that are valued in human society. They reverse or revise the valued traits that have been held to belong especially to (white) males and for which white males have been socialized. An elaborate science develops that teaches that men are overly controlled by their genitals and the emotion of anger; their so-called rational abilities are now seen as rationalizations to support their biological and emotional demands. Male achievement in the arts, literature, philosophy, and sport are expunged from the pages of history and the media or treated as trivial accomplishments. The new set of valued traits installed as human making include many of the traits in which men have not traditionally excelled; for example, being a caregiver. A crisis ensues in which men lose confidence in themselves and strive to live up to the new concept although hardly any are seen as doing so. Men, by socialization, are simply not prepared to excel in this new world. As a result even when they are given the opportunity they do not fare nearly as well as the new humanoids and/or women. Men in fact do have the traits to excel in this world, but they are systematically kept from the kinds of achievements and opportunities to develop those abilities and when they do they are exceptionalized or ignored. In short, men are dehumanized and therefore oppressed.

The hypothetical world which I describe could come about; it could come about without an invasion of aliens. In fact, in our present world the standards are changing. The norms by which people are judged to be worthy are no longer so uniformly (white) male. It is this change that men fear and it is this changing standard that leaves some men less prepared for this world. Instead of welcoming a new and more humane conception of what is truly human, these men resist that change. They attack the revolutionaries as oppressors.

Feminist theorists have made the case that women are dehumanized; that is, women as an identifiable group are seen as defective relative to men whose talents and achievements constitute a norm. In fact, much of the history of Western science is a debate as to whether women have the requisite abilities, needs, wants, and achievements, be it in medicine, sports, artistic expression, music, religion, or science itself. On the negative side women have been found wanting by male political theorists, scientists, and political leaders; wanting in genius, creativity, spirituality, and political ability. On the positive side women have made important gains against their exclusion by simply demonstrating that they do have the requisite abilities and talents to do the very things from which they have been excluded. Feminists have also demanded a new set of valued traits for all persons; it is a set that is without preference for sex or race. Hopefully it is a conception that will not readily lend itself to the dehumanization of any group.

Among theories of social oppression, the dehumanization theory alone meets the minimal criteria of adequacy. When applied it does not support the claim that men are oppressed as men. The arguments to that conclusion have been found wanting; at best they rest on a philosophically inadequate theory of social oppression; at worst they are disingenuous and self-serving.

Notes

1. The dehumanization theory of oppression used in this essay was developed jointly with Mark Walstead. I owe Mark thanks for supporting me in this paper and making substantive theoretical and historical contributions.

2. New Society Publishers, *Off Their Backs . . . and on Our Own Two Feet* (Philadelphia: New Society Publishers, 1983), pp. 3, 12.

3. Roy Schenk, *The Other Side of the Coin: Causes and Consequences of Men's Oppression* (Madison, WI: Bioenergetics Press, 1982).

4. Marilyn Frye, *The Politics of Reality: Essays in Feminist Theory* (Trumansburg, NY: The Crossing Press, 1983), p. 33. Jonathan H. Turner, Royce Singleton, Jr., and David Musick, *Oppression: A Socio-History of Black-White Relations in America* (Chicago: Nelson-Hall, 1984), p. 1. Iris M. Young, "Five Faces of Oppression," *The Philosophical Forum* 19:4 (Summer 1988), p. 275.

5. Frye, op. cit., p. 8.

6. Frye, op. cit., p. 4; Turner, Singleton, and Musick, op. cit., p. 1; Young, op. cit., p. 273.

7. Frye, op. cit., p. 33; Turner, Singleton, and Musick, op. cit., p. 1; Young, op. cit., p. 275.

8. Judith Tormey, "Exploitation, Oppression, and Self-Sacrifice," *Women and Philosophy: Toward a Theory of Liberation,* eds. Carol C. Gould and Marx W. Wartofsky (New York: G. P. Putnam's Sons, 1980), pp. 206–21.

9. Turner, Singleton, and Musick, op. cit., pp. 1–2.

10. Bell Hooks, *Feminist Theory from Margin to Center* (Boston: South End Press, 1984), p. 5.

11. Alison M. Jaggar, *Feminist Politics and Human Nature* (Totowa, NJ: Rowman & Allanheld, 1983), p. 6.

12. Frye, op. cit., p. 4.

13. Ibid., p. 10.

14. Ibid., p. 13.

15. Young, op. cit.

16. Ibid., pp. 270–71.

17. Paulo Friere, *Pedagogy of the Oppressed* (New York: The Continuum Publishing Corporation, 1970), p. 28.

18. Frye, op. cit., p. 50.

19. Daniel C. Maguire, *A New American Justice: Ending White Male Monopolies* (Garden City, NY: Doubleday, 1980), pp. 129–30.

20. Sandra Lee Bartky, "On Psychological Oppression," *Philosophy for a New Generation*, eds. A. K. Bierman and James A. Gould (New York: Macmillan, 1981), pp. 418–29.

21. John Boswell, *Christianity, Social Tolerance, and Homosexuality: Gay People in Western Europe from the Beginning of the Christian Era to the Fourteenth Century* (Chicago: University of Chicago Press, 1980).

22. Cedric J. Robinson, *Black Marxism* (London: Zed Books, 1983), p. 105.

23. Stephen Jay Gould, *The Mismeasure of Man* (New York: W. W. Norton, 1981).

24. Turner, Singleton, and Musick, op. cit., pp. 15–17.

25. John F. Dovida and Samuel L. Gaetner, eds., *Prejudice, Discrimination, and Racism* (Orlando, FL: Academic Press, 1986), p. 6.

26. Gould, op. cit., pp. 158–74.

27. L. M. Terman, *The Measure of Intelligence* (Boston: Houghton Mifflin, 1916).

28. Ibid., pp. 91–92.

29. Andrew Carnegie, *Triumphant Democracy* (New York: Scribner's, 1893), p. 176.

30. Ibid., pp. 111, 113, 121, 122, 192, 200, 205.

31. Frederick Douglass, *Life and Times of Frederick Douglass* (New York: Macmillan, 1962), p. 96. See also Frantz Fanon, *The Wretched of the Earth* (New York: Grove Press, 1963), p. 42.

32. Kenneth Clatterbaugh, *Contemporary Perspectives on Masculinity: Men, Women, and Politics in Modern Society* (Boulder, CO: Westview: 1990), p. 52.

33. Betty Friedan, *The Feminine Mystique* (New York: Dell, 1963); Jack Sawyer, "On Male Liberation," *Men and Masculinity*, eds. Joseph Pleck and Jack Sawyer (New York: Prentice-Hall, 1974), pp. 170–73.

34. Jeff Keith, "My Own Men's Liberation," *Men and Masculinity*, eds. Joseph H. Pleck and Jack Sawyer (New York: Prentice-Hall, 1974), pp. 81–88.

35. Berkeley Men's Center, "Berkeley Men's Center Manifesto," *Men and Masculinity*, eds. Joseph H. Pleck and Jack Sawyer (New York: Prentice-Hall, 1974), pp. 173–74.

36. Joseph H. Pleck, *The Myth of Masculinity* (Cambridge, MA: MIT Press, 1981), pp. 143–44.

37. James Doyle, *The Male Experience*, 2nd ed. (Dubuque, IA: Wm C. Brown, 1989), p. 103.

38. Mary Roth Walsh, *"Doctors Wanted, No Women Need Apply": Sexual Barriers in the Medical Profession, 1835–1975* (New Haven: Yale University Press, 1977).

39. Herb Goldberg, *The Hazards of Being Male: Surviving the Myth of Masculine Privilege* (New York: Signet, 1976).

40. Ibid., pp. 181–82.

41. Ibid., p. 3.

42. Ibid., p. 4.

43. Ibid.; Herb Goldberg, *The New Male* (New York: Signet, 1979), p. 141.

44. Goldberg, *The Hazards of Being Male*, op. cit., p. 5.

45. Ibid., p. 2.
46. Schenk, op. cit., p. 66.
47. Warren Farrell, *Why Men Are the Way They Are* (New York: McGraw-Hill, 1986), p. 237.
48. Francis Baumli, ed., *Men Freeing Men: Exploding the Myth of the Traditional Male* (Jersey City, NJ: New Atlantis, 1985).
49. Cf. Schenk, op. cit., pp. 78–79; Ibid., pp. 120–21, 262, 306.
50. Sara E. Rix, ed., *The American Woman 1990–91* (New York: W. W. Norton, 1990).
51. Marc Feigen Fasteau, *The Male Machine* (New York: McGraw-Hill, 1974), and Jon Snodgrass, ed., *A Book of Readings for Men Against Sexism* (Albion, CA: Times Change Press, 1977).
52. Myriam Miedzian, *Boys will be Boys: Breaking the Link Between Masculinity and Violence* (New York: Doubleday, 1991).
53. Dan Logan, "Woman in Combat," in Baumli, op. cit., p. 239.
54. Farrell, op. cit., p. 229.
55. Farrell, op. cit., p. 228.
56. R. L. McNeely and Gloria Robinson-Simpson, "The Truth about Domestic Violence: A Falsely Framed Issue," *Social Work* (November–December 1987), pp. 485–90.
57. Lucy Berliner, "Domestic Violence: A Humanist or Feminist Issue," *Journal of Interpersonal Violence,* 5:1 (March, 1990) 128–29, and Michele Bograd, "Why We Need Gender to Understand Human Violence, *Journal of Interpersonal Violence,* 5:1 (March 1990), 132–35. See also: Tamar Lewin, "Battered Men Sounding Equal-Rights Battle Cry," *The New York Times* (April 20, 1992, A12).
58. Fredric Hayward, "We Who are About to Die," in Baumli, op. cit., pp. 238–39.
59. Mark Gerzon, *A Choice of Heroes: The Changing Face of American Manhood* (Boston: Houghton Mifflin, 1982), pp. 30–45.
60. New York Times byline, "Troop Cuts Make Army a Harder Place to Start," in *Seattle Post-Intelligencer* (May 7, 1990).
61. Schenk, op. cit., p. 37.
62. Clatterbaugh, op. cit., pp. 52, 61–83. The men's rights perspective is usually distinguished from profeminist perspectives that try to offer an analysis of the male experience within the confines of some feminist theory. It is also distinct from the mythopoetic perspective, which is neither profeminist nor antifeminist in its basic assumptions.

11

Honor: Emasculation and Empowerment

Leonard Harris

Honor is almost universally accorded men over women within social entities such as classes, ethnic groups, nations, or racial communities. Honor is a social good, i.e., a form of reverence, esteem, and deference an individual receives from others. Persons excluded from a moral community, however, are also generally excluded from honor independent of gender. Exceptions to this generality of particular concern are well-established cases that an individual's will is subservient to the will of the dominant community. Conferring honor on groups excluded from a moral community is inimical to a core feature of honor—the possession of qualities that "relate existence to certain archetypal patterns of behavior."[1] Honor involves the imposition of wills, an imposition that often uses threats, demands, pressure, and aggressive behavior. The expression of such traits by members of subjugated communities is, however, normally considered a sign of insurrection or belligerence. Racism, I believe, helps account for why honor has been an elusive good for African-American males despite occasional examples of individually honored African Americans. The honor accorded Dr. Martin L. King, Jr., and the general subjugation of the African-American community, does not defeat the idea, I suggest, that membership in the moral community is crucial for the possibility of an individual to be honored.

In the first section, "A Conception of Honor," I provide a working definition of honor. In "Honor and Emasculation" I explore the meaning of dishonor. I discuss eunuchs, lynching, and castration as

191

exemplary of forms of emasculation and exclusion from the moral community. In "Honor and Masculinity" I consider the character of honor as a masculine good. In "Honor and Dr. King" I consider the traits that warrant honoring Dr. Martin L. King, Jr. The honor accorded Dr. King, and the lack of honor accorded the African-American community, does not defeat the idea, I contend in "Dr. King as Counterexample" that membership in the moral community is essential for an individual to be socially honored. There is, I believe, an ambivalence in the American cultural fabric over what honor means. I suggest in "Honor and Empowerment" that the honor accorded Dr. King is different from the kind that we often rely on in normal social life as vicarious conduits representing archetypal behavior. The traits of love, care, compassion, and sacrifice are considered different from such traits as tenacity and aggressiveness, but no less significant as features of social normality and sources of honor.[2]

A Conception of Honor

Parenting normally includes teaching children how to impose their wills—wiping their noses, deciding not to eat candy, exercising their preference for clothes, and discussing, arguing, and using body language in ways that help convince. Parents are authorities whether they use tyrannical means of domination or discourse as a form of coercing and shaping behavior. Analogously, children's play includes means for children to impose their wills on one another. It may be that the play of boys evinces a greater concern for competition, rules, and winning than that of girls; the play of girls may be more concerned with cooperation, sharing, and keeping a game enjoyable rather than determining who wins. Nevertheless, both forms of play share the project of will imposition; the first through verifiable results and the second through a cohesion that allows deciding who is included and who is excluded from the shared bonds. Threats, demands, pressure, and aggressive behavior are features integral to the imposition of wills in both parenting and play.

There are tremendously varied ways and purposes through which individuals seek to have their wills imposed on others. However, the fact of imposing one's will is cross-culturally important as a way of securing regard from others and developing a sense of self-worth. The personalization of politics is telling in attitudes of children toward race, war, and social identity.[3] Caring, loving, and nurturing children to become soldiers or to be supportive of soldiers has occurred generation after generation in American history.[4] The imposition of wills through a variety of techniques is a feature of the normal daily lives of children and parents, but it is hardly definitive or exhaustive of what is involved in either. The features of parenting and play that I have mentioned are also, however, important bases of honor.

Honor is a good often accorded because virtues and meritorious traits are assumed to be embodied by an agent. The willful obedience of children to their parents' most cherished expectations, for example, is a form of honoring one's parents. Honor reflects discrete and explicit social rankings and boundaries between agents. Failure to accord appropriate deferential behavior or appropriate regard for social rankings and boundaries, such as children cursing adults, bespeaks dishonor. Persons can be honored it they have no accomplishments, such as persons of noble birth, and honor can be bestowed on epic heroes as well as the dead. There are tremendously different forms of honor, different conceptions of what is required for a person to be honored, and different views about what counts as degradation. The above features of honor are certainly not exhaustive.

Peter Berger argues that honor in the modern world is no longer prevalent. He associates honor with socially imposed roles, chivalrous codes of behavior, and laws against insults to honor. However, for Berger, "A return to institutions will be *ipso facto* a return to honor" because institutions impose roles and establish hierarchies.[5] Contrary to Berger, normal social life has an array of hierarchies to support informal codes of honor. Moreover, the royal houses of Austria, England, Japan, and Saudi Arabia are faring well in modernity. A visit to nearly any multinational corporate headquarters, military barracks, or schoolyard might dispel academicians of the illusion that conceptions of honor are not prevalent in modernity. Nonetheless, I intend to mean by honor a variety of forms of exalted accord. One way to see that honor is a social good, and to present a sample of its many forms, is by considering what it is to be dishonored.

Honor and Emasculation

According to Orlando Patterson in *Slavery and Social Death*, slavery is the condition of being generally despised and natally alienated; incapable of defining descending generations or directing the course of ascending generations. "The dishonor the slave was compelled to experience sprang instead from that raw, human sense of debasement inherent in having no being except as an expression of another's being."[6] Contrary to Hegel and Marx on Patterson's account, slaves were not necessarily workers; they were never accorded the status of moral persons. Moreover, male and female slaves, no matter how rich, were always under the threat of harm from any member of the slave-holding class—child, homeless free person, woman, man, or even pets of the free. "The absolute ruler . . . requires the ultimate slave; and the ultimate slave is best represented in the anomalous person of the eunuch."[7]

Eunuchs were absolutely incapable of redemption—they could father no future generations and they were usually despised. They were emasculated, not only because as a group they could not function as normal biological parents, nor hold the respect of their relatives if these were known, but because they lacked the possibility of empowerment over other men and dominance over women. As tax collectors, for example, they could shape the life chances of a tremendous range of wealthy as well as poor persons; but they could never participate in shaping the next generation as their surrogates, vassals of their values, or as testaments to their love; nor could they dictate the flow of wealth from one generation to the next. As a group, eunuchs could not stop the children of their masters from becoming adults that would despise eunuchs any more than African-American "nannies" could stop the children they raised on behalf of their masters from selling them or their children, beating their husbands, raping their daughters, or castrating their sons. Eunuchs existed completely for the other—bodies for sport, sex, status, guards, servants, and administration—irredeemable physically, spiritually, and socially. The dishonor of eunuchs was conditioned on the exclusion of the eunuch community from the moral community, i.e., the embodiment of virtues and meritorious traits by an individual eunuch was always tainted because individual eunuchs were members of, or perceived as members of, a generally despised community.

Thomas More's *Utopia* provides an excellent example of the importance performed by the boundary between membership in or exclusion from the moral community and the way that membership establishes which individual is potentially due deference. More considered slavery a substitute for death and an improvement in the life of the spiritually or virtue-dead person. In More's *Utopia* there are no singular positions of exalted honor. Rather, the society of Utopia itself is an honorable social entity. Utopia is reached only by accident or luck. Almost no one ever leaves Utopia. Slaves and colonized aliens are voluntary subjects or ones subjugated for their own benefit. In either case, they are always pleased to have been saved from their previous state of decadence. Everyone that lived outside of Utopia could be ranked as more or less degraded in comparison to the life in Utopia. Persons were or became honored because they identified with, had the sentiments of, and conducted themselves in accordance with the norms of the social order in Utopia. That order is what More constructs as honorable. That is, social normality in *Utopia* is coterminous with nobility—everyone is in an exalted station and utopia itself is the highest earthly form of excellence.

The same is the case in *Ethopia Unbound*, an idealized depiction of

Africa by the noted Ghanian nationalist J. E. Casely Hayford (1866–1930).[8] Hayford's *Ethiopia Unbound* has a hierarchical character that functions to promote egalitarianism; polygamy, chiefs, and provincial villages are grounded in Hayford's eyes on egalitarianism. The elite are exalted models of the best norms perceived as definitive of normality.

Utopias characteristically require the perfect ability of the utopianites to impose their wills—wills that are coterminous with perfect virtue. Normal social life is thereby coterminous with exalted character virtues.[9] A utopia is thus the best, or best possible, social world. That is, honor and normality are coterminous in conceptions of the best, or the best possible, world; the abnormal, inferior, and irredeemably lost souls exist outside of the honor of utopia's normality, i.e., outside the moral community.

Social entities excluded from the moral community are also generally excluded from the social good of honor. Wealthy eunuchs, for example, were treated honorably although the poorest members of the caste enslaving eunuchs were empowered to demean them without reprimand. As a group, they could not be honored. Free American Blacks prior to 1865, regardless of their color, social graces, wealth, or stature in a military unit, for example, were always subject to the possibility of being enslaved and their progeny enslaved; a possibility that was not one any white person faced, regardless of class, status, or gender. The threat of being lynched is an example of the exclusion of African Americans from the moral community—a threat faced most often by African-American males and a threat that existed independent of their virtues and merits.

Decapitation, torture, burning, and starvation were some of the common practices used in the process of forming and controlling slave communities in the Americas. The vast majority of persons treated as cargo, chattel, and fodder for plantations in the Americas were initially Black men. Moreover, it has been argued that "It was threat of honor lost, no less than slavery, that led them [southern American states] to secession and war."[10] Long after the formal end of American slavery in 1865, however, the project of exclusion of African Americans from the moral community continued. Trudier Harris, in *Exorcising Blackness*, describes an American mode of excluding Blacks from the moral community by its practice of lynching. Vicksburg, Mississippi, *Evening Post*, 1904:

When the two Negroes were captured, they were tied to trees and while the funeral pyres were being prepared they were forced to suffer the most fiendish tortures. The blacks were forced to hold out their hands while one finger at a time was chopped off. The fingers were distributed as souvenirs. The ears of the murderers were cut off. Holbert was beaten severely, his skull was fractured, and one of his eyes, knocked out with a stick, hung by a shred from the socket. . . . The most excruciating form of punishment consisted in the use of a large corkscrew in the hands of some of the mob. This instrument was bored into the flesh of the man and woman, in the arms, legs and body, and then pulled out, the spirals tearing out big pieces of raw, quivering flesh every time it was withdrawn.[11]

Quivering flesh, taken by avid corkscrewers, was thrown to the crowd for souvenirs. The bodies were burned, and after cooling, pieces of charred flesh were taken from the ashes by men, women, and children for souvenirs. Shopkeepers and women of class occasionally used severed hands as ornamentation. This ritual of violence was not isolated to Mississippi: in almost every case of lynching Blacks in America, a similar ritual was followed. With the increased accessibility of cameras, photographs of the crowd gloating over the body became a common feature of the ritual.

Approximately 25 percent of the lynchings studied by the NAACP in 1927 involved accusations of sexual harassment of white women as the justification for the lynching—the rest involved accusations of belligerence and property theft. When couples were lynched, the woman might be clubbed, hair cut and thrown to the crowd, fingers thrown to the crowd, corkscrewed through the breast and her flesh thrown to the crowd while the man was forced to watch what awaited him immediately upon completion of her torture. His genitals might be removed during his torturing and his "balls" later pickled as souvenirs.

Lynching bespeaks the importance of the body as an object for degradation to substantiate the submission of persons excluded from a moral community; experiments on Black men are another example of the Black male body as a site for degradation.[12] In an excellent book, *Bad Blood: The Tuskegee Syphilis Experiment*, James Jones describes the "moral astigmatism" that allowed white government administrators, nurses, military personnel, entrepreneurs, doctors, news reporters, and poor Black and white workers to participate in a study for over forty years on the "effects of untreated syphilis on [399] Black men in Macon County, Alabama."[13] An experiment without procedures, an experiment predicated on the intentional withholding of known effective treatments, an experiment about which generation after generation of well-intentioned but astigmatic white physicians presented papers at professional conferences, is an experiment that suggests why there should be a basic distrust of professionals and unreflective workers. Both may be ready practitioners of moral astigmatism if for no other reason than that they performed their duties, following precedents, or pursued professional self-promotion in approved utilitarian fashions. Neither an unvirtuous character, an authoritarian personality, or evil intentions are necessary facets of persons deeply involved in perpetuating treatable pain and preventable misery. This is so because moral astigmatism often pervades relationships with persons excluded from the moral community. Consequently, individuals from social entities excluded from the moral community are burdened with raising the status of their community or finding some way to distance themselves absolutely from identification with their community in order to secure honor.

The above forms of terror most often confronted by African-American males are not intended to suggest a well-designed conspiracy. They do suggest, however, a persistent pattern of immiseration and exclusion from the moral community. Honor is an elusive good for African-American males in a world dominated by male codes of honor.

Honor and Masculinity

Honor has been most often a masculine good in the sense that the ability to kill, destroy, compel others to subordinate themselves, and control resources either necessary for survival or status has been most often a power held by men. Men, for example, are most often the symbols of a nation's warriors, regardless of the roles played by women. Neither the women warriors of North Vietnam nor the women guerrillas of Algeria and Zimbabwe are memorialized in nearly as vast an array of statues, street names, or government-sponsored ceremonies as are the men. Men have most often accorded the rewards and rituals of honor to other men within their communities.

Honor is not a masculine good when women accord women exalted regard independent of men or when the accord of exalted regard is not gender specific. Queens, women warriors, free women in slaveholding societies and women of upper classes and statuses, for example, may be honored for similar reasons as men—they are empowered in ways in which persons lower on the scale of membership in the moral community, or persons exiled from that community, are excluded. Even if exalted regard is itself considered a masculine trait, it is nonetheless a trait that has been held by women as women, e.g., as goddesses and czarinas. The wife of any citizen of Athens held power over Aristotle because Aristotle, an outsider, a mete, could have become a slave but he could almost certainly never have ascended to citizen. Any Athenian that might have married Aristotle, regardless of how rich or wise he might have become, would have lowered her status. Citizenship, as a family-based good, excludes persons outside of its network. Whether considered immoral, demented, irredeemably inferior, a witch, or a tramp, any white woman held power over every Black, whether the Black was a model mother, husband, father, mistress, Christian, servant, or entrepreneur. Race, class, status, gender, and citizenship can bifurcate who, and in what form, honor is accorded. Marriage is an example of a social institution that provides men honorable regard across these lines.

Honor through marriage is accorded to males in societies that practice patrilateral parallel cousin marriage (i.e., the marriage of one brother's son and another brother's daughter) as well as societies that practice exogamy.[14] Patrilateral parallel cousin marriage provides for a family and the male in these marriages a form of community respect for the family unit that can only be achieved through such marriages; their embodiment of spiritual, family, and communal leadership qualities are intoned by the marriage, not by any particular achievement otherwise. The poor as well as the rich gain status through such marriages. In Western societies, however, parallel cousin marriages are discouraged. Spiritual, family, and communal regard is frequently gained in Western societies by men through marriages with persons of the same or higher status as defined by wealth and education. Whether family solidarity is emphasized through affinal or agnate ties, honor is a good situated in social bonds. The family continues to be an important route by which men gain deference and regard from their affiliates.

The status men gain by virtue of marriage, however, does not mean that all married men are held above all women: married men of Turkish heritage are not held above German women in Germany, married or single; married French Muslim men of Arabic heritage face prejudice in France although under less suspicion than single Muslim men of Arabic heritage; white American married men are not held in greater regard than Japanese women in Japan; married Muslim Palestinian men are not held above Jewish women in Israel. The increase of honor in marriage for men is tied to their community. There may be a greater respect for married men over single men within as well as outside of their communities. However, neither marital status nor gender defeats status designation by nationality, ethnicity, or race. Community membership and relationships between communities, I believe, are extremely important in situating the type of regard available to a person.

It would seem to follow that an individual from a generally subjugated community could not be honored by society in general because, as I have argued, honor is a good tied to perceptions of the moral community. Dr. Martin L. King, Jr., is honored, however, although the African-American community has not ascended to exalted regard. The honor accorded Dr. King, I suggest in the following, does not defeat the idea that honor is a social good tied to moral communities.

Honor and Dr. King

Dr. King followed a principle of communal love; that principle was central to a protest movement that permanently transformed the world.[15] He imposed his will, a will that was simultaneously associated with the will of a large community of immiserated persons. The Aristotelian concept of honor requires that an individual embody virtues. This embodiment affords them the right to demand deference from others. The Aquinian concept of honor requires that an agent temper claims to deference with the recognition that ultimately good virtues and good acts are made possible by God. Both concepts require that agents impose, or be capable of imposing, their will, and both require that agents to some degree embody virtues.[16] I suggest that a defensible depiction of the honor accorded Dr. King rests on an Aquinian conception of honor and an idea that was inconceivable in the Middle Ages: the idea that persons are nodally equal across lines of religion, nation, race, gender, and age.

The honor accorded Dr. King excludes the possibility of moral astigmatism because it is founded on an ideal that includes the necessity of moral reflection and commitment. We are enjoined in articles, sermons, and lectures to reflect on everyday moral concerns. An unjust law or practice, for Dr. King, is no law and not a practice we are compelled to follow. Rather, we are morally bound to evaluate social practices that define normality and required to pursue the change of unjust laws and immoral practices.

Dr. King embodies a crusade and a vision of a community, a herculean struggle of the ostensibly weak overcoming the misguided strong; the fundamental transformation of the descendants of slaves—a dreadful heritage of humanity—to the status of free person; not a mystical, dialectical becoming through a Hegelian movement of spirit but a radical, this-worldly transformation. The song "We Shall Overcome," for example, has been sung by protesters in China, Russia, Germany, and South Africa. Its meaning has resonated with the dreams of millions. There are very few songs, dreams, or morally packed messages rooted in American history emulated by a greater diversity of peoples than the songs, dreams, and messages associated with Dr. King. Unlike the condition of president, soldier, entrepreneur, noble, or least well off, the honor accorded Dr. King is exalted because he represents ideals that are not expressed by granting accord to fairly circumscribed social roles.

Ironically, the honor accorded Dr. King is associated with his promotion of communal love: an ideal that is also associated with femininity, passivity, and emotional abandon. It is certainly arguable that Dr. King's life contributed to a redefinition of masculinity: commitment to *agape,* strength through compassion, caring even at the expense of self-harm. Dr. King is not required to have lived some mystically perfect moral or normatively sanguine life—only that the life he did live was extraordinarily magnanimous. Dr. King is perceived as embodying virtues such as courage and tenacity, but these are subordinate to his image as a champion of non-violence and collective love. Arguments for a King memorial holiday, for example, do not rest on the family life of Dr. King as a model father or husband, a model minister, divine prophet, courageous savior of the polity, or fearless defender of the nation.

Even if after a thorough research of white attitudes it is found that whites accord Dr. King honor because they perceive his will as one totally subservient and non-threatening to their will, it is still the case that the courage and magnanimous character required to love, care, be compassionate, and sacrifice should have an important place in the social fabric of Americans. The difficulty of according honor to such traits is considered below.

Dr. King as Counterexample

If honor is a social good accorded to members of a moral community, and the African-American community is often excluded from membership, it would seem to follow that Dr. King could not be generally honored unless his will was clearly subservient to the will of the dominant community. It is arguable that Dr. King's pacifism (non-violent direct action) helped make it possible for him to be honored in a way in which Malcolm X could not be honored. This is plausible if Dr. King's ideas and non-violent methods are perceived as being or functioning in ways subservient to the will of the dominant community, e.g., loving enemies, promoting the interests of the rich by non-violent civil disobedience among the poor, promoting Black identity as "American" in the face of Black exclusion from equal treatment, etc. If his ideas and methods are also perceived as "feminine" in the sense in which that which is feminine is considered somehow compliant, weak, and submissive to that which is masculine, then the view of Dr. King's pacifism as consonant with the will of the dominant community gains further warrant. However, I suggest that the above perception of Dr. King's ideas and methods fails to appreciate the specificity of race, the ambivalence in the American cultural fabric over the meaning of honor and the character of communal love.

A perception of Dr. King as submissive is simply misguided. Dr. King prevailed, for example, despite attacks by the U.S. government's COINTELPRO (Counterintelligence Program) under J. Edgar Hoover's FBI, orchestrated to blackmail Dr. King into committing suicide, and despite the attacks on his life by segregationists. Even if his ideas and methods functioned in ways subservient to the will of the dominant community they were instrumental in bringing substantive change. The laws and institutional rules of segregation, as well as avowed prejudicial beliefs, have all declined in direct response to the civil rights movement in which Dr. King was a major actor.

A perception of Dr. King as feminine, when feminine is construed as compliant, weak, and submissive, expurgates Dr. King from being perceived as Black (already stereotyped inferior by race). Such a perception also requires erasure of the character of his pro-active approach, i.e., civil disobedience, non-violent direct action, and courageous resistance to injustice.

The character of racial and gendered forms of oppression are not identical.[17] African-American males, for example, do not face date rape or spouse abuse in anywhere near the proportion of women, Black or white. They are more likely to be the perpetrators of date rape and spouse abuse. They face, more than Black or white women, the likelihood of being unemployed. The minuscule group of middle-class Black males fares better than Black females, far worse than white males, and is far smaller in relation to their numbers than white females. Black males face the greatest likelihood of incarceration, regardless of guilt. For such reasons it is not intrinsically confusing to write about African-American women and men facing multiple jeopardy (race, sex, gender, and class)—the character of the jeopardies is interlaced yet distinct.

If the specificity of the subject is not taken seriously, the victim is ignored. For example, if the abuse of children is simply subsumed under the abuse of spouses, children become effectually erased. Abused children are frequently under the care of abused mothers; however, an appropriate array of such abuses would allow for children as subjects with their own experiences—including experiences that warrant interests and rights against parents whether the parent is an abusing mother, father, relative, or stranger. The specificity of the subject does not reside outside of a social network—who are the abusers, who has remained silent about the abuse, who is empowered to aid the abused? A perception of Dr. King as submissive without remainder fails to take account of the specificity of his community; a community despised by the other.

In one sense Dr. King is not a counterexample to the generality that honor is a social good accorded to members of a moral community—in the sense that his pacifism is perceived as completely in the service and interest of the dominant community. The federal government and most states have instituted a Martin L. King, Jr., national holiday, for example, but they are under no pressure to disband their armies or militia thereby. The non-violent message of Dr. King's pacifism is selectively applied according to the will of the agents intoning his message. However, his pro-active method for imposing his will and his inclusion of African-American people as full members of the moral community are sources of ambivalence for the larger community. One feature of the ambivalence involves honoring Dr. King as an agent that promoted love *and* change, when change is often accompanied by unkindly threats, pressure, and aggression.

If there is a difference between the way Dr. King and Malcolm X can be honored, the difference may rest on our evaluation of their different views of communal love. When Dr. King and Malcolm X intoned "I love my people," their views of how that love was best actualized differed. Love, in both cases, was a form of "empowerment" in a direct sense, i.e., it was a good through which one engenders, among other things, the ability of others to impose their will. Parents, for example, help empower their children by caring, nurturing, and guiding; partners empower one another by support, dialogue, and aid; relatives empower one another by functioning as information networks, sites of belonging, and sources of encouragement. Loving is empowering but its form and content may differ.

Dr. King's form of love allowed for an acquiescence to the culture of America as a combined entity and Malcolm X's did not. The *two nations* are for Dr. King at their best when conjoined in communal love; the two nations are at their best for Malcolm X when each is allowed its own cultural legitimacy and self-controlled empowerment.[18] Dr. King's form of love is empowerment in competition against the dominant order for the reformation of the society through the aegis of love, care, compassion, and sacrifice. Malcolm X's form involved empowerment in competition against the dominant order for the reformation of the society through aggression.

The ideals of communal love and non-violent resistance have long histories in African-American culture. Vincent Harding's *There Is a River* is a moving history of African-American forms of resistance.[19] In addition, Harding's response to *Habits of the Heart* is an exploration into the difference between the norms defining the African-American community and the white community.[20] Abolitionists, Reconstruction moral suasionists, civil rights activists, and various nationalist movements have promoted a notion of communal love and non-violent resistance as moral imperatives. In the contemporary era, *Nation Conscious Rap*, for all of its aggressive, uncompromising, and sexually charged themes, has a major chord of communal love and non-violent resistance.[21] The ideal of communal love and non-violent resistance consequently reflects cultural ambivalence about the relationship of love and change and a similar ambivalence about the meaning of honor.

Honor and Empowerment

Honor, as one among many social goods, is a function of community. Analogously, power, in the way Jennifer L. Hochschild uses it to depict a variety of goods (economic, political, and internal motivation) affecting means and prospects regarding equal opportunity, is a function of community.[22] That is, the possibility of honor for an individual is integrally tied to the possibility of his or her community having, or potentially having, honorable status. The African-American community gained because of the civil rights era symbolized by Dr. King in the sense that it gained status within the moral community of America. Its ability to protect its members from wanton attacks by the Ku Klux Klan or advance its members through legal redress, for example, is suggestive of its empowerment.

One difficulty with honoring Dr. King through the aegis of love, care, compassion, and sacrifice is that such traits do not readily bespeak other equally important sources of honor. Moreover, the imposition of wills through threats, demands, pressure, and aggressive behavior are not neatly separated from love, care, compassion, and sacrifice. (The parenting examples used earlier suggest the sort of intermeshing linkage that I mean.) Nor, it seems to me, are the traits of love, caring, compassion, or sacrificing reducible to a neat category of "affective." However, even if love and aggressiveness fit in separate trait categories, normal social life involves imposing wills through the aegis of both trait categories.

An inference from socially normal activity to the activity of an individual is an important inference because honor is a form of deference to individuals sustained by social groups—families, citizens, African Americans, Americans, peace-loving people, etc.—which sustain the bond between the individual and the existence that a social group perceives itself as embodying. Moreover, archetypal behavior is archetypal because it represents an inward nature only intimated by actual normal behavior. There is, in a sense, a two-way street between the individual and the social; between the socially normal and the exalted. If we honor, for example, a president, whether of NOW or of the United States, one reason is because he or she embodies, stands for, or represents some traits that we hold in regard. It is not required that we agree with everything representatives do, nor even that we like the organizations they head; what is required is that they embody traits that we hold in regard.

The moral community of America is most often conceived in ways that exclude the African-American community. A perception of the African-American community as capable of imposing its will, ranking above others, commanding deference—crucial features of normality— is contrary to America's perception of one of its least favored groups. Dr. King certainly imposed his will through tremendous labor, sacrificial love, and non-violent resistance. A good deal of social normality is, however, the imposition of wills through threats, demands, pressure, and aggressiveness.

One reason parents, soldiers, entrepreneurs, the poor, teachers, and the elderly can be held in high regard is because they are perceived as persons who successfully manage exigencies against pressures to fail—exigencies that include, but are not restricted to, performances that have little or nothing to do with affective goods such as love, caring, compassion, or sacrificing. Parents, for example, clean, cook, wash, pay bills, and are often blamed for the atrocities that their children commit but are rarely applauded if their children perform laudable acts. There are no national holidays, however, dedicated to good parenting. Even if parenting in the modern world can be said to be in some sense "caused" by love, as distinct from the medieval view of parenting as a duty, the performances of generating income, paying bills, cleaning up, and spending time that directly takes away from other enriching adult activities require tenacity, diligence, thrift, aggressiveness, and discipline. There are, for example, more African-American male single parents than white American male single parents in proportion to their numbers in society—but single fathering is hardly an image located in any social group's perception of African-American males. Single parenting, for African-American males, requires a willingness to do so despite the certainty that popular social media such as television, newspapers, novels, or church services will not offer much encouragement or recognition.

Parenting also requires tremendous aggressiveness and self-assurance for African Americans in general, and African-American males in particular, to protect their children. Many grade school administrators, primarily male and white, and grade school teachers, primarily female and white, harbor and impose a daunting array of demeaning and destructive prejudices toward African Americans in general, and especially African-American males. The history of research on administrator and teacher attitudes, detailing their prejudicial practices toward African-American males, is simply overwhelming: researchers may disagree on which array of prejudices and precisely how daunting, but they almost invariably portray a dismal picture of African-American males receiving less attention, lower grades, harsher punishment and fewer awards than white children with identical or similar performance.[23] Successful parenting requires diligence: persistently arguing, demanding accountability, and defending one's child against a barrage of prejudices against the very persons parents depend on for educating their children.

One of the most distressing features of aggressiveness and threatening behavior is that they are also implicated in the harms facing African-American males. Black males receive harms in part because of the way they are socialized, not simply because of their sex.[24] Black on Black homicide, for example, is the cause of far more deaths than white on Black homicides. Black males physically inflict more harms on themselves than anyone else—it is improbable that this has nothing to do with their socialization and form of being nurtured. The imposition of wills through uncompromising or nearly uncompromising demands, mutually unpleasant encounters, aggressiveness, pressure, and threats may function well or horribly. Honor is often accorded the powerful—for example, presidents, entrepreneurs, nobles, and soldiers—through the conduits of their successful use of aggression and pressure for causes considered laudable. This, it seems to me, is true whether the honored are conceived as pure egalitarian pacifists ruled by affective emotions or absolute monarchical warlords ruled by meanness. Aggressiveness and threatening behaviors—traits that ruling groups tend to reserve as legitimate forms of behavior for themselves—may be tools in Malcolm X's sense, i.e., traits that can help defend a person against an onslaught of social tyranny or help lift a person from the degradation of social death. Survival tools are invaluable in a chronically racist society that confronts obstacles from the improbability of prenatal care or fair treatment in grade school to the improbability of employment or income even nearly commensurate with others of similar endowment. Whether the traits of aggressiveness or threatening behavior are sources of harm or conduits for survival, they are features of social normality through which some forms of honor are obtained. Emasculation, however, is most assuredly not a basis for honor.

The attack on the African-American male is arguably a sex-specific emasculating attack in the sense that African-American men are the object, or at least African-American men have received an undue array of harms, by virtue of their sexual socialization and race. It is a feminist issue in Ida B. Wells's sense—lynching for her was an issue for the nation and Africans as a people, yet it was particularly a feminist issue because Black men, sons and husbands, were its most frequent object. It is also fruitfully characterized as more than sex specific: it can be characterized as a part of an attack on the body of a people—a people long excluded from the moral community and continually under duress. This is so not because Black men are breadwinners (except for a small sector of middle-class Black men, Black men have less income than Black women), or because Black men are leaders (the percentage of Black elected officials has radically improved, but it hardly corresponds to the percentage of the Black U.S. population; civil rights leadership has been notoriously male dominated and almost completely chauvinist—there are no reasons why this should continue).

It is an attack on the body of a people because in a certain sense "men" do not exist in social normality outside the context of associations, relations, networks, parents, and ascending and descending generations of persons. Men do not exist in the sense of their sharing identical material assets, powers to command deference from persons outside their communities, or ability to shape and execute life plans. Men of subjugated communities, for example, are characteristically emasculated. To be emasculated is to be disjoined from the possibility of empowerment across generations—a possibility that exists only in social connection.

The idea that in a certain way "men" do not exist as a social entity does not mean that "men" cannot be treated as an independent variable.[25] Without so doing it would be difficult to see chauvinist forms of gender oppression practiced by men across social entities of class, race, and ethnicity. It would also be difficult to see specifically gendered forms of male association. However, one of the limitations of treating "men" as an independent variable is the tremendous difference concerning what happens to men because of race, class, status, and culture. Native American men, for example, are hardly in the same position as American men of any ethnicity or race—the former are not a part of the American nation nor do they have as a nation standing armies; it is not reasonable for native American mothers and fathers to instill in their children an expectation of soldiering in an existing army as a possible future career. The disempowerment of African-American men is, analogously, integrally tied to the status of the African-American community.

There is little doubt that the African-American community gained status as members of the moral community in the world because of Dr. King—it is debatable to what degree African Americans are accorded the status of full persons in America. That status, as Americans, conditions the possibility of empowerment and the negation of emasculation. It is certain that African-American males are in multiple jeopardy—one part of which is the *elusive* good of honor of the kind that we can easily identify with through normal social life—a social life the character of which is due for substantive change.

Notes

1. John K. Campbell, *Honour, Family and Patronage* (Oxford: Oxford University Press, 1964), p. 271. Also, according to Julian Pitt-Rivers, "the claim to honor depends always in the last resort, upon the ability of the claimant to impose himself. Might is the basis of right to precedence, which goes to the man who is bold enough to enforce his claim, regardless of what may be thought of his merits." Julian Pitt-Rivers, "Honor," in *Encyclopedia of the Social Sciences*, 2d ed. (New York: Macmillan, 1968), vol. 6, p. 505. The general idea that honor is a social good is not particularly unique, although the way I argue for this view and its application is hopefully of interest.

2. An implication of my view of honor as a social good is that generally honoring an individual woman for virtues and merits associated with women

as such is a function of whether "women" as a social group have status in the moral community and the sort of status that they have as a group. The analog for this is an African-American male (Dr. King) and the African-American community, i.e., social status in the moral community, is the crucial factor shaping the possibility of honor for an individual.

3. See, for example, Robert Cole, *Political Life of Children* (Boston: Atlantic Monthly Press, 1986); Janice E. Hale-Benson, *Black Children* (Baltimore: The Johns Hopkins University Press, 1986).

4. See Bertram Wyatt-Brown, *Southern Honor: Ethics and Behavior in the Old South* (Oxford: Oxford University Press, 1982). Honor was an important variable shaping the cohesion of Southerners; a cohesion sufficiently strong to compel tremendous sacrifice in defense of a segregated way of life. Also, see Julian Pitt-Rivers, *Mediterranean Countrymen* (Paris: Mouton, 1953), p. 80. Also see J. Pitt-Rivers, J. G. Peristiany, *Honor and Grace in Anthropology* (Cambridge: Cambridge University Press, 1992).

5. Peter Berger, "On the Obsolescence of the Concept of Honour," in Michael Sandel, ed., *Liberalism and its Critics* (New York: New York University Press, 1984), p. 158.

6. Orlando Patterson, *Slavery and Social Death* (Cambridge, MA: Harvard University Press, 1982), p. 78. I am indebted to Patterson's work for comparing honor and degradation.

7. Patterson, *Slavery and Social Death*, p. 315.

8. J. E. Casely Hayford, *Ethiopia Unbound* (London: Frank Cass, (1911) 1969); *Gold Coast Native Institutions* (London: Sweet and Maxwell, 1903).

9. This is the case even if the utopia consists solely of women, imposing their wills on one another or imposing their wills on men, e.g., C. Gilman's *Herland* (New York: Pantheon Books, 1978), or S. S. Tepper's's *The Gate to Women's Country* (New York: Foundation Books, 1988).

10. Wyatt-Brown, *Southern Honor*, p. 5.

11. Trudier Harris, *Exorcising Blackness* (Bloomington: Indiana University Press, 1984), p. 2. This quote has been used in the literature on lynching as a fairly standard example of the elements involved in the ritual.

12. See, for examples of honor accorded various body parts and expressions, Michel Feher, ed., *Fragments for a History of the Human Body*, Part One, Part Two, Part Three (New York: Urzone, Inc., 1989). Also see Philomena Essed, *Everyday Racism* (Claremont, CA: Hunter House, 1990).

13. James Jones, *Bad Blood: The Tuskegee Syphilis Experiment* (New York: Free Press, 1981).

14. See Ladislav Holy, *Kingship, Honour and Solidarity* (Manchester: Manchester University Press, 1989), p. 125.

15. See John Ansbro, *Making of a Mind* (New York: Orbis Books, 1982); Carson Clayborne, ed., *Eyes on the Prize* (New York: Penguin Books, 1991); James M. Washington, ed., *A Testament of Hope: The Essential Writings of Martin L. King, Jr.* (San Francisco: Harper & Row, 1986).

16. For comparison and contrast of Aristotelian and Aquianian concepts of honor see Maurice B. McNamee, S.J., *Honor and the Epic Hero* (New York: Holt, Rinehart and Winston, 1960).

17. See, for example, Bill Lawson, ed., *The Underclass* (Philadelphia: Temple University Press, 1992); A. Zegeye, J. Maxted, and L. Harris, eds,

Exploitation and Exclusion (London: Hans Zell, 1991); Elizabeth Fox-Genovese, *Within the Plantation Household* (Chapel Hill: University of North Carolina Press, 1988); bell hooks, *Yearning* (Boston: South End Press, 1990); David Goldberg, *Anatomy of Racism* (Minneapolis: University of Minnesota Press, 1990).

18. Andrew Hacker, *Two Nations: Black and White, Separate, Hostile, Unequal* (New York: Charles Scribner's Sons, 1991). Also see Haki R. Madubuti, *Black Men* (Chicago: Third World Press, 1990).

19. Vincent Harding, *There is a River* (New York: Harcourt Brace Jovanovich, 1981); *The Other American Revolution* (Los Angeles: Center for Afro-American Studies, 1980). Also see Donald Yacovone, "Abolitionists and the 'Language of Fraternal Love,' " Mark C. Carnes, Clyde Griffen, eds., *Meanings for Manhood* (Chicago: University of Chicago Press, 1990), pp. 85–94.

20. Vincent Harding, "Toward a Darkly Radiant Vision of America's Truth: A Letter of Concern, An Invitation to Re-Creation," in *Community in America: The Challenge of Habits of the Heart* (Berkeley: University of California Press, 1988), pp. 67–83; also see Robert Bellah et. al., *Habits of the Heart* (Berkeley: University of California Press, 1985).

21. J. D. Eure and J. G. Spady, eds., *Nation Conscious Rap* (New York: PC International Press, 1991).

22. Jennifer L. Hochschild, "Race, Class, Power, and Equal Opportunity," in *Equal Opportunity*, ed. Norman Bowie (Boulder, CO: Westview Press, 1988).

23. See for example Jonathan Kozol, *Death at an Early Age* (Boston: Houghton Mifflin, 1967); Jonathan Kozol, *Savage Inequalities* (New York: Crown, 1991).

24. I am indebted to Trudier Palmer, University of Pittsburgh, for the importance of noting the influence of socialization here.

25. For examples of the fruitfulness of so doing, despite problems of how much to weigh the variable as a cause, see M. C. Carnes and C. Griffen, eds., *Meanings for Manhood*. See, for my ideas of community and agency, "Historical Subjects and Interests: Race, Class, and Conflict," Michael Sprinkler et al., eds., *The Year Left* (New York: Verso, 1986), pp. 91–106; "Columbus and the Identity of the Americas," *The Annals of Scholarship* (New York: Annals of Scholarship, Inc., forthcoming).

12

Men, Feminism, and Power[1]

Victor J. Seidler

Feminism deeply challenges the ways that men are and the ways that men relate. It draws attention to the power men sustained in their relationships with women and shows that what liberalism conceived of as a relationship of equality with men and women operating in different spheres is in reality a relationship of power and subordination.[2] Recognizing this involves more than a change of attitude on the part of men towards women, for it becomes clear that it is not simply enough to think of someone as an equal with equal respect, but it also has to do with the organization of the relationship of power that exists between men and women in relationships. It is a material issue, though there has been considerable difference about how to conceptualize the nature and character of this materialism. Feminism seems to challenge too narrow an economistic version of materialism but the extent to which feminism and feminist theory have allowed for a reformulation of Marxist conceptions of materialism is still very much an open issue.

If men have to change they have to do this for themselves, for they can no longer rely on women to "pick up the pieces." Men are left to explore and investigate the nature and character of their inherited forms of masculinity. The crucial point is that feminism does not simply present a theoretical challenge to the ways that men understand the world but it also presents a personal and practical challenge to who we are as men and how we relate as men both to ourselves and to others.

It was this personal challenge that men sought to meet in consciousness-raising groups, but often they were difficult situations because as men we were often so used to intellectualizing and rationalizing our experience, rather than sharing it. Sometimes these groups died after a few weeks when it was not clear what men were supposed to talk about. It was difficult for men to *share* their experience with other men because we have been brought up to treat other men as competitors in a way that makes it easy to feel that showing our vulnerability would only be used against us. It was not uncommon for many heterosexual men to say that they did not need consciousness-raising because they felt closer to women anyway, and did not find it difficult to talk to them. Often this would cover over a fear of sharing ourselves with men, a suspicion of men that had deep roots connected to homophobia and a fear of intimacy. This allowed men a certain identification with feminism while being able to disdain men who involved themselves in consciousness-raising. This allowed men to sustain a feeling of superiority in relationship to other men and also to avoid the charges of feminists who would say in the early days that consciousness-raising was simply another form of male bonding that could so easily lead to a reassertion of male power.

Rejecting Masculinity

Another significant strain in the response of men to feminism has been a negation by men of their own masculinity. Masculinity was taken to be *essentially* oppressive to women and as being a structure of oppression. This touches something significant in sexual relationships, for it is a movement of denial that involves a self-rejection, often a loss of vitality and even sexuality. It is this response to feminism that was challenged in the writings of "Achilles Heel,"[3] that sought a reworking of masculinity as part of the project of men involved in consciousness-raising. In fact, this self-rejection is often because men have failed to explore the contradictions of their masculinity. Rather they have learnt that masculinity is essentially a relationship of power, so that you could only give up your power in relationship to women, and so no longer collude in women's oppression, if you were prepared to "give up" your masculinity. This is a part of guilt and self-denial that was not an uncommon male response to feminism. In the end it is self-destructive but nevertheless it has to be understood.

It has often meant that men, having often found no way through them, have given up these issues and concerns completely. In some cases this has possibly fuelled a kind of anti-feminist politics, a threat or fear that women are somehow out to take away men's potency, and this has fuelled the politics of the Right. The move towards a men's rights position has grown to enormous strengths in the United States, often being larger than any men's movement grouping. This is in part why it is so important to rework and rethink men's relationships to feminism.

It was an important part of the "Achilles Heel" project in England to look for more affirming and positive visions of masculinity, and so to challenge some of the sources of guilt and self-denial that had sometimes been part of men's responses to feminism. This involves a personal and theoretical quest. It could also be that "men's studies," as developed in the United States, is a move away from this difficult personal terrain and an attempt to deal theoretically, so that we will not need to deal more personally, with the challenges of feminism. This suspicion is partly fuelled by the strength of a positivist social science methodology within "men's studies," which probably is related to the disciplinary strength of psychology and the ways that these issues can become "topics" within a reworked social psychology. It is as if the claims of feminism, say, around issues of pornography, could be "tested" so that we could know what the "effects" of pornography are on men, whether it makes them more violent or not, and whether it influences the nature and character of their relationships with their partners. Women have grounds to be nervous about the testing of feminist claims within this kind of framework.

Of course there has to be a relationship between empirical research and feminist theory, but we have to be very careful about it. It is too easy given the struggle of social science methodologies to imagine that the causal claims can be "neutrally tested."[4] For what about the fact that we grow up as men within a culture that is deeply imbued with pornographic images? How does this affect us? And is this not the larger context in which these "experiments" are taking place? At the same time it might be argued that men have to be able to set their own agendas and, if this is the way they seek to investigate the issues, it has to be left to men to be responsible for the exploration of men and masculinity. But this raises questions and issues about the challenges that feminist theory makes to different forms of social science methodologies and the ways these are marginalized by claiming that they are only relevant in the exploration of women's experience, that will inevitably be troubling.

On the other hand, what about the radical feminist assumption "that all men are potentially rapists"? What does this mean about the conception of masculinity that underpins some feminist theoretical work? Is this something that men can challenge? If men are seen as an ontological category fixed within a particular position within a "hierarchy of powers," what space is left for men to explore their masculinity? This is a question that feminists may wish to take seriously. It is also raised for men who would consider themselves as "male feminists"; or, in a different way, as "pro-feminists." A crucial question is who "sets the agenda" for research on men and masculinity. These are difficult issues to resolve, for it is crucial to keep in mind that it has been the challenges of feminism that have made the dominant conceptions of masculinity problematic. In this sense men's studies has to have a close relationship to feminism, while the extent to which feminism can "set the agenda" for all studies into men and masculinity remains unclear. It is not unusual these days for men to pay lip-service to feminism and to women's struggles in their opening paragraphs, only to go on to ignore the implications of these studies for the work that they are engaged in.

It needs to be taken seriously that many men have responded to feminism by internalizing a particular conception of their masculinity as "the enemy." Since this masculinity was said to be "essentially" a position of power in relationship to women, there was little for men to do but to reject their masculinity. So it seemed that to identify with feminism and to respond to the challenges of feminist theory involved an abandonment of masculinity itself. Sometimes the analogy is made, which I think is misleading, with the position of whites in South Africa, the idea that the only way that whites could abandon their privilege was to identify completely with the black struggle. So analogously it could seem that there is no point for men to work with other men, for this would be to work with the "oppressor" and the only thing that could be justified would be to "give up" our position of oppression.

Here again there is a resonance with an orthodox Marxist frame of mind. Just as middle-class people could "betray their class" and identify themselves with the struggles of working-class people against capitalistic oppression, so it seems as if men can be asked to forsake their masculinity. In part it is possible to change our class position and identify ourselves within a proletarian position, though there are difficulties with this vision of political struggle. This has often involved denial of our "education" and of our understanding of how capitalist institutions crush and distort working-class life and culture. But why does an identification with feminism have to involve a *rejection* of our masculinity? If we adopt a conception of masculinity which simply defines it as a relationship of power, or as the top place within a hierarchy of powers, then we are tempted into thinking that it is "possible to abandon our masculinity." Similarly if we conceive of "heterosexuality" as simply a relationship of power that fixed straight men in a position of power and enforces the subordination of gay men and lesbians, then it can seem that "heterosexuality" can equally simply be abandoned. This has often gone along with the idea of sexuality as being "socially constructed," with the implication that it can equally be "deconstructed" and different choices made. This fosters the view that sexual orientation is in the last analysis a matter of political choice. At another level this reconstructs a rationalistic project that assumes that our lives can be lived by reason alone and that through will and determination, as Kant has it, we can struggle against our inclinations to live according to the pattern that we have set for ourselves through reason.[5]

These are difficult and complex questions and they need to be handled with care and sensitivity. It might be that heterosexuality is a structured institution and that it enforces the conception of "normality" that is taken for granted within the culture. This establishes important relationships of power that marginalize and work to criminalize the sexuality of gay men and lesbians. It has been crucial to understand sexuality not as a "given" but as the outcome of a series of personal relationships, so bringing out the precarious character of all our sexualities. This is part of the importance of recognising "differences." But it is one thing to understand the institutional power of heterosexuality and another to think that sexual orientation is a matter of "political choice."

In part it has been our sharp dichotomy, inherited as a defining feature of modernity and further inscribed within a structuralist tradition, between "nature" and "culture" that has fostered this way of thinking, as if "culture," in opposition to "nature," as an outcome of reason, is within our conscious control. This is one of the difficulties with the prevailing conceptions of "social construction" deeply embedded within the human sciences, which help foster a form of rationalism that gives us the idea that our lives are within our rational control and that through will and determination alone we can determine our lives. It forms our vision of freedom and morality which within a Kantian tradition are identified with reason.

This is part of an Enlightenment rationalism and develops a particular vision of self-determination, as if we *should* be able to control our lives by reason alone. So we begin to think that to say that our sexuality is "natural" is either to say that it has been "given" or that it is somehow beyond our conscious control. But this is to create too sharp an opposition. Freud helps us understand the organization of our sexuality, how it has come to be what it is. He does not thereby think that it can be "rationally reconstructed." For Freud change comes through some form of *self-acceptance* of our sexual feelings and desires, even if these do not take the form that we would want or even that would be regarded as legitimate within the larger society. Rather than judging these feelings and desires by external standards, we learn to acknowledge them for what they are and we learn to suspend judgment. This is part of a psychoanalytic process. It is crucial for Freud that within a rationalistic culture we learn to judge and often condemn our feelings and emotions because they do not fit in with the ideals that we have set ourselves. Part of the originality of Freud, despite all the difficulties, is his break with the idealization of culture and his recognition of the importance of validating our experience for what it is.

Similarly we cannot simply *reject* our masculinity as if it is "wrong" or "bad," or "essentially oppressive to women." This is not to say that we cannot *change* the ways that we are. What is at issue is the model of change that we inherit within our culture, and in this respect Freud is critical of a Kantian-Protestant tradition that says that we can *cut out* or eradicate those parts of ourselves, of our feelings and desires, that we judge as wanting, as if reason provides some kind of neutral arbiter or legislator for determining what is to be regarded as *unacceptable* to us. This was also part of a 1960s inheritance, that said that our anger or jealousy was "unreasonable" and therefore unacceptable, and that therefore it should be eradicated. It was assumed that we could somehow cut our feelings of jealousy out and behave as if they did not exist at all. Jealousy was socially and historically constructed and so equally it could be reformulated according to our wills. If we insisted on our jealousy this just showed a failure of will and determination.[6]

Such a Protestant tradition is still very much with us in the idea of "mind over matter," in the idea that if you take your mind off what is troubling, then the feelings of despair or sadness will somehow disappear. Because we live in a secular culture we are often unaware of the Protestant sources of many of our ideas and values. Freud and psychoanalytic theory move against this aspect of our inherited culture. It was part of the project of "Achilles Heel" to say that you could not *reject* your masculinity, but you could work to *redefine* it. We would work to change what we are by first accepting the nature of our emotions and feelings rather than judging ourselves too harshly. This is to come to terms with the self-critical voice which too often stands in the way of our changing.

Possibly it is because the culture puts such great force on the idea of "self-rejection" that so few men have really taken up these issues. In part it is also up to a theoretical grasp of men and masculinity to reject the idea that men cannot change and to show the ways that men can change might be an important way of unfreezing the notions that make masculinities seem unredeemable. In working towards a transformed understanding of men and masculinity we have to recognise the injuries that were done by the idea that men should be guilty *as men*. At the same time we have to take responsibility for how underdeveloped the theoretical grasp of men and masculinity remains and how long it has taken for men to explore more openly and honestly their relationship to feminism.

Men, Power, and Feminism

If we think about the question of whether feminism is in men's interests we can say that clearly at one level it is not, in the sense that it is a challenge to the power men have to make the larger society in their image. Liberal theory argues that men and women should have equal rights in society and to the extent to which women are denied these rights, the society is unequal and unjust. So it is that men have been able to support the claims of liberal feminism without having to bring into question the inherited forms of masculinity. The women's movement has gone further in its challenge to the power men have to make society in their own image. It also challenges the dominance of masculine values and aspirations which are largely taken for granted in the institutional organization of society. Feminism in its new phase presents a challenge to men's power in society and also to the sources of men's power in sustaining personal relationships. It is a challenge to the ways that both public life and private life are largely organized around the value of men's time and interests, so devaluing and failing to recognize, or giving equal value to, women's time, values and aspirations. So the women's movement has encouraged women to recognize how much they have been forced to give up in themselves in order to see themselves through the eyes of men. It recognizes the difficult tasks that women have of rediscovering their own values and relationships in the context of a patriarchal society.

So it is important to keep in view the ways that feminism remains a threat to the ways that men are, without thereby insisting that it is up to feminism to somehow set the agenda for the reworking of dominant forms of masculinity. In this context, it is quite common for men "sympathetic" to feminism to find some kind of security in the ideas that feminism should be left to women to do, and that women should be given space to set down their ideas and projects free from the interferences of men. This is not an uncommon response but it fails to take account of the challenge that feminism presents to the prevailing forms of masculinities. Briefly, we learn to say "the right thing" when we are around feminists; we feel that we are walking on thin ice and we learn to be careful. It is important to keep in view the ways that feminism remains a challenge to the character and organization of men's power in society, since this challenges the parallelism that can so easily be drawn when we talk about "men's studies" in relationship to "women's studies." The idea that "in the last analysis" or at some deeper level feminism is in fact in the interests of men, has to be handled with great care, for this too can foster a kind of parallelism, where it is also possible for men to assimilate certain feminist insights which they can then use against women.

It also becomes possible to give deference to feminism and to talk about the power which men have within the larger society without fully grasping the power of sociology to co-opt a feminist challenge. Even though a "men's studies" paradigm has challenged the pervasive influence of role theory, the idea that gender exists as a pre-existing set of expectations of what "men" and "women" are supposed to be and do in the larger society is very current. It is easy, and the literature shows it, to fall back into a much more refined form of role theory, which allows for greater flexibility in gender expectation but loses a grip on issues of power and subordination, because this is such a dominant paradigm within psychology and the human sciences generally. It is the methodology of the social sciences, largely unchallenged, which comes to provide the legitimacy for these areas of intellectual study. The critique that feminism can make of an Enlightenment tradition and the forms of social theory and methodology that have emerged from it tend to get lost. An empirical sociology tends to take charge and begins to set the terms in which "gender studies" are to prove themselves as valid and legitimate.

A different approach to power is provided by recent developments in post-structuralist theory. Here we have a vision of power as all-pervasive, that can undermine our sense of the nature of interpersonal power. This insight into the pervasiveness of power can be used to question whether it is right to say that men have power in relationship to women, because it can be argued that both "masculinity" and "femininity" are interpolated within a particular relationship of power. This could be another support for a kind of parallelism being set up between men's studies and women's studies, because both genders are embedded or organized within particular relationships of power. We are offered the notion of identity as being articulated through particular relationships of discourses of power. This is the way that the notion of "social construction" is conceived within a post-structuralist framework. It rejects the idea of power as a thing-like "commodity" that some people have over others, for it wants to insist that the pervasiveness of power means that all identities are articulated with particular discourses of power. In part this accounts for the difficulties which Foucault[7] has in illuminating gender relationships of power. In this sense the influence of Foucault's work has tended to subvert some crucial insights into the relationship among power, identity and experience.

On the other hand, part of what is appealing in this move is that it brings out into the open the idea that men are not all-powerful in all spheres of their lives and that women are not always completely powerless or subordinate. It helps challenge the pervasive picture of a hierarchy of powers with white men sitting on the top of the pile. But this means listening to the experience of men and taking seriously the terms in which they present themselves. A structuralist framework undermines its own insight into the complexity of power by seeing experience as itself the outcome or product of particular discourses. The dialectic that exists between experience and identity and the continuous struggle that people are involved in, in trying to clarify their needs and desires, gets lost. The complexities and tensions of experience are lost as they are presented as the effects of language.

Nevertheless, the picture of the "hierarchy of powers" so easily places woman in a position of victim, as being subordinated and oppressed, and so denies her her own activity and power to shape her own history. At one level a similar problematic can be identified within post-structuralist theory because it assumes that subjects or identities are the products or results of discourses. It tends to present people as passive. The vision of people as victims has a powerful hold within different traditions of social theory. Sometimes the theory can be part of the problem, for it can place, for instance, women in a position of subordination and powerlessness that seems impossible to break. It can create its own forms of dependency and submissiveness and it can stand in the way of women being able to empower themselves. In this sense, structuralism has found a way of talking about identities, but it has been difficult to identify the ways in which it sustains a particular form of rationalistic theory. It sees identities as being provided externally and thereby tends to reinforce a vision of women as being passive. We are back to the idea that the powerless have to be rescued or that there has to be some kind of external intervention, by the state say, to save them. Even if this process of identity formation is seen as an ongoing active process within certain post-structuralist writings, it is difficult to make sense of this because experience itself is taken to be a product of discourse.

It was an insight of the early women's movement to stress the self-activity of women and to focus on the ways that women can retain power in their lives. But this vision remains theoretically in tension with a vision that draws on the "hierarchy of powers," as well as with a more general structuralist/post-structuralist tradition, as if we have to work for the whole structure to be turned upside down before there is going to be any movement.

Men, Power, and Social Theory

As already noted, the dominant paradigm in much academic work on men and masculinity has in fact been provided within a revised and flexible form of social psychology. A competing conception has been provided by sociology whereby social theory has begun to talk of the social construction of masculinity, whether positivist, structuralist or post-structuralist, to point out that masculinity is not simply given or provided for by biology but is sometimes constructed within particular social relationships. Both conceptions can operate within a particular social science methodology. They can both present themselves as being "objective" and "impartial." Crucially they avoid issues of method that have been acutely raised within feminist theory. It might be useful to set out some of the issues which this "gender perspective" framework, as it is often called, tends to avoid. This begins to set the ground for a different kind of exploration of men and masculinity, which is more sensitive to historical and philosophical sources.

First, these theories avoid the tension between the experience that men have of themselves and the way they are supposed to be within the dominant culture. If they illuminate the pain and confusion that are often felt, this is put down as transitional, as part of the movement from one social role to a newly defined and more flexible social role. Second, by talking about this tension in terms of "social construction," we undermine people's trust in their own experience, in the ways that they might come to define what they want for themselves both individually and collectively.

Third, it displaces the issue of *responsibility*, for the role, like the construction, is provided for me "by society." It is not anything that I can help, nor is it anything that I can be held individually responsible for. This is important for men because it is important for men to learn to take responsibility for a masculinity that is so often rendered invisible. It is also important for men to think about the dominant position of masculinity. Responsibility might well turn out to be a crucial issue for men, especially in relationships, for it can be seen that, even though men are "responsible" in the public world of work where it can be a matter of following established rules and procedures, often in relationships men can be controlling, constantly finding fault with what their partners are doing, and feeling somehow estranged or outside of the relationship.

Fourth, these conceptions of masculinity make no sense of the contradictions within men's experience. For instance, there is little sense that it is because men identify with their reason, because of the Enlightenment identification between masculinity and reason, that they are thereby estranged from their emotions and feelings. This is systematically organized and structured. It is a matter of the way a particular dominant form of masculinity and male identity is organized. So this sets up a particular tension between what men grow up to want for themselves, for example, to do well at work, to be successful, to achieve, and their feelings for what matters most to them in their lives.

In the light of these complications, one way forward might be that we have to take more seriously the idea of sexual politics, particularly the idea that the "personal is political," as the basis for a renewed conception of the dialectic among experience, identity and history, or of a reformulated historical materialism. Feminists have long recognized that there is no way of squaring the contradiction whereby women have struggled for an autonomy and independence which are being constantly challenged and negated within the larger society. This is a contradiction that women have learnt to live with, recognizing the importance of the support they can receive from others. In this sense it is no different from men who are struggling to change the patterns of behaviour that have been institutionalized. In both contexts we have to recognize the importance of a social movement for change, as part of a redefinition of values and relationships, so that "the micro" and "the macro" have to be brought into relationship. They cannot be separated off as independent levels of analysis as is often done within the human sciences.

So as men change it will have to be part of a movement for change which will transform the organization of institutional powers and the forms of personal relationships. So it is that the "micro" cannot be separated from the "macro," nor can they be reduced to one another. This is an important feminist insight that men are in danger of losing if they take their theoretical starting point not from within sexual politics or from within a developing male sexual politics but from within the established social scientific frameworks. It is understandable that this temptation will be strong because the movements for change have been relatively weak for men, understandably so because men have been so closely identified with prevailing relationships of power, dominance, and authority. This also serves as a warning against thinking that the "speculative claims" of feminist theory can somehow be tested against the causal claims that they seem to be making, say, in the case of the effects of pornography on men's values and behaviour. This would be for men to take the high ground of a refined positivist methodology, thinking that this is neutral and provides a secure base from which feminist claims can be evaluated.

If this temptation is to be resisted it will be because men have learnt their own complicity with the dominant forms of social theory. They have learnt to question the universality of these theories and methods, recognizing the masculinist assumptions which they carry. They are set within a rationalist framework that recognizes reason as the only source of knowledge and invalidates feelings and desires as being legitimate sources of understanding, insight and knowledge. It is a constant danger for new areas of studies, whether it be women's studies or men's studies, somehow to seek legitimacy in terms of the prevailing paradigms of scientific investigation. This is a tendency to be watched because it can easily lead to losing the crucial power and the value of feminist insight.

But this is not to say that a sexual politics of masculinity will not yield new questions that might challenge some of the notions of some feminist methodologies. A study of men and masculinity will yield its own methodological concerns. These questions will not always lie within feminist theory, nor can we say in advance what they might be. They cannot necessarily be judged according to pre-existing feminist standards but if they are firmly grounded they will deepen our understanding of the sources of women's oppression and subordination. They will also illuminate the conditions and possibilities of changing conceptions of masculinity, if not also the conditions for the liberation of men.

Notes

1. This commentary is an extract from a much longer paper entitled "Men, Feminism and Social Theory," part of a forthcoming text on masculinity and social theory. The full paper includes the discussion of several other questions, including the historical relationship of men and feminism, men's studies, and the "hierarchy of powers." Many of these thoughts were stimulated by discussions that were going on throughout a conference. That it provoked such excitement and opposition can only be a tribute to the occasion and to the sense of lively exploration it helped create.

2. Victor Seidler, *Kant, Respect and Justice: The Limits of Liberal Moral Theory* (London: Routledge, 1986).

3. Achilles Heel is a men's publishing collective that produced the journal of the same name from 1977 to 1983, and again in 1987, as well as a number of pamphlets. While the political position of the collective developed over this time, it was broadly concerned with the relationship between men's sexual politics and socialism. See Achilles Heel Collective, "By Way of an Introduction. . . ," *Achilles Heel*, vol. 1, 1978, pp. 3–7; and P. Morrison, "Our Common Ground," *Anti-Sexist Men's Newsletter*, vol. 10, 1980, reprinted in Jeff Hearn, *The Gender of Oppression: Men, Masculinity and the Critique of Marxism* (New York: St. Martin's Press), pp. 203–204.

4. See Sandra Harding, *The Science Question in Feminism* (Ithaca, NY: Cornell University Press, 1986); C. Ramazanoglu, *Feminism and the Contradictions of Oppression* (London: Routledge, 1989); H. Roberts, *Doing Feminist Research* (London: Routledge & Kegan Paul, 1981); D. Smith, *The Everyday World of the Problematic* (Milton Keynes: Open University Press, 1987); L. Stanley and S. Wise, *Breaking Out: Feminist Consciousness and Feminist Research* (London: Routledge & Kegan Paul, 1983).

5. L. Blum, *Friendship, Altruism and Morality* (London: Routledge & Kegan Paul, 1981); Victor Seidler, *Rediscovering Masculinity: Reason, Language and Sexuality* (London: Routledge, 1989).

6. Seidler, ibid., Ch. 3.

7. Michel Foucault, *The History of Sexuality*, I: *An Introduction* (Harmondsworth: Penguin, 1976).

Selected Recent Bibliography

Abbott, Franklin, editor. *New Men, New Minds: Breaking Male Tradition*. Freedom, CA: The Crossing Press, 1987.

Altman, Dennis. *AIDS in the Mind of America: The Social, Political and Psychological Impact of a New Epidemic*. New York: Anchor Press, 1986.

August, Eugene R. *Men's Studies: A Selected and Annotated Interdisciplinary Bibliography*. Littleton, CO: Libraries Unlimited, 1985.

Barrett, Robert L. *Gay Fathers*. Lexington, MA: Lexington Books, 1990.

Baumli, Francis, editor. *Men Freeing Men: Exploding the Myth of the Traditional Male*. Jersey City, NJ: New Atlantis, 1985.

Beneke, Timothy, editor. *Men on Rape*. New York: St. Martin's, 1982.

Benjamin, Jessica. "The Bonds of Love: Rational Violence and Erotic Domination." *Feminist Studies*, vol. 6, 1980.

Berliner, Lucy. "Domestic Violence: A Humanist or Feminist Issue." *Journal of Interpersonal Violence*, vol. 5, March 1990.

Bettelheim, Bruno. "Fathers Shouldn't Try to Be Mothers." *Feminist Frameworks*, edited by Allison Jaggar and Paula Rothenberg. New York: McGraw-Hill, 1984.

Blum, Lawrence A. *Friendship, Altruism and Morality*. London: Routledge & Kegan Paul, 1981.

Bly, Robert. *Iron John*. Reading, MA: Addison-Wesley, 1990.

Boose, Linda, and Betty Flowers, editors. *Daughters and Fathers*. Baltimore: Johns Hopkins University Press, 1989.

Bordo, Susan. "The Cartesian Masculinization of Thought." *Signs*, vol. 11, Spring 1986.

Boswell, John. *Christianity, Social Tolerance, and Homosexuality: Gay People in Western Europe from the Beginning of the Christian Era to the Fourteenth Century*. Chicago: University of Chicago Press, 1980.

Brittan, Arthur. *Masculinity and Power*. Oxford: Basil Blackwell, 1989.

Brod, Harry, editor. *The Making of Masculinities: The New Men's Studies.* Boston: Allen & Unwin, 1987.

——, editor. *A Mensch Among Men: Explorations in Jewish Masculinity.* Freedom, CA: The Crossing Press, 1988.

——. "The New Men's Studies: From Feminist Theory to Gender Scholarship." *Hypatia*, vol. 2, Winter 1987.

——. "Work Clothes and Leisure Suits: The Class Basis and Bias in the Men's Movement." *Men's Lives: Readings in the Sociology of Masculinity*, edited by Michael Kimmel and Michael Messner. New York: Macmillan, 1989.

Brown, Wendy. " 'Suppose Truth Were a Woman . . .': Plato's Subversion of Masculine Discourse." *Political Theory*, vol. 16, November 1988.

Cancian, Francesco. *Love in America: Gender and Self Development.* Cambridge: Cambridge University Press, 1987.

Carnes, Mark C., and Clyde Griffen, editors. *Meanings for Manhood.* Chicago: University of Chicago Press, 1990.

Clatterbaugh, Kenneth C. *Contemporary Perspectives on Masculinity: Men, Women and Politics in Modern Society.* Boulder, CO: Westview Press, 1990.

Connell, R. W. *Gender and Power.* Stanford, CA: Stanford University Press, 1987.

Craib, Ian. "Masculinity and Male Dominance." *Sociological Review*, vol. 35, November 1987.

Dellamore, Richard. *Masculine Desire: The Sexual Politics of Victorian Aestheticism.* Chapel Hill: University of North Carolina Press, 1990.

Doyle, James. *The Male Experience.* 2nd ed. Dubuque, IA: William C. Brown, 1989.

Dyer, Kate, editor. *Gays in Uniform: The Pentagon's Secret Reports.* Boston: Alyson Publications, 1991.

Ehrenreich, Barbara. *The Hearts of Men: American Dreams and the Flight from Commitment.* Garden City, NY: Anchor Press, 1983.

Ehrensaft, Diane. *Parenting Together: Men, Women, and Sharing the Care of Their Children.* New York: Free Press, 1987.

Farrell, Warren. *Why Men are the Way they Are.* New York: McGraw-Hill, 1986.

Finn, Geraldine. "Nobodies Speaking: Subjectivity, Sex and the Pornography Effect." *Philosophy Today*, vol. 33, Summer 1989.

Foucault, Michel. *The History of Sexuality, Vol. I: An Introduction.* Translated by R. Hurley. New York: Vintage Books, 1978.

Franklin, Clyde W. *The Changing Definition of Masculinity.* New York: Plenum Press, 1984.

——. *Men and Society.* Chicago: Nelson-Hall, 1988.

Gerzon, Mark. *A Choice of Heroes: The Changing Faces of American Manhood.* Boston: Houghton Mifflin, 1982.

Gilmore, David D. *Manhood in the Making: Cultural Concepts of Masculinity*. New Haven, CT: Yale University Press, 1990.

Glass, Leonard. "Man's Man/Ladies' Man: Motifs of Hypermasculinity." *Psychiatry*, vol. 47, August 1984.

Goodwin, Joseph P. *More Man Than You'll Ever Be: Gay Folklore and Acculturation in Middle America*. Bloomington: Indiana University Press, 1989.

Hacker, Andrew. *Two Nations: Black and White, Separate, Hostile, Unequal*. New York: Charles Scribner's Sons, 1991.

Halperin, David M. *One Hundred Years of Homosexuality and Other Essays on Greek Love*. New York: Routledge, 1990.

Hamilton, Mykol C. "Masculine Generic Terms and Misperception of AIDS Risk." *Journal of Applied Social Psychology*, vol. 18, November 1988.

Harris, Trudier. *Exorcising Blackness*. Bloomington: Indiana University Press, 1984.

Hartmann, Heidi. "The Family as the Locus of Gender, Class, and Political Struggle." *Signs*, vol. 6, 1981.

Hartsock, Nancy. *Money, Sex and Power: Toward a Feminist Historical Materialism*. New York: Longman, 1983.

Haug, Wolfgang Fritz. *Critique of Commodity Aesthetics: Appearance, Sexuality and Advertising in Capitalist Society*. Translated by Robert Bock. Minneapolis: University of Minnesota Press, 1986.

Hearn, Jeff. *The Gender of Oppression: Men, Masculinity, and the Critique of Marxism*. New York: St. Martin's, 1987.

Hearn, Jeff, and David H. J. Morgan, editors. *Men, Masculinities, and Social Theory*. London: Unwin Hyman, 1990.

Held, Virginia. "The Equal Obligations of Mothers and Fathers." *Having Children*, edited by Onora O'Neill and William Ruddick. New York: Oxford University Press, 1979.

Herdt, Gilbert H. *Guardians of the Flutes: Idioms of Masculinity*. New York: McGraw-Hill, 1981.

Herek, Gregory. "On Heterosexual Masculinity: Some Psychical Consequences of the Social Construction of Gender and Sexuality." *American Behavioral Scientist*, vol. 29, May/June 1986.

Hirsch, Marianne, and Evelyn Fox Keller, editors. *Conflicts in Feminism*. London: Routledge, 1990.

Hoberman, John. *Sport and Political Ideology*. Austin: University of Texas Press, 1984.

Hoch, Paul. *White Hero, Black Beast: Racism, Sexism, and the Mask of Masculinity*. London: Pluto Press, 1979.

Holden, Jonathon. "American Male Honor." *TriQuarterly*, no. 73, Fall 1988.

Hutchins, Lorraine, and Lani Kaahumanu, editors. *Bi any other Name: Bisexual People Speak Out*. Boston: Alyson Publications, 1991.

Ingoldsby, Bron B. "The Latin American Family: Familism vs. Macho." *Journal of Comparative Family Studies*, vol. 22, Spring 1991.

Jardine, Alice, and Paul Smith, editors. *Men and Feminism*. New York: Methuen, 1987.

Johnson, Robert A. *Transformation: Understanding the Three Levels of Masculine Consciousness*. San Francisco: Harper, 1991.

Jones, Gerald, and Carol Nagy Jacklin. "Changes in Sexist Attitudes Toward Women during Introductory Women's and Men's Studies Courses." *Sex Roles*, vol. 18, May 1988.

Kaufman, Michael, editor. *Beyond Patriarchy: Essays by Men on Pleasure, Power and Change*. Toronto: Oxford University Press, 1987.

Keen, Sam. *Fire in the Belly: On Being a Man*. New York: Bantam Books, 1991.

Kimmel, Michael S., editor. *Changing Men: New Directions in Research on Men and Masculinity*. Newbury Park, CA: Sage Publications, 1987.

Kimmel, Michael S. "Toward Men's Studies: Introduction." *American Behavioral Scientist*, vol. 29, May/June 1986.

LaFollette, Hugh, and George Graham, editors. *Person to Person*. Philadelphia: Temple University Press, 1989.

Laqueur, Thomas. "The Facts of Fatherhood." *Conflicts in Feminism*, edited by Marianne Hirsch and Evelyn Fox Keller. London: Routledge, 1990.

Lauritzen, Paul. "A Feminist Ethic and the New Romanticism—Mothering as a Model of Moral Relations." *Hypatia*, vol. 4, Summer 1989.

Little, Roger. "Friendships in the Military Community." *Research in the Interweave of Social Roles*, vol. 2, edited by Helena Znaniecka and David Maines. Greenwich, CT: JAI Press, 1981.

Lisak, David. "Sexual Aggression, Masculinity and Fathers." *Signs*, vol. 16, Winter 1991.

Lloyd, Genevieve. "Selfhood, War, and Masculinity." *Feminist Challenges*, edited by Carole Pateman and Elizabeth Gross. Boston: Northeastern University Press, 1986.

McGill, Michael E. *The McGill Report on Male Intimacy*. New York: Holt, Rinehart and Winston, 1985.

MacKinnon, Catherine. "Pornography, Civil Rights and Speech." *Harvard Civil Liberties–Civil Rights Law Review*, 1985.

May, Larry. *Sharing Responsibility*. Chicago: University of Chicago Press, 1992.

Messner, Michael. "Boyhood, Organized Sports, and the Construction of Masculinities." *Journal of Contemporary Ethnography*, vol. 18, January 1990.

———. *Power at Play: Sports and the Problem of Masculinity*. Boston: Beacon Press, 1992.

Messner, Michael, and Donald Sabo, editors. *Sport, Men and the Gender Order*. Champaign, IL: Human Kinetics Books, 1990.

Metcalf, Andy, and Martin Humphries, editors. *The Sexuality of Men*. London: Pluto Press, 1985.

Miedzian, Miriam. *Boys Will Be Boys: Breaking the Link between Masculinity and Violence*. New York: Doubleday, 1991.

Miles, Rosalind. *Love, Sex, Death, and the Making of the Male*. New York: Summit Books, 1991.

Mirande, Alfredo. "Que Gaucho Es Ser Macho: It's a Drag to be Macho." *Astlan*, vol. 17/2, 1988.

Mitchell, Cary L. "Relationship of Femininity, Masculinity and Gender to Attribution of Responsibility." *Sex Roles*, vol. 16, February 1987.

Mohr, Richard. *Gays/Justice*. New York: Columbia University Press, 1988.

Money, John. *Gay, Straight, and In-Between: The Sexology of Erotic Orientation*. Oxford: Oxford University Press, 1988.

Murphy, Peter. "Toward a Feminist Masculinity." *Feminist Studies*, vol. 15, Summer 1989.

Pagels, Elaine. *Adam, Eve, and the Serpent*. New York: Vintage Books, 1988.

Parker, William. *Homosexuality: A Selected Bibliography*. Metuchen, NJ: Scarecrow Press, 1971; second supplement 1985.

Pedersen, Loren E. *Dark Hearts: The Unconscious Forces that Shape Men's Lives*. Boston: Shambhala Publications, 1991.

Plant, Richard. *The Pink Triangle: The Nazi War Against Homosexuals*. New York: Henry Holt and Company, 1986.

Pleck, Joseph H. *The Myth of Masculinity*. Cambridge, MA: MIT Press, 1981.

Poole, Ross. "Modernity, Rationality, and the 'Masculine.' " *Feminine/Masculine and Representation*, edited by Terry Threadgold and Anne Cranny-Francis. Sidney: George Allen & Unwin, 1990.

———. "Morality, Masculinity and the Market." *Radical Philosophy*, vol. 39, Spring 1985.

Pronger, Brian. *The Arena of Masculinity: Sports, Homosexuality and the Meaning of Sex*. New York: St. Martin's, 1990.

Puka, Bill. "The Liberation of Caring: A Different Voice for Gilligan's 'Different Voice'." *Hypatia*, vol. 5, Spring 1990.

Raphael, Ray. *The Men from the Boys: Rites of Passage in Male America*, Lincoln: University of Nebraska Press, 1988.

Redekop, Paul. "Sport and the Masculine Ethos: Some Implications for Family Interaction." *International Journal of Comparative Sociology*, vol. 25, September/December 1984.

Rhode, Deborah, editor. *Theoretical Perspectives on Sexual Difference*. New Haven, CT: Yale University Press, 1990.

Rowan, John. *The Horned God: Feminism and Men as Wounding and Healing*. London: Routledge & Kegan Paul, 1987.

Ruddick, Sara. "Thinking About Fathers." *Conflicts in Feminism*, edited by Marianne Hirsch and Evelyn Fox Keller. London: Routledge, 1990.

Schenk, Roy. *The Other Side of the Coin: Causes and Consequences of Men's Oppression*. Madison, WI: Bioenergentics Press, 1982.

Scott, Charles E. "The Pathology of the Father's Rule: Lacan and the Symbolic Order." *Thought*, vol. 61, March 1986.

Sedgwick, Eve Kosofsky. *Between Men: English Literature and Male Homosocial Desire*. New York: Columbia University Press, 1985.

Segal, Lynne. *Slow Motion: Changing Masculinities, Changing Men*. London: Virago, 1990.

Seidler, Victor J. *The Achilles Heel Reader: Men, Sexual Politics and Socialism*. London: Routledge, 1991.

――. *Recreating Sexual Politics: Men, Feminism, and Politics*. London: Routledge, 1991.

――. *Rediscovering Masculinity: Reason, Language and Sexuality*. London; New York: Routledge, 1989.

Snell, William, Rowland Miller, and Sharyn Belk. "Men's and Women's Emotional Disclosures: The Impact of Disclosure Recipient, Culture, and the Masculine Role." *Sex Roles*, vol. 21, October 1989.

Soble, Alan. *Pornography: Marxism, Feminism and the Future of Sexuality*. New Haven, CT: Yale University Press, 1986.

Staples, Robert. *Black Masculinity: The Black Male's Role in American Society*. San Francisco: Black Scholar Press, 1982.

Stoltenberg, John. *Refusing to be a Man*. Portland, OR: Breitenbush Books, 1989.

Strauss, Sylvia. *Traitors to the Masculine Cause: The Men's Campaigns for Women's Rights*. Westport, CT: Greenwood Press, 1982.

Thompson, Edward H. Jr. "The Maleness of Violence in Dating Relationships: An Appraisal of Stereotypes." *Sex Roles*, vol. 24, March 1991.

Tiger, Lionel. *Men in Groups*. New York: Marion Boyars, (1969) 1984.

Tjiattas, Mary, and Jean-Pierre Delaporte. "Foucault's Nominalism of the Sexual." *Philosophy Today*, vol. 32, Summer 1988.

Tong, Rosemarie. "Feminism, Pornography and Censorship." *Social Theory and Practice*, vol. 8, 1982.

Vetterling-Braggin, Mary, editor. *Femininity, Masculinity and Androgyny: A Modern Philosophical Discussion*. Totowa, NJ: Littlefield & Adams, 1982.

Waters, Malcolm. "Patriarchy and Viriarchy: An Exploration and Reconstruction of Concepts of Masculine Domination." *Sociology*, vol. 23, May 1989.

Whitney, Catherine. *Uncommon Lives: Gay Men and Straight Women*. New York: Plume, 1990.

Wideman, John Edgar. *Brothers and Keepers*. New York: Holt, Rinehart and Winston, 1984.

Williams, Dorie Giles. "Gender, Masculinity-Femininity, and Emotional Intimacy in Same-Sex Friendship." *Sex Roles*, vol. 12, March 1985.

Williams, Walter L. *The Spirit and the Flesh: Sexual Diversity in American Indian Culture*. Boston: Beacon Press, 1986.

Wolf, James G. *Gay Priests*. New York: Harper and Row, 1989.

Woodhouse, Annie. *Fantastic Women: Sex, Gender and Transvestism*. New Brunswick, NJ: Rutgers University Press, 1989.

Young, Iris. *Throwing Like a Girl and Other Essays*. Bloomington: Indiana University Press, 1990.

Index

abuse, of children, 83
Achilles Heel collective, 210–11, 214, 220n3
aesthetic delight in war, 26–29
African Americans: males, xvii–xix, 191–206; oppression of, 179–80
aggression, 3, 61; perceptions of, 5–6; social response to, 14
aggressiveness, 203–5
alienation: from male culture, 81; male, xv, 151–63; women's, 143
Amin, Idi, 52
anagnorisis, 50–51
androgyny, xiii, 127
anti-feminism, 169, 170–71, 210
anti-pornography movement, 162
Aquinas, St. Thomas, 199
Aristotle, xvii, 101, 104–6, 197, 199
Athens, 105, 106, 197
athletics, xvi, 41–53, 54n2, 104
Augustine, Saint, 35

Bartky, Sandra Lee, 178
Beauvoir, Simone de, 162
Berger, Peter, 193
Berkeley Men's Center, 181
Bettelheim, Bruno, 85–86, 87
Bing, Stanley, 99
biological drives, 150
Bloom, Allan, 85–86

Bly, Robert, xii, xiv–xv
body: desensitization of, xvii, 138; dualism with mind, 52; imperialism of, 159; male, 124–25; objectification of, 152–53
Booth, Wayne, 49
breast-feeding, 84–85
Brod, Harry, xii, xviii
Buchanan, Pat, 122
Byron, George Gordon, 135–36

callousness, emotional, 102–3
Campbell, Joseph, 131n34
capitalism, 135, 138, 156, 159, 212
care, 59–60, 67–68, 79, 106
Carnegie, Andrew, 180
childbirth, 84
childcare, 62, 64, 83–84, 87–88; *see also* parenting
children, xvii, 83, 192–93, 201, 204; *see also* father
civil libertarians, 159
civil rights movement, 199–200
Clatterbaugh, Kenneth, xii, xviii
Chodorow, Nancy, 84
commodification of sexuality, 136, 154
community, 30–33; *see also* moral community
competition, as model, 103

229

About the Contributors

Harry Brod has taught philosophy and gender studies at the University of Southern California and Kenyon College. He is the author of *Hegel's Philosophy of Politics* (Westview, 1992). He has edited *The Making of Masculinities: The New Men's Studies* (Routledge, 1987), *A Mensch Among Men: Explorations in Jewish Masculinity* (Crossing Press, 1988), and *Theorizing Masculinities* (Sage, forthcoming in 1993).

Kenneth Clatterbaugh teaches philosophy at the University of Washington, Seattle. He is the author of *Contemporary Perspectives on Masculinity* (Westview, 1990).

J. Glenn Gray taught philosophy for many years at Colorado College. He was the author of *The Warriors* (Harper & Row, 1959), *The Promise of Wisdom* (J. B. Lippincott, 1986), and *On Understanding Violence* (Harper & Row, 1970). He also edited and translated a number of Martin Heidegger's works.

Patrick Grim teaches philosophy at the State University of New York, Stony Brook. He is the author of *Incomplete Universe* (MIT, 1991). He has edited *Philosophy of Science and the Occult* (SUNY, 1982).

Leonard Harris teaches philosophy and African-American studies at Purdue University. He is the editor of *Philosophy Born of Struggle* (Kendall/Hunt, 1983), *The Philosophy of Alain Locke* (Temple, 1989), and *Exploitation and Exclusion: The Question of Race and Modern Capitalism* (Hans Zell, 1991).

Patrick D. Hopkins is a graduate student in philosophy at Washington University in St. Louis. His research interests lie in the areas of social theory, gender studies, and the philosophy of technology.

Hugh LaFollette teaches philosophy at East Tennessee State University. He has co-edited *World Hunger and Moral Obligation* (Prentice-Hall, 1977), *Whose Child?* (Littlefield Adams, 1980), and *Person to Person* (Temple, 1989). He is completing a book on personal relationships entitled *Just Good Friends*.

Larry May teaches philosophy at Washington University in St. Louis. He is the author of *The Morality of Groups* (Notre Dame, 1987) and *Sharing Responsibility* (Chicago, 1992). He has co-edited the anthologies *Collective Responsibility* (Rowman & Littlefield, 1991) and *Applied Ethics: A Multicultural Approach* (Prentice-Hall, forthcoming in 1993).

Brian Pronger teaches in the school of physical and health education at the University of Toronto. He is the author of *The Arena of Masculinity: Sports, Homosexuality and the Meaning of Sex* (St. Martin's, 1990).

Victor J. Seidler teaches philosophy at the University of London. He is the author of *Kant, Respect and Justice* (Routledge, 1986), *Rediscovering Masculinity* (Routledge, 1989), and *Recreating Sexual Politics* (Routledge, 1991). He has co-authored *A Truer Liberty: Simone Weil and Marxism* (Routledge, 1989), and he has edited *The Achilles Heel Reader: Men, Sexual Politics and Socialism* (Routledge, 1991).

Alan Soble teaches philosophy at the University of New Orleans. He is the author of *The Structure of Love* (Yale, 1990) and *Pornography: Marxism, Feminism and the Future of Sexuality* (Yale, 1986). He has edited *Eros, Agape and Philia* (Paragon, 1989) and *The Philosophy of Sex*, 2nd ed. (Rowman & Littlefield, 1991).

Robert Strikwerda teaches philosophy at Indiana University, Kokomo. He has written on topics in the history and philosophy of social science and in applied ethics.